The Training Evaluation Process

Evaluation in Education and Human Services

Editors:

George F. Madaus, Boston College,
  Chestnut Hill, Massachusetts, U.S.A.
Daniel L. Stufflebeam, Western Michigan
  University, Kalamazoo, Michigan, U.S.A.

A selection of previously published books in the series:

Kelleghan, T., Madaus, G., and Airasian, P.:
  The Effects of Standardized Testing
Madaus, G., Scriven, M., and Stufflebeam, D.:
  Evaluation Models: Viewpoints on Educational and Human Services Evaluation
Hambleton, R., and Swaminathen, H.:
  Item Response Theory
Stufflebeam, D., and Shrinkfield, A.:
  Systematic Evaluation
Cooley, W. and Bickel, W.:
  Decision-Oriented Educational Research
Gable, R.:
  Instrument Development in the Affective Domain
Sirotnik, K. and Oakes, J.:
  Critical Perspectives on the Organization and Improvement of Schooling
Wick, J.:
  School-Based Evaluation: A Guide for Board Members, Superintendents, Principals, Department Heads, and Teachers
Glasman, N. and Nevo, D.:
  Evaluation in Decision Making: The Case of School Administration
Gephart, W. and Ayers, J.:
  Teacher Education Evaluation
Madaus, G. and Stufflebeam, D.:
  Educational Evaluation: Classic Works of Ralph W. Tyler
Mertens, D.:
  Creative Ideas for Teaching Evaluation
Hambleton, R. and Zaal, J.:
  Advances in Educational and Psychological Testing

The Training Evaluation Process

*A Practical Approach to Evaluating
Corporate Training Programs*

David J. Basarab, Sr.
Darrell K. Root

Kluwer Academic Publishers
Boston/Dordrecht/London

Distributors for North America:
Kluwer Academic Publishers
101 Philip Drive
Assinippi Park
Norwell, Massachusetts 02061 USA

Distributors for all other countries:
Kluwer Academic Publishers Group
Distribution Centre
Post Office Box 322
3300 AH Dordrecht, THE NETHERLANDS

658, 3/2404
B29t

Library of Congress Cataloging-in-Publication Data

Basarab, David J.
    The training evaluation process : a practical approach to evaluating
corporate training programs / David J. Basarab, Darrell K. Root.
        p.   cm. -- (Evaluation in education and human services)
    Includes index.
    ISBN 0-7923-9266-3
    1. Employees--Training of--Evaluation.   I. Root, Darrell K.
    II. Title.   III. Title: Training programs.   IV. Series.
    HF5549.5.T7B294   1992
    658.3'12404--dc20   92-25675
                                                                       CIP

MB

Printed on acid-free paper.

Printed in the United States of America

Contents

Preface

Acknowledgment

Preface

This book details a unique training evaluation approach developed by David J. Basarab, Sr. currently the Manager of Evaluation at Motorola University. This approach was developed in part based on information from his graduate coursework with Dr. Darrell K. Root, professor of program evaluation and educational administration at the University of Dayton. It enabled Motorola to evaluate their corporate training programs to determine whether money spent on training was an investment or an expense. This evaluation approach is also significant in determining either the effectiveness of or the opportunities to improve corporate training programs.

In this text, *The Training Evaluation Process*, David Basarab and Darrell Root provide commercial industry training with a step-by-step approach to use when evaluating training programs, thus allowing training to be viewed as an investment rather than an expense. This text focuses on assessing training programs, so that they may be improved. This approach provides a successful procedure to use when evaluating training programs.

Included in the text is a comprehensive explanation of the evaluation model developed by D. L. Kirkpatrick (Kirkpatrick, D. L., November 1959) in which he described four levels of evaluating training programs:

Level 1 - Reaction: Evaluate to learn participants' perception to the training program.

Level 2 - Learning: Evaluate to determine whether participants have learned the course subject matter.

Level 3 - Behavior: Evaluate participants' use of newly acquired job skills on the job.

Level 4 - Results: Evaluate the organizational impact of training on company's workforce.

The rationale for performing these evaluation levels is to collect data, to analyze it and use it to make sound business decisions which would serve as an indicator to improve training where necessary. In other words, these processes support the purpose of program evaluation, *not to prove but to improve.* A five-step process is used in this text to describe each of the four levels of evaluation. The five steps are:

1. Planning an evaluation.
2. Developing appropriate data collection instruments and associated data analysis models.
3. Obtaining data to evaluate training.
4. Systematically compiling and analyzing information.
5. Reporting results and making recommendations.

These five steps are the components of *The Training Evaluation Process.* Each step is a point within the process that is documented, definable, measurable, and repeatable, to always produce the same outcomes. The end of each step contains a set of control points with measures. Before the next step can be taken, the measures must affirmatively meet defined criteria. As each step is repeated, the ultimate goals of reducing training related problems will be achieved. Within each evaluation level and step within the process, examples of actual work are provided to help explain what is required to perform each step.

This book is for you if . . .

1. You know you want to do a training evaluation by you're not sure how to start, proceed, or finish.
2. You're not sure if your training programs are having the desired impact.
3. You've been given a large undefined project to assess the success of your training department.
4. You need a process that will help you improve your training programs.
5. You're eager to learn about training evaluations.
6. You have been conducting training evaluations but there is no pattern or procedure that consistently is followed and supplies valuable information.
7. You want to document the quality of your training programs.

We believe that *The Training Evaluation Process* will be useful to evaluation practitioners by providing tangible descriptions and examples of evaluation studies. The text serves the profession by showing our experience in using evaluation in practice. Using this text, evaluators and students of evaluation will be able to expand their knowledge and skills into new and better evaluation practices. We hope the book enhances your professional evaluation activities and is beneficial in improving your company's Training Program.

David J. Basarab, Sr.
Darrell K. Root

Acknowledgment

We were fortunate when writing this book to have the cooperation, support, along with constructive feedback, from various organizations and individuals.

Motorola in Schaumburg, Illinois U.S.A. is greatly appreciated for the in-process text and the use of Motorola University examples within this book. The examples of evaluation practices are important to show that the Training Evaluation Process does work. Brenda Sumberg, Director of Quality at Motorola University gave not only for her support but also for her insights on how training evaluation supports Motorola's quality initiatives.

To the Department of Educational Administration at the University of Dayton, Dayton, Ohio, for its sponsorship of the text by providing clerical staff and editing staff as well as other resources necessary for the completion of this text.

The authors particularly want to thank Mary Lou Andrews and Marla Dwyer, of the Department of Educational Administration, for the many hours they devoted to editing the book and for scheduling and inspiring us to continue our work. They started with us from the very beginning by assisting with preparing and sending proposals to publishers and continuously worked with us during the writing process. Also, a warm thank you to J. Ann Basarab who spent many hours proof reading the final draft. Their support made the writing of the book a much more pleasant and doable task.

1. INTRODUCTION TO EVALUATION

Purpose of This Chapter

This chapter provides a general overview of training evaluation and its usefulness in corporate training programs. By understanding the underlying purpose of training evaluation, a methodology can be established upon which to build when applying the Training Evaluation Process and its components to meet business needs.

Evaluation levels and techniques used in determining training effectiveness and areas for improvement will be discussed in this chapter. The techniques for using the Training Evaluation Process to document quality of training also will be provided. With this information, evaluation can be used to improve training offerings, document training process success, and strive to satisfy customer's requirements which are the ultimate reason for training.

Objectives of This Chapter

At the conclusion of this chapter you can:

1. Define evaluation as it relates to training within today's business environment.
2. Discuss formulation of the goals of a training evaluation that compliment the mission, goals and subsequent objectives of a business unit.
3. Understand how training evaluation affects the decision-making process as it relates to training effectiveness, document areas for improvement, provide data for process improvement, articulate the quality of training, and achieve customer satisfaction.

4. Address the purposes and uses of evaluation to meet business needs.
5. Discuss two types of training evaluation and when it is appropriate to use each type.
6. Explain four evaluation levels and which level to use when designing, developing, and delivering a training model.
7. Discuss the implementation of training evaluation standards so that an evaluation is proper, ethical, useful, and feasible.

Understanding Evaluation

Before evaluating training programs, the evaluator should understand the Training Evaluation Process so that it can be used to its greatest advantage. This understanding is essential when designing and implementing training evaluation. Without it, training evaluation may fail. When initial training evaluation activities fail it decreases the chances for a second opportunity to perform an evaluation. Understanding the evaluation process, therefore, is essential to ensure training evaluation success.

It must also be understood what evaluation is not. It is not, as many companies have been led to believe, a company policy with a standard end-of-class form where all participants rate various components of training. It is not a sheet of paper or a policy. It is not a series of techniques applied to only selected courses and performed differently from one course to another. It is not limited to writing and administering tests. Nor is it a method of collecting data and creating numbers to justify the expense of training.

Evaluation is a <u>systematic process</u> by which pertinent data are collected and converted into information for measuring the effects of training, helping in decision making, documenting results to be used in program improvement, and providing a method for determining the quality of training. It is important to remember that evaluation is a set of interrelated work tasks where each task builds upon the previous one. Evaluation is essential and should be considered a value-added endeavor to a business. In its simplest form, the Training Evaluation Process addresses the design of evaluation plans, development of data collection instruments, collection of data, analysis and interpretation of results, and generation of evaluation reports.

The process assesses the total value of a training system and the actual training or program with respect to the needs of the participants, the cost/benefits to the corporation, and the requirements of stakeholders. The result of this assessment provides the information for senior management to view training as an *investment in their employees* rather than *as an expense.* Typically, management views training as a bottom-line figure in terms of the number of training days, the number of employees in training, and the number of dollars expended in the design, development, and delivery of training. Training should be viewed as an investment that yields a return and increases a company's market share and profitability. The Training Evaluation Process can provide the steps a company can take to increase market share and profitability by increasing the effectiveness of its training programs.

THE TRAINING EVALUATION PROCESS

Evaluation will not only document that training is an investment in a business but will also provide other valuable information. The Training Evaluation Process described in this book will show how to measure the effectiveness of the knowledge gained in a training program by the participants and how to measure the participants' improved job performance. By systematically planning for, collecting, analyzing, and reporting evaluation results, sound business decisions can be made with respect to training design, development, delivery, and maintenance of corporate training programs. This information, when viewed in an open, non-hostile manner, will lead to an environment in which improvements to current training programs along with modification of the design processes can easily occur. An environment similar to this fosters high quality training.

Information from the Training Evaluation Process must satisfy needs of the stakeholders. Stakeholders are any persons affected by the training. Sponsors of training programs are called key stakeholders because they have a vested interest in the program. If their needs are not met, training has no value to them. Some things stakeholders look for when sponsoring training programs are:

1. Reduction in cycle time.
2. Improved Quality.
3. Increased Performance.
4. Reduced Errors.
5. Increased Sales.

As in any business, mangers have defined sets of goals and objectives. To meet these goals they hire personnel and equip them with the tools and resources to do the job as employed. At times gaps exist between employees' skills and job knowledge and those required to do their jobs. It then becomes the responsibility of the manager to decrease or eliminate that gap. Managers have two basic choices when it comes to providing employees with new skills and knowledge: to train the employees themselves or to send the employees to a training program.

When employees begin a training program, their managers become stakeholders and the training must meet the managers' requirements by providing appropriate training delivered expeditiously at the proper skill level. When the stakeholders' requirements have either been fully met or exceeded, high quality training has been achieved. The Training Evaluation Process provides a method to track and measure training against stakeholders' requirements.

To be successful, evaluation must be considered a process that, when rigorously followed, yields a result that is repeatable, expected, consistent, and measurable. By viewing evaluation as a process rather than an activity, training evaluation becomes a professional, valuable endeavor to the company.

Evaluation does not exist within business solely for evaluation; it supports the function of designing and improving training. Successful evaluation operations are important as value-added resources to all training. Evaluators are not quality control experts but rather are knowledgeable on the theory and practices of training evaluation. This book contains information on the theory and practice of some evaluation training programs that were successfully implemented over a period of years at several corporations.

To become competent in evaluation practices, it is suggested that corporate personnel become familiar with training evaluation by reading, by attending seminars and corporate evaluation training programs, and by going to evaluation and training conventions. They learn from those who have been successful and from those who have not. Evaluation must be valued by business leaders since it adds time and money to the training budget. The value gained from training evaluation must outweigh the cost of conducting it. To persuade business leaders to appropriate the money, the benefits and value that evaluation will yield must be outlined in terms of satisfying stakeholder requirements and how results will be used to make course improvement. Business leaders must be convinced to pilot the Training Evaluation Process in order for them to see the value of evaluation. These results should prove that the value received outweigh the cost. This would be shown in terms of:

1. The effects of training.
2. How it helps in decision making.
3. What needs to be done to satisfy stakeholder requirements and achieve highest quality.

EVALUATION PHILOSOPHY

To embrace the idea of training evaluation and obtain all the benefits the training program has to offer, a company must establish and publish a **philosophy** associated with evaluation. A philosophy statement, at times called a mission statement, is a guide to the development, implementation, and maintenance of training evaluation. The philosophy is a testimony to company practices concerning evaluation. A typical training evaluation philosophy for a fictitious company could be:

> *"This corporation strives to provide a workforce that is highly skilled in all aspects of its job requirements. To meet that need, the company provides job-related, performance-based training. To ensure training is effective and meets the needs of the individual and the company, a training evaluation process for all training is used to measure the effectiveness of training, identify areas for improvement, and satisfy all stakeholder requirements."*

Any philosophy, to be meaningful, has to be accepted and endorsed by senior management, middle management, as well as the employees.

Goals of Evaluation

Once an evaluation philosophy or mission has been adopted and endorsed, evaluation goals must be set according to the evaluation philosophy. Evaluation goals are written so that they compliment training goals which are determined at the inception of the training program. As with any goals, training goals are statements written so that those responsible for evaluation of training programs and implementation can use them as guidelines to achieve a particular purpose. Goals spring from the corporate philosophy statement. Using a corporation philosophy statement as a starting point, the goals for its training evaluation process could be:

> *"A well-designed and executed training evaluation will provide evidence of 1) the training program's success in achieving its objectives, 2) how training can be improved, 3) to what degree the course program maximizes return-on-investment, and 4) the techniques used to document training quality."*

Evaluation goals are the end toward which work efforts are directed. The Training Evaluation Process offers the techniques to move toward and eventually achieve these goals. By following the process, evaluators enhance their chances of realizing their goals.

TRAINING EVALUATION AND DECISION MAKING

Training evaluation is not conducted for its own sake but to help in decision making. The primary purpose of training evaluation is to provide information to decision makers. The following are the types of decisions that evaluation supports:

1. Decisions regarding whether a training program is continued, cut back, or eliminated. In industry, the requirements of technology often change. In one industry, due to ever changing technology, training is required every year. However, this would not be true in a stable industry where evaluation of training takes place when the need is identified. Evaluation would help determine the "shelf-life" of a training program.
2. Decisions regarding whether elements of the training program (such as materials, activities, delivery method, objectives, etc.) should be changed and if so how. These changes usually revolve around issues such as: modifications of content, changes in instructional

strategies, and validation and possible enhancements to the defined needs.

3. Decisions regarding whether the type and number of participants being sent through the course should be modified, and if so, in what way. For instance, a training manager decides that a training program initially developed for experienced sales people is more applicable to entry-level sales personnel. Through the evaluation process, decisions can be made to determine revisions to the training program to meet the needs of a new audience.

4. Decisions regarding how can the effectiveness of a training program in meeting its stated objectives can best be summarized and described in terms of return-on-investment to the company.

5. Decisions regarding whether all stakeholders' requirements have been satisfied.

6. Decisions regarding whether training met or exceeded stated quality goals. If quality goals were not met, then the actions that need to be put into place to increase quality and therefore meet stakeholders' requirements must be determined.

These concepts, along with systematic evaluation design, collection, and analysis for the express purpose of generating information that is useful in decision making, are the major purposes of the Training Evaluation Process.

PURPOSE AND USES OF TRAINING EVALUATION

The Training Evaluation Process is an effective process to follow because it is flexible enough to address multiple purposes and uses. The following is a list of typical reasons for using the Training Evaluation Process:

1. To identify whether a training program is accomplishing its objectives. Objectives may not only be learning objectives but may also be behavioral changes in personnel, monetary effects on the company, and quality results.

2. To benefit those who sponsor training programs. Sponsoring training programs can mean funding development of the course program or sending employees through the program.

3. To decide if participants are behaving more effectively on the job and if that behavior is a result of the training.

4. To identify whether training contributed directly to the participants' improved job performance or whether the improved job performance was due to environmental changes in the work situation.

5. To identify learning from the course program that is actually being used in the work situation or to identify learning that is not-applicable to the work situation and should be eliminated.

6. To find if training contributed to a more effective and efficient business organization.
7. To identify strengths and weaknesses in the training process and the reasons or causes of those strengths and weaknesses.
8. To find the cost/benefit ratio of a training program.
9. To decide who should participate in future training programs.
10. To identify which participants benefited the most and which benefited the least from the course program.
11. To decide if the course program has both merit and worth.
12. To establish a data base that can help management in making decisions.

This list will never be complete as the wants and needs of business change from year-to-year due to modification of corporate strategies and objectives. The Training Evaluation Process, with its built-in flexibility, allows the evaluator to easily and cost effectively meet new and expanding corporate strategies and objectives.

TYPES OF TRAINING EVALUATION

Formative Evaluation

Formative evaluation provides information to staff for purposes of improving the course program during its development and implementation. This methodology is performed to assure that the program has been implemented as designed and to assure that it is working during a training cycle. The basic purpose for formative evaluation is to measure progress and to use this information for program improvement during the life of a program. In formative evaluation, the audiences are those individuals who design, develop and deliver training. This type of evaluation provides information for designers and developers to ensure that the program: 1) meets or exceeds defined quality standards, 2) provides a positive learning environment for the participants, and 3) meets stakeholder requirements. (Course implementation individuals use formative evaluation to ensure that the train-the-trainer and initial course offerings are being executed as planned).

Summative Evaluation

Summative evaluation provides information to show the merit and worth of a training program. This evaluation is followed after participants have completed the course so that appropriate recycling decisions can be made. The basic purpose for summative evaluation is to provide a summary report of the training results. In summative evaluation, the audiences include those from formative evaluation as well as the funding and training stakeholders. These individuals are concerned with the results from the course program as a whole and use evaluation data to document the results and net effect from training.

Typically, formative evaluation is conducted first followed by summative evaluation. Findings from the formative process directly affect the decisions made in the summative process. Exhibit 1 shows the fundamental difference between formative and summative training evaluation.

Exhibit 1: Formative vs. Summative Evaluation

	Formative	Summative
Audience	Course designers Course developers Course design managers Course development managers Instructors Course implementation managers	Funding department Stakeholders Course designers Course developers Course design managers Course development managers Instructors Course implementation managers
Emphasis	Clarification of goals Course design, development, and delivery processes Clarification of problems Documentation of outcomes Documentation of implementation	Documentation of outcomes Documentation of implementation
Role of evaluator	Interactive	Independent and interactive
Typical methods used	Quantitative and qualitative	Quantitative and qualitative
Frequency of data collection	Ongoing monitoring	Limited

EVALUATION LEVELS

One widely used method of evaluating corporate training programs comes from Donald Kirkpatrick[1]. In his evaluation framework, he has developed a series of levels to use when deciding the type of data to use and the time line for collecting evaluation data. His model uses levels of evaluation that will be described in the next portion of this chapter. It will be shown that Levels 1 and 2 are formative and Levels 3 and 4 are summative.

Level 1: The Reaction Level

The first level of evaluation is the "reaction" level and provides information concerning what the participants thought of the training program including materials, instructor(s), facilities, teaching methodology, delivery mechanism, content, etc. It *does not* include a measure of learning that took place. Level 1 evaluation has response from all participants not just from a few satisfied or a few disgruntled participants. Responses to Level 1 evaluation may pinpoint possible problems within the course program. Level 1 evaluation is the most frequently used methodology for evaluating training but is not an effective technique when making program improvements. It provides evidence of possible problems but supplies no concrete indicators of what the problems are or how to correct them.

To draw an analogy, if a forest ranger saw a fire, Level 1 would only tell him that there was smoke. It would not tell him the extent (size) of the fire, what caused it, how to put it out. Level 1 evaluation is similar to this analogy. It is only an indicator of a problem. It does not give a solution to fix the problem or assurance that there is a problem.

The following suggestions are generally followed when conducting a Level 1 evaluation of a training program.

1. Identify evaluation questions.
2. Design a comment sheet/interview so reactions can be tabulated and quantified. Obtain honest reactions by making the forms anonymous.
3. Distribute a written comment sheet or survey or conduct class interviews covering those items determined in the previous step.
4. Allow participants to write additional comments in addition to answering the questions.

Level 2: The Learning Level

The second level of evaluation determines the course's effectiveness in providing the participants with the ability to show attainment of the principles, facts, techniques, and skills presented in a training program. Level 2 evaluation is not the testing of participants and/or the giving of grades. Rather, it takes participants' learning results and determines how well the course achieves its learning strategies. The results are objective and produce indicators of how well the participants understood and absorbed the material.

Level 2 evaluation measures cognitive learning and behavioral skills. Cognitive learning is measured by administering a pre-test given before training begins and a post-test given at the conclusion of the training. The pre-test and post-test must be *exact* or *equivalent to one another*. They are two different tests that ask the same questions and measure the same abilities. The difference between the results of the pre- and post-tests provides evidence as to the learning gained in the training. The perfect training program would have a 0% participant mean score on the pre-test and a 100% participant mean score on the post-test. The pre-test identifies the entry level skills possessed by the participants and the post-test identifies how well the course program succeeded in teaching the participants the desired knowledge. If the scores show that participants did not gain the desired knowledge, then the trainers know their program is ineffective in reaching the outlined course quality goals and learning objectives.

Pre-test and post-test results are analyzed to improve training. The items on the knowledge checks are keyed to course objectives.

An item analysis is performed on each pre-test question that was answered correctly by several participants. For example, when the knowledge check item is a valid and reliable question and participants completing the knowledge check were a representative sample of the defined population, a business decision can be made to either eliminate the course objective and its associated instructional activities or to retain the objective but to reduce time expended during training related to the objective.

An item analysis is performed on post-test questions on training objectives that were answered incorrectly by many participants. Assuming the knowledge check item is a valid and reliable question and participants completing the knowledge check are a representative sample of the defined population, a business decision can be made to enhance instructional activity associated with the objective.

Behavioral training skills are measured by using a performance-based check administered during a workshop or practical exercise. The performance-based check depicts all tasks a participant must exhibit to show knowledge of a particular skill. Results of the check are analyzed to identify which of the desired skills were not learned by a significant number of participants. Assuming that the workshop or exercise is a valid and reliable measure of necessary skills and participants completing the activity are a representative sample of the defined population, a business decision can be made to enhance the instructional activity that will yield more effective participant results. If they have not mastered the skill in the training session, employees will not apply skills on the job.

The following guidelines are generally followed when conducting Level 2 evaluation:

1. Participant's learning will be measured so results can be determined.
2. Knowledge is measured using pre- and post-course skills are measured by performance based checks.
3. Pre- and post-test are analyzed to decide which cognitive objectives were learned and can be attributed to training.
4. Learning is measured on an objective basis.
5. Evaluation results are analyzed so learning can be shown in terms of correlation or level of confidence.

Level 3: The Behavioral Level

The third level of evaluation measures how well participants training skills or behaviors from the training programs have been "transferred" to their job. Level 3 compares participant skills gained in the training session to those behaviors that were observed during their job performance. Level 3 determines which training skills were being used on the job, the success of the training in establishing those skills, what needed training skills were not being used on the job and the reason, and what necessary job skills were not a part of the training. For instance, environmental issues may prevent use of newly learned training behaviors. A participant returning to his office may be faced with a "stop-training" attitude. This can happen when the participant's manager ignores what the trainee has learned and insists on the same work behavior used before training.

Results from Level 3 evaluations are used to help make decisions associated with training modifications or identification of the need and content of "update" training. Administration of Level 3 evaluation can be carried out using a combination of the following four activities: (1) questionnaires mailed to participants, their managers, and peers/subordinates, (2) on the job action plans created in training and later reviewed, (3) interviews with participants, their managers, their peers/subordinates, or (4) observation of participants performing job skills before and after the training. To avoid or eliminate any biases, at least two of the four methods should be used. This will also lend validity to evaluation findings. The ideal Level 3 evaluation is designed at the same time the training program is developed. The first step is to survey the participants to determine their current skill level. The survey would then become a needs analysis used for course design/development. The final step would be to deliver the course and resurvey the participants with the same instrument to determine changes in behavior.

The following guidelines are generally followed when performing a Level 3 behavioral evaluation:

1. Level 2 evaluation has been completed and the results are positive.
2. A systematic analysis is made by observing on-the-job performance before-and-after training.

3. Data collected from one or more of the following depending on time resources and needs related to participant's job performance:

    A. The participant.
    B. The participant's superior or superiors.
    C. The participant's subordinates.
    D. The participant's peers.

4. An analysis is made to compare before-and-after performance and relate changes to training.
5. Post-training evaluation is made some time after training so that participants would have had an opportunity to put their learning into practice. A fine line exists between applying evaluation too soon or too late. If it is applied too early, participants will not have had an opportunity to practice the new skills; and if it is applied too late, other factors will have had an influence on participants' job performances. The decision of when to apply evaluation is a judgment call and should be based on content of training as well as the type of participant. Typically two evaluations are necessary, one about three months after completing training and a second after six months.

Level 4: The Results Level

Evaluations at level 4 are used to measure results of training with organizational improvement based upon the company's return-on-investment. In order for a Level 4 evaluation to be conducted and to be appropriate, three conditions must exist: 1) Level 3 evaluation is completed and the results are positive, 2) records to compare company profits before and after the training, and 3) the use of control and experimental groups to compare business results. If these three conditions do not exist, the program will not be a candidate for a Level 4 evaluation. At this level the evaluator does not create an evaluation instrument or conduct a data collection procedure. The data (for example accounting records) used to determine return-on-investment must already exist before training to provide a comparison of before-and-after dollar figures on return-on-investment. Some results that can be examined are:

1. Cost savings.
2. Improvement work output.
3. Quality changes.

Applying Evaluation to a Corporate Training Program

Exhibit 2:   Curriculum Design Process and Evaluation Application

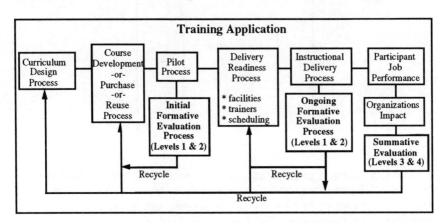

The Training Evaluation Process is complimentary to the design, development, and delivery of training programs. When training programs do not exist or if they do exist but are not being implemented as designed, the Training Evaluation Process will have little chance of success. Exhibit 2 shows the typical setting where training is designed, developed, delivered, evaluated, and maintained. Please note that this setting is intended as a typical scenario for a training function. It is not intended to necessarily portray the best methodology for executing training. It shows how training evaluation, specifically the four levels of evaluation, compliment and enhances a training operation. Boxes in the diagram describe the training evaluation processes. Each process feeds the next process with the output of one process becoming the input to the next process. The Training Evaluation Process activities are positioned below the course process they compliment. As in Exhibit 3, the formative evaluation during Level 1 and 2 evaluations are applied to corporate training programs in the following way: formative evaluation is applied to both the curriculum design process and the course development process as well as later during the Delivery Readiness and Instructional Delivery Processes. After completing a cycle of a training program, organizational impact is measured by applying summative evaluation. Each process within a corporate training program environment will be briefly investigated.

Exhibit 3: The Curriculum Design Process

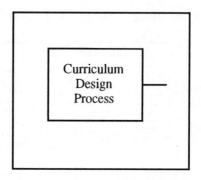

   The <u>Curriculum Design Process</u> defines the training that is required for a given need. The need may be for a single course to meet a defined deficiency in employee performance or the need may be so great that a series of courses or a curriculum may be created. The <u>Curriculum Design Process</u> begins with a training requirement from some business unit within the company. This requirement may be real or perceived. To validate the real need, a <u>needs analysis</u> conducted by someone such as an instructional systems designer is performed. The needs analysis documents the discrepancy between what is and what ought to be. This discrepancy is stated in terms of the knowledge, skills, or attitudes necessary to perform a job or a series of tasks.
   The following procedures are generally followed when conducting a needs analysis:

1. Assess current employees' knowledge, skills, or attitudes.
2. Identify performance problem(s), (if any).
3. Identify the knowledge, skills, or attitudes necessary to perform a specific job.
4. Design analysis instrumentation.
5. Apply data collection techniques.
6. Analyze findings from the needs analysis.

   The intent is to determine the current level of employees' knowledge, skills, or attitudes and compare it to the expectations of company officials. When a discrepancy appears between the two, then the instructional systems designer conducts a <u>training analysis</u> to find: 1) where training can help improve employees' knowledge, skills, or attitudes, and 2) the best type of training to achieve the company's expectations. The primary output of the <u>Curriculum Design Process</u> is an Instructional Design Document that states: the course methodology, the objectives to be achieved, budget (cost) for course development, and a timetable for completion of the training.
   The <u>Curriculum Design Process</u> may also be initiated when the findings of

the evaluation of a training program <u>already</u> exist. The Process, when used as shown in exhibit 2, will produce information that can be used in <u>recycling decisions</u> associated with training. These decisions are the direct result of conducting on-going formative evaluation or summative evaluation. Recycling decisions address the following issues:

1. Changes in course content to meet target population needs.
2. Changes in instructional design strategy to further enhance participant learning and organizational impact.
3. Additions or deletions to the curriculum to satisfy employee and business needs.

Exhibit 4: The Course Development Process

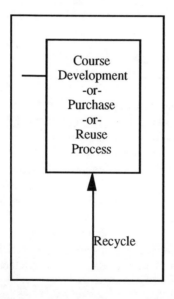

The output of the <u>Curriculum Design Process</u> (Instructional Design Document) is the input to the <u>Course Development Process.</u> This process uses the Instructional Design Document to create training materials that satisfies training requirements. The name <u>Course Development Process</u> is at times misleading. When it makes sound business sense, the course developer or the user of the <u>Course Development Process</u> may elect to purchase off-the-shelf training materials or reuse existing materials. Whether training is newly developed, purchased from the outside, or from existing materials, the final products or course materials must meet requirements specified in the Instructional Design Document.

Exhibit 5: The Pilot Process

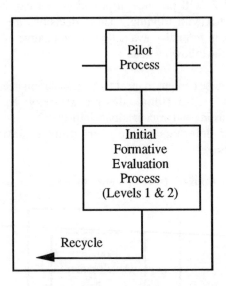

Course development may also be initiated due to formative training results (Levels 1 and 2) from the <u>Pilot Process</u>. In the <u>Pilot Process</u>, the course is "tested" with participants from the target population or anyone who would be an applicant for the training program. Good pilot formative evaluation is used by implementing Levels 1 and 2 evaluation techniques. Participant reaction and level of learning within the pilot are used to determine what changes are necessary to the course before it can be implemented. The quality goals to determine program successes are articulated during the <u>Curriculum Design Process</u>. Level 1 and Level 2 evaluation results are compared with these quality goals and the following decisions can be made: 1) implementation of the program as designed or 2) improve the program and then implement.

Exhibit 6: The Delivery Readiness Process

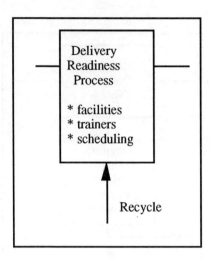

Before the course that requires changes is implemented, a second pilot is conducted using the same formative evaluation techniques. Analysis of evaluation results dictate changes to be made to the training program or dictate the release of the program for general implementation. Once the course has met or exceeded quality goals in the Pilot Process, the course is released for general attendance. In order for the course to be implemented effectively, the suggestions below are generally followed:

1. Arrange facilities to conduct training according to specifications detailed during the curriculum design process.
2. Prepare the trainers. This activity includes running train-the-trainer sessions where trainers are certified to teach the new course.
3. Enroll and schedule participants.

Exhibit 7: The Instructional Delivery Process Using Formative Evaluation

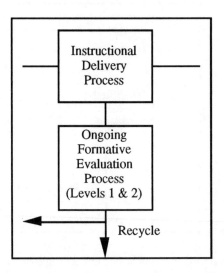

When the facilities, trainers, and schedules are prepared, delivery of the course begins. During the training, Level 1 and Level 2 evaluations are conducted. This is on-going formative evaluation where results are used to improve the <u>Delivery Readiness Process</u> and the <u>Instructional Delivery Process</u>. The intent is to find any deficiencies in the processes or their delivery and to correct them.

The evaluation data are also used for recycling decisions for the <u>Curriculum Design Process</u>. This activity gathers Level 1 and Level 2 evaluation data for all courses being implemented to help decide changes, if any, to the curriculum design.

Exhibit 8: Summative Evaluation

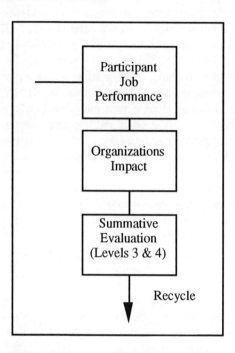

During the <u>Instructional Delivery Process</u>, the desired outcome is improved employee on-the-job performance that will have a positive impact on the organization. Summative evaluation using Levels 3 and 4 determines the effectiveness of on-the-job performance and organizational impact.

Output from the evaluation studies is input to the decision making process that will be used to define the curriculum. Types of decisions made because of these evaluations are:

1. Changes to the curriculum structure such as the addition of supplemental courses, ordering of courses in a training program or discontinuing the courses.
2. Specific changes to individual courses within the curriculum.

The application of formative and summative evaluations using Levels 1 through 4 in a complimentary role fosters program improvement in a positive way for purposes of improvement, documents training quality, and is measurable, definable, and repeatable. The benefit of a training environment of this nature is that it supplies all the steps necessary to achieve a world-class training function.

Evaluation activities, follow specific standards to ensure that the evaluation is practical, feasible, proper, and accurate. In the text, <u>Standard for Evaluation of</u>

Educational Programs, Projects and Materials, the Joint Committee on Standards for Educational Evaluation constructed standards for all types of studies used to evaluate of educational materials, programs and projects. These standards are excellent and are used to monitor all evaluation including the Training Evaluation Process. They will be discussed in chapter 8.

Two assumptions are made when writing a training program. The first assumption is that certain skills and knowledge are needed by a participant. The second assumption is that there are certain entry-level skills and knowledge that participants already possess. The skills and knowledge that they do not possess become the job-performance requirements. The difference between entry-level skills and job-performance requirements determines the course program content. Before a company decides to train 500 employees a training program is tested (Pilot Process) on a sample of the target population and assessed through use of the evaluation. Training evaluation data (Levels 1 and 2) are used to decide what constitutes a successful pilot. Level 1 determines how well participants enjoyed the class and Level 2 determines what they learned. From the evaluation findings, decisions are made to assure training effectiveness. The following are examined when determining if a pilot training session was effective:

1. That training was delivered in the manner in which it was designed. If a class was designed for hands-on training and only lecture format was used, the course was not delivered in the manner in which it was designed. This standard assures that the learning experience is being evaluated in the context in which it will eventually be delivered.
2. That participants completing the program are from the defined target population. This assures that the evaluation results (Levels 1 and 2) represent the effectiveness of the instructional design. Non-target participants are not included in the evaluation study.
3. That a significant number of participants must be involved in the evaluation.
4. That all components of the training session were used during the pilot. A pilot cannot be considered successful if one of the components was not used during training. A missing component invalidates the results.

When the above are all met the following measures can be used to predict the success of training programs and therefore set the criteria for course (program) release:

1. **Level 1:** A quality rating of ninety percent is achieved on the Level 1 instrumentation. Quality ratings portray the amount of good responses to all responses, thus supplying an indicator of the acceptability of the course.
2. **Level 2:** Eighty percent or more of the participants' mean scores are eighty percent or greater.

Requirements for Level 3 Training Evaluations

The requirements for Level 3 evaluations are intentionally sparse so as not to inhibit the implementation of it. Due to cost and significance, however, Level 3 cannot be conducted on only a few participants. The following five criteria to determine if a course is a Level 3 candidate are:

1. At least fifty participants within the course population have completed training.
2. The participants who respond are significant enough in number to predict with a confidence level of 90% or better.
3. The behaviors that are expected to be successfully transferred to the job are established, agreed upon, and documented.
4. As defined in the Evaluation Plan, evaluations are not administered until participants who have been trained have had an opportunity to practice the behaviors on the job.
5. Level 2 is complete and the results are positive.

Requirements for Level 4 Training Evaluations

To administer and analyze a Level 4 training evaluation, the following conditions are met:

1. A control group (set of employees who do not receive training) and an experimental group (set of employees who receive training) of similar sizes are established. The differences in the results of the two groups in terms of business results and money are tracked over the same period.
-or-
2. A baseline of pre-training results must be available and established before the course is used. This functions as a before-and-after approach where pre-training results are the control group and post-training results are the experimental group.
3. Level 3 is conducted and the results are positive.
4. The keys to Level 4 evaluation is that accounting records already exist and that the evaluator has access to them. The evaluation results of training are tracked, compared to accounting records, and turned into a dollar value (return-on-investment).
5. Return-on-investment is then calculated by dividing the value of training expressed in dollars by the cost of designing, developing, and delivering training.

In theory, control and experimental groups are ideal to find the effectiveness of training. In reality however, they are not always practical. Because it may be impractical, some business may not allow the use of control groups. For such reasons, quasi-experimental designs are often used. Although one may not be able to predict with the desired level of confidence, this practice is acceptable. Whether true experimental design is used or not, evaluation should provide evidence to the success of the course, the effect it had on employee's behavior, and the evaluation of bottom-line impact on the company. The data received from an evaluation will enable a company to make judgment and business decisions concerning the future of its training programs.

ENSURING A SUCCESSFUL TRAINING EVALUATION

A successful and useful training evaluation does not just happen. It is a result of certain conditions being met, such as enough time, budget, resources, and expertise to design and carry out valid and reliable evaluation. Evaluation cannot be combined with other daily responsibilities of a full-time job, rather it is recommended that your company hire a full-time evaluator. In addition to a full-time evaluator, there must be enough resources, e.g., money to travel, to hire consultants, to duplicate and mail materials, as well as proper training for becoming competent in evaluation. To train a present employee to be an evaluator, the following suggestions should be followed:

1. A well-documented planned Training Evaluation Process has to be in place.
2. Training on the process must occur.
3. The necessary tools, computer software, guidelines, reference materials and examples to follow must be supplied.
4. The employee must have access to a supervisor or competent evaluator.

For evaluations to be successful, the objectives of the course programs under evaluation study must be clearly stated and include reactionary objectives, learning objectives, behavioral on-the-job objectives, and return-on-investment objectives. The course objectives are stated in terms specific enough for the evaluator to know whether they have been accomplished. For example, if the objective states that a participant must be able to conceptualize a certain practice, the evaluator would have no means of being able to decide if the participant has achieved that objective. In other words the objectives must be measurable.

The evaluation must be well planned so as not to threaten the personnel involved. Trainers, their managers, and participants must cooperate. Typically evaluators deal with the "evaluation phobia" of personnel who don't want to be evaluated because they are afraid they will lose their job. The purpose, however, is to evaluate the program not the personnel. Therefore, full cooperation must be achieved for proper program evaluation. Otherwise the mission will fail. Finally, there must be a commitment to act on results of the evaluation, otherwise the evaluation is pointless.

References

1. Kirkpatrick, D. L., <u>Techniques for Evaluating Training Programs.</u> A four part series beginning with the 1959 issue of the *Training Director's Journal*
2. Sullivan, R. L., Wircenski, J. L., and Sarkes, M. D., <u>A Practical Manual for the Design, Delivery, and Evaluation of Training</u> (1990), Aspen Publications, Inc., pp CD:1 - CD:3
3. The Joint Committee on Standards for Educational Evaluation. <u>Standards for Evaluation of Educational Programs, Projects, and Materials</u> (1981), McGraw-Hill, New York, NY. pp 7

2. TRAINING EVALUATION PHASES

Purpose of this Chapter

This chapter provides an overview of the Training Evaluation Process phases that are used when evaluating corporate training programs. As stated in chapter one, the Training Evaluation Process is the central focus for successful evaluation and consists of five phases. To implement the process, each phase must fit and work together. Each phase of the Training Evaluation Process compliments the other phases. Within each phase is a set of defined and interrelated functions. If properly followed, the result would be a successfully evaluated training program that produces high quality training.

Objectives of this Chapter

At the conclusion of this chapter, you will be able to:

1. Name the five phases of the Training Evaluation Process.
2. Understand the purpose of each phase.
3. Identify the user of a particular phase.
4. Identify the input needed to perform a particular phase.
5. Establish the process to determine the output from each phase.
6. Identify the customer for each phase.

The Training Evaluation Process is designed to collect data from a company's training program and relate it to the needs and objectives of the company and from that data determine the program's merit, worth, and quality aspects. A training program has merit or intrinsic value if it provides a learning experience that meets the program's objectives and trainees respond favorably to the course. A training program has worth or extrinsic value if the training results add value to the company's operations and business success. A training program achieves high quality if it satisfies all customer requirements.

Within the Training Evaluation Process, Levels 1 and 2 evaluations provide evidence of the merit of the course by documenting participants' feelings toward the course and the program's capability to allow them to master the learning objectives. The data, if positive, show the intrinsic value of the course. Evaluation Levels 3 and 4 provide evidence of the worth of the course by documenting the impact the course had upon employee performance and the organization. Since these effects are outside the course they demonstrate extrinsic value or worth. Finally, all four levels of evaluation describe the quality aspects of the course by documenting whether all customer requirements have been satisfied. Successful training programs have merit, worth, and quality. At times a program may have merit and not worth.

For example, a group of insurance sales personnel attend a training program designed to train them to make pizza (highly unlikely - but useful for our example). At the end of the class they are all skilled at pizza making and have enjoyed the program. The training, therefore, has merit because it taught them to make pizza, which is the intent of the course, and they enjoyed it. The program, however, lacks worth because as insurance salespeople, the trainees would never be required to make pizza while performing their jobs.

Besides merit and worth, all training evaluations need to have utility, feasibility, propriety, and accuracy as defined by the Joint Committee on Evaluation Standards and discussed in detail in chapter eight. Utility standards ensure that an evaluation will be informative, timely, and influential. Feasibility standards ensure an efficient and viable evaluation with easy implementation procedures. Propriety standards require that evaluations be conducted legally, ethically, and with due regard for the welfare of evaluators and evaluation stakeholders. Finally, accuracy standards require the use of technically accurate findings and formation of logical conclusions based on the data. It must be remembered that the purpose of the Training Evaluation Process is not to prove wrong doing or incompetence but to improve the course. If any of these standards are not followed, the result will be a poorly evaluated program that leads to unsound business decisions.

It must also be remembered that training evaluation is not personnel evaluation. It is program evaluation conducted for the improvement of programs. Therefore data collected, both quantitative and qualitative, should not be used to judge the effectiveness or ineffectiveness of course designers, developers, trainers, or participants but rather to show the effectiveness of the program and to make any necessary decisions for improvement of the program.

Every program within a corporation is related to the corporation's decision-making process. The Training Evaluation Process assists company officials to continue, terminate, modify, recycle, or refocus a training program. It also provides data showing how the training effects decision-making regarding business objectives, problems, and opportunities. Companies often tend to teach skills or old concepts that have become outdated and no longer needed by either the business or its personnel. If a training program no longer has worth, it should be discontinued.

The Training Evaluation Process also provides an <u>Evaluation Report</u> that effects product and service improvement processes. The Training Evaluation Process supports human resource development (HRD) activities by relating HRD program success to the course(s) involved. The Training Evaluation Process also benefits decision-making by providing quantitative and qualitative data that include quarterly and annual reports. Most companies only report on dollars spent on training, hours personnel are in training, and the number of persons trained. The reports, however, should be balanced by giving the value of the training to the company, the learning gained by the participants, and the return-on-investment due to the training. In times of cutbacks, one of the first items to be cut is usually the training budget. If corporate decision-makers consider the revenue and value gained due to successful training programs, they would realize that by reducing training activities, corresponding amounts of value and revenue from training also would be reduced.

Programs to be Evaluated

Companies should have specific criteria regarding what should be evaluated and, just as importantly, what should not. This criterion should be documented and closely followed. Companies who make statements such as, "We *evaluate all training . . .* " or " *We don't need to evaluate at all . . .* ," are simply not in touch with realistic corporate training evaluation.

Listed below are examples of criteria for companies to use to determine which training programs should be evaluated:

1. The dollar amount spent on program development, procurement, or delivery equals or exceeds a set amount. For example, at company "A" anything less than $100,000 (development plus delivery) does not have to be evaluated.
2. When the required development time of a course is three months or more, the course is evaluated.
3. The course is important to company initiatives. When the cost of training may not be significant but the course results could be vital to a company's success, an evaluation is necessary.
4. A company's training program would benefit more than one group, division, or business unit. Many large companies have smaller business units that act as individual companies. If one unit conducts a training program that could benefit another unit, an evaluation is conducted.

5. If a training program was initiated to facilitate a change within the company or if a company foresees a great change, an evaluation is conducted for information with which to support the change.

Level of Evaluation to be used

When a training program meets the criteria for evaluation, the question of what level of evaluation (1, 2, 3, or 4) to be performed must be addressed. A workable approach is given below:

> *All training that meets one or more of the stated evaluation criteria will require at least a Level 1 (Reaction) and Level 2 (Learning) evaluation. Programs that support major company initiatives or are deemed essential to company success will require Level 3 (Behavior) evaluation. Selected critical programs or course content will require Level 4 (Results) evaluation.*

Due to the expense of evaluation, Levels 3 and 4 are only performed on those programs that are imperative to business success. For instance, if a training program was conducted to reduce the amount of employee turnover, the company probably would want training results to be evaluated to determine employee effectiveness and morale that are essential to a company's success. The key factor to consider when deciding if a Level 3 or Level 4 evaluation is necessary is to find **whether the amount of existing information is sufficient to make a business decision and the change in a training program is large enough to justify the expense.** The Training Evaluation Process provides the techniques for successful evaluation that adds value to the company through its most important resource -- its people.

To conduct a Level 1 evaluation, the training program must be a course with defined objectives, instructional materials, and defined participant population. It must not consist of just meetings, reading brochures, or a conference.

Criterion for Level 2 evaluations are:

1. The course must meet the requirements for a Level 1 evaluation.
2. The course must contain learning objectives that state the skill the participant must be able to master, the context within which the skill will be performed, and the standard by which the mastery of the skill is measured. For example, an incomplete objective could be:

Given a map of the building, the student will label the reception desk, auditorium, and meeting room A.

A better objective would be:

Given a map of the building, the student will label the reception desk, auditorium, and meeting room A. All sections will be labeled correctly, from memory, within 2 minutes.

3. The course content must match the objectives being evaluated.
4. The test mechanisms (Pre-test, Post-test, and Performance-Tests) must match the learning objectives.

Criteria for a Level 3 evaluations are:

1. All Level 2 evaluation requirements are met.
2. Level 2 evaluation results are positive. (Please note that if the results from Level 2 do not show the desired learning gained, then it is quite difficult to draw any correlation between on-the-job performance and the training event.)
3. The skills to be evaluated can be agreed upon and documented including the following:

   A. An exact description of the skill.
   B. The expected duration of the skill when being performed in normal work conditions.
   C. The expected outcome or results from executing the skill.
   D. Anticipated resources such as additional personnel, tools, office supplies, scrap rate, etc.
   E. The average number of opportunities a typical employee will have to put the skill into practice.
   F. The number of times the skill is performed in relation to the number of opportunities to perform the skill.

Criteria for a Level 4 evaluations are:

1. The course meets all Level 3 evaluation requirements.
2. Level 3 evaluation has been conducted and the results were positive. (As with Level 2 evaluation, when the Level 3 evaluation results are not positive, it is very difficult to correlate organizational impact and return-on-investment due to training.)
3. Control and experimental groups are used. The control group is a set of employees who have not received training. The experimental group is a set of employees who have successfully completed training. Both groups are of similar size and perform the same job function. Each group's results are tracked using the same accounting records over the same period. (Note: In an ideal situation random

sampling is used to establish the control and experimental groups. With this technique each employee has an equal chance of being in either group. However, in the real world of training evaluation, this rarely happens. Typically control and experimental groups exist due to the way employees attend courses. Even though employees may not have had an equal chance of being in both groups, when this occurs and is explained in the Evaluation Plan, it is acceptable.

4. Accounting records must exist that measure the training results (such as sales order value, scrap rate, words typed per minute, accounting journal entries, etc.) and the evaluator must have access to them.

When these criteria are followed, the chance of conducting successful evaluations are greatly enhanced. The result would be courses evaluated at the correct level thus maximizing the evaluation resources.

Five Phases of the Training Evaluation Process

The Training Evaluation Process follows five defined phases. This process is designed to enhance whatever standard Curriculum Design and Course Development Process exist and link with other product and personnel processes. In order for an evaluation to be successful it must follow a set of guidelines and practices known as a process. A process is a series of sequential tasks with defined and measurable outcomes that, when performed correctly, will result in expected and measurable work - in this case properly evaluated training programs. Shown in Exhibit 9 in flowchart form are the five defined phases of the Training Evaluation Process.

Exhibit 9: The Phases of the Training Evaluation Process

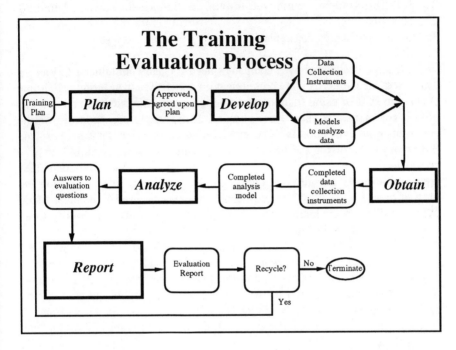

As shown in Exhibit 9, the Training Evaluation Process consists of five distinct phases:

1. The Plan phase
2. The Develop phase
3. The Obtain phase
4. The Analyze phase
5. The Report phase

Each of phase of the Training Evaluation Process includes the following elements:

1. User
2. Input
3. Supplier
4. Output
5. Customer

The user is the person executing a given phase of the Training Evaluation Process. Users of the Training Evaluation Process typically will be:

1. Full-time company employed evaluation personnel.
2. Full-time company employed training personnel who evaluate training programs.
3. Outside evaluation consultants.

Users are designated by a company's need for and commitment to training evaluation. If the needs and commitment are extensive, then hiring a full-time evaluation staff or using training personnel on a part-time basis is probably the best investment. If, however, evaluation activities are sporadic or the commitment to evaluation is weak, employing outside consultants may provide the greatest return for the investment. Outside consultants should also be considered as company evaluators may have a vested interest in programs they are evaluating. An outside consultant could lend credibility to an evaluation and prevent biased reporting. Outside consultants may be used to conduct Meta-evaluations or an evaluation of training evaluation to give credibility to an evaluation. Meta-evaluations are discussed in detail in chapter eight.

Each phase of the Training Evaluation Process has input or the resources, information, data, etc. the user needs to complete each phase of the Training Evaluation Process. Without well-defined input, the process will fail. Input may be a product or a service from a previous phase within the process or a product or a service from a completely different process. Input conforms to requirements specified by the process and is predictable, consistent, and measurable.

The supplier furnishes the input to the Training Evaluation Process in each phase. In order for a process to be successful, a designated supplier, which may be a person, organization, or another process, is essential for providing input to a specific phase of an evaluation. The supplier and user are partners in achieving conformance to process requirements.

The output is the product of the work completed by the user. Output conforms to requirements that are established by the process and, similar to input, is predictable, consistent, and measurable. Output from one phase of a process becomes input to the next phase.

The customer may be an individual but also could be an organization, the next phase of a process, or another process entirely. The customer receives the output from a phase. The customer sets requirements that the output must meet. These requirements are the control measures necessary for output to be used as input to the next phase.

Exhibit 10: Process Information Flow

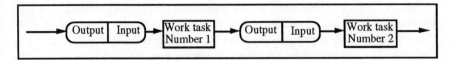

Exhibit 10 shows the flow of information from supplier to customer. Successful execution of step in Exhibit 10 demand well defined input, output, and supplier-customer relationships. If followed in a process form, the time needed to complete the process is reduced therefore diminishing chances for error.

The Training Evaluation Process is a repeatable, sequential set of phases with control measures at each phase. The measures are used to decide the success of each phase and to decide whether to go on to the next phase. In summary, every process contains the following elements:

Exhibit 11: Process Elements

Element	Description
User	Individual who executes the phase of the Training Evaluation Process.
Input	Information, resources, data, etc. necessary for the user to execute the Training Evaluation Process.
Supplier	The individual, organization, or process that provides the input to the Training Evaluation Process.
Output	The actual work produced by the user during the specific phase of the Training Evaluation Process.
Customer	The individual, organization, or process who will acquire the output from the specific phase of the Training Evaluation Process.

Each phase of the Training Evaluation Process contains these elements that allow the evaluator to list the necessary requirements to complete the Training Evaluation Process, to select the approach when conducting the evaluation, and to show successful completion of the evaluation.

The idea of process components and relationships can be simplified by an example. Assume Sally has asked her mother to make a pitcher of lemonade so that Sally can sell it on the front lawn. The user in this task is Sally's mother. She is using a recipe to make lemonade. The input of this phase includes all the necessary items to make a pitcher of lemonade: clean, cold, drinkable water, lemonade mix, a pitcher, and a spoon (stirring instrument). The suppliers in this phase are the organizations who have furnished the input: the water company, the grocery store, and the manufacturer of the lemonade mix. The output is a pitcher of cool, drinkable lemonade. The customer of this phase is Sally. She now has the required output (lemonade) that becomes input to the next phase of this process - the selling of lemonade. During each of these steps, control measures were successfully met, otherwise, the required output, (the drinkable pitcher of lemonade), would not have been possible.

The Training Evaluation Process compliments a company's training design, development, and implementation processes. In other words, evaluation that is designed as an integral part of the training will always generate greater and more meaningful data than an evaluation that is initiated after a training program has already been implemented.

The Plan Phase

Exhibit 12:   The Plan Phase

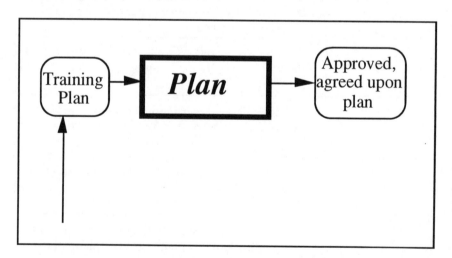

The Plan phase is the starting point of the Training Evaluation Process. Planning an evaluation is specifying what and how you are going to evaluate by reviewing a training plan or strategy developed by the company's <u>Curriculum Design Process</u> and identifying and interviewing the key stakeholders in the evaluation. The <u>user</u> of this phase is the course designer or the evaluator. <u>Input</u> can either be a <u>Training Plan</u>, a <u>Plan of Action</u>, or <u>questions from stakeholders</u> (individuals or organizations who have a vested interest in the course and its outcomes).

Training Plans initiate design and development of training along with evaluation. A Training Plan is created by a department within the company who has requested the need for a training program or an instructional systems designer. A Training Plan contains the following elements:

1. Preliminary definition of training need which is the reason for training. The reason could be a deficiency in job performance, introduction of a new product, initiation of a new company strategy, etc. The training need is either real or perceived. Instructional design validates this need and generates specific plans for the development or purchase of course materials. Evaluation is an integral part of this planning process.
2. Description of the typical participant or the intended audience to receive the training. This would include a description of the existing skills and knowledge, job descriptions, and prerequisite course completion or experiences. This data allows the evaluator to focus on different techniques for different audiences. For example, participants for the engineering division could complete a Level 3 questionnaire, but when the audience is factory personnel and the training involves basic literacy training, a questionnaire may not be appropriate.
3. Number of participants or the estimated number of individuals who will complete training from the beginning through the life of the course.
4. Date training will begin drives evaluation schedules from the delivery courses. Initial pilot tests require Level 1 and Level 2 evaluation to be in place before conducting the course. This deadline is an essential element when developing the Evaluation Plan.
5. Description of the deliverables from the course development activity. This datum is important because it focuses on the evaluation effort. For instance, if the course is to be delivered by self-paced computer based training, then a whole class interview is out because no classes exist.
6. Topical outline of proposed content which allows the evaluator to decide what level 2 techniques (Pre-testing, Post-testing, Performance-Based Tests) are needed. Also included are decisions on what on-the-job skills to track (Level 3 evaluation).

The Training Evaluation Process takes this training plan as input and uses the data to begin formulation of techniques, methods, and levels of evaluation.

A Plan of Action uses evaluation data from a previous training evaluation to improve a training program. It identifies course modification(s) or additional needed course development. For example, due to evaluation results, the participants' behavior on-the-job is not up to expectation and an update or "booster training" is required (i.e., the sales strategy proposed by the industry director is not working -- the students are implementing the strategy as trained, but not producing the desired results). The Plan of Action will trigger the Training Evaluation Process just as the Training Plan does.

After reviewing a <u>Training Plan</u> or <u>Plan of Action</u>, the evaluator needs further information to formulate an Evaluation Plan. This information is gathered by interviewing evaluation stakeholders.

The evaluation stakeholders, those individuals or organizations who have a vested interest in the course and its results, provide the questions they want the evaluation to answer which will be the <u>input</u> to the planning phase. These evaluation questions are the heart of the whole evaluation and set the tone for the remainder of the process. They control what will be evaluated, how it will be evaluated, and they facilitate the phase of analyzing and understanding collected evaluation data. In customer satisfaction terms they are the requirements that must be fulfilled. By using the Training Evaluation Process you can satisfy these requirements and achieve a high quality evaluation.

It is imperative that users of the Training Evaluation Process interview evaluation stakeholders. If users do not, the effectiveness of evaluation questions (requirements) may satisfy only the evaluator's needs and requirements but may not satisfy those of some very important individuals. For example, in one evaluation of a new sales training program, the Industry Marketing Director stated, "I want to know what the students thought of the new sales strategy we are teaching in this course." The evaluator had already compiled a list of pertinent evaluation questions and had not included this one in the list. After further inquiry, the director explained that he needed early feedback from the experienced sales force to validate his decision to implement the new strategy. If the evaluator had not questioned the stakeholder, an important evaluation question would have been overlooked, and the evaluation would not have met the needs of that stakeholder and possibly of the company.

Identifying stakeholders and their role in training evaluation is a critical step for the successful formulation of an <u>Evaluation Plan</u>. Not every stakeholder needs to be interviewed. The evaluator must weigh the time, money, and resources expended to gather data from stakeholders. However, enough stakeholders must be interviewed to provide a broad range of viewpoints to create an accurate and complete evaluation plan.

Output of the Plan phase is an <u>Evaluation Plan</u> that becomes <u>input</u> to the second phase of the Training Evaluation Process, the Develop phase. The Plan phase provides data to decide whether to continue with the development phase. An <u>Evaluation Plan</u> is developed by the evaluator and submitted to the organization funding the evaluation as well as to right-to-know audiences. Copies to the following company organizations should be considered:

1. Product management
2. Product marketing
3. Sales groups
4. Course implementing organizations
5. Organizations requesting the course
6. Manufacturing

7. Management
8. etc.

Essentially, an Evaluation Plan is developed, discussed, and accepted by all stakeholders and identifies the following elements of the evaluation:

1. Identification of what will be evaluated. This is a list of the curriculum, courses, or a single course to be evaluated. Included in the identification are the levels at which each course will be measured. This list must be accurate and complete so that stakeholders have a complete view of what the evaluation entails.
2. Evaluation questions. These are the questions the evaluation will answer. They must satisfy stakeholder requirements and be in line with corporate evaluation goals and practices.
3. Purpose of the evaluation or the reason for evaluating. In other words, the use of the evaluation data once it is provided to evaluation clients.
4. Design of the evaluation levels to be implemented, data collection instruments, instruments and procedures, data analysis models, and analysis techniques. This is the major focus of the evaluation plan. It details what will be done by which person.
5. Implementation. This encompasses the schedule of evaluation activities. It gives a time frame for conducting Level 1 and Level 2 evaluations and executing Level 3 and 4 evaluations.
6. Reporting Schedule which lists when reports will be written and who will receive them. The output of the Training Evaluation Process are evaluation reports. The reporting schedule describes when they will be completed, who will complete them, and who will receive them.
7. Expected benefits and results or what a company can expect to achieve from an evaluation. This gives the expectations from the evaluation studies. Companies only spend money when the expected value is larger or equal to anticipated costs. This section must be truthful and list what company funds will buy and, more importantly, what they will bring.
8. Budget-estimated funds required to develop and implement an evaluation. This is the cost of the evaluation. This cost must be in line with evaluation benefits. Cost must be realistic and relate directly to courses and evaluation levels within each course.

It is imperative that an approved formal written agreement (Evaluation Plan) is in place before performing the subsequent phases of the Training Evaluation Process. At times, depending upon the importance of the course development effort and upon the budget, an Evaluation Plan will not call for evaluation efforts. Evaluation is not always necessary and should never be conducted just for the sake of evaluating. If enough information already exist to make a business decision concerning training, then an evaluation is not conducted. If more information is needed to make decisions, then an evaluation is appropriate.

Once the control measure of phase 1 has been met (an approved, agreed upon Evaluation Plan), the Training Evaluation Process continues with the next phase - the Develop phase.

The Develop Phase

Exhibit 13:   The Develop Phase

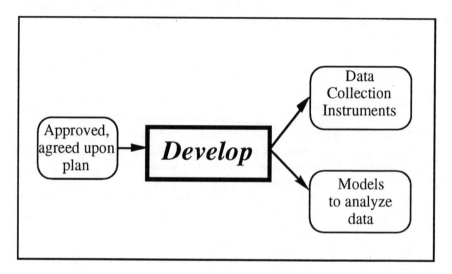

Developing an evaluation is using the output from the Plan Phase as input and drafting the techniques, procedures, and instruments necessary to implement evaluation. Instruments, such as data collection instruments and data analysis models, are developed at this stage. Ideally, the data collection instruments and the analysis models are developed simultaneously to facilitate proper summation of data and appropriate collection of data. During the Develop phase, all levels of evaluation are addressed in order to determine which level(s) would be needed in the evaluation. The outputs of the Develop phase would be:

1.   Instruments to collect data.
2.   Models to analyze collected data.

Both the collection instruments and analysis models are designed simultaneously. Data collection cannot progress without forming proper analysis models. Evaluators must first propose the collection instruments to be used, design the appropriate analysis models to support the collected data, and then finalize the collection instruments to be used.

In other words, this is not a simple two-step procedure. The first step (design of collection instruments) cannot be completed until the second step (design of analysis models) has been agreed upon. Once the analysis models to be used are confirmed the evaluator would complete step one. Simultaneous development of these instruments ensures the existence of appropriate models to analyze collected data.

The data collection instruments are designed to collect the data that will be analyzed in order to answer the evaluation questions. The instruments could be designed in a variety of forms depending upon the intent and level of evaluation. For example, Level 1 evaluation instruments are typically questionnaires and Level 2 instruments are usually pre- and post- test measures. The instruments are then used by the implementing organization as input to the next phase - the Obtain Phase. Either the evaluator or trainer will collect evaluation data depending on the situation. If the trainers are responsible for collection of data, they must refer to the Evaluation Plan for times and types of tools for data collection.

Instruments are specified in the evaluation plan and must be appropriate for the course. Otherwise collected data will not provide answers to the evaluation questions. Data collection instruments may be reused from a previous evaluation or may be specifically for a given evaluation. If an instrument has previously been successful and it is appropriate for the given training program, reusing it will save time and money. At times evaluators may use specific data collection instruments with which they are comfortable or familiar. Exhibit 14 depicts some typical data collection instruments by evaluation level.

Exhibit 14:   Data Collection Instruments

Evaluation Level	Data Collection Instrument
Level 1: Reaction	Questionnaire Whole class interview
Level 2: Learning	Pre-course test Post-course test Performance check Role play Lab work Simulations
Level 3: Behavior	Questionnaire Action plan Work log Observation Accounting records Interview Focus group
Level 4: Behavior	Accounting records Training cost model

The data analysis models are determined before data collection procedures because analysis methods determine data collection procedures. The analysis models can be designed in a variety of forms by the evaluator and are a method of summarizing collected data. Models are created by course developers or the evaluator and are provided to course implementation organization(s). Models may range from simple paper and pencil tabulation tools to spreadsheets, databases on a personal computer, or sophisticated computer programs.

The Develop phase cannot end until its control measures, the analysis models and collection instruments, are agreed upon and have been reviewed by key stakeholders as time allows. Once data collection instruments and corresponding analysis models have been designed and agreed upon, the Training Evaluation Process continues with the Obtain phase.

The Obtain Phase

Exhibit 15:   The Obtain Phase

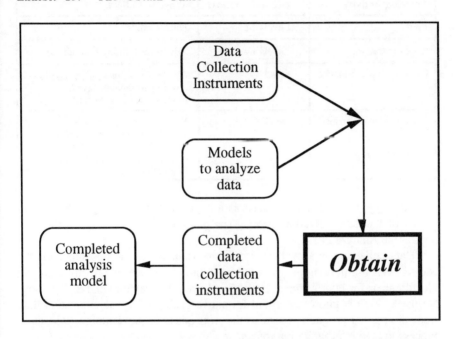

The Obtain Phase of the Training Evaluation Process involves gathering information to address the evaluation questions from Plan phase 1 using data collection instruments from the Develop phase. Data is systematically collected during the Obtain phase to prevent loss of data and to ease analysis of data. The user of this phase is typically the course implementation organization(s) or the evaluator depending on the situation. Collection of the evaluation data also depends upon the level of evaluation being executed. When data from evaluation levels 1 and 2 are being collected, it is usually done by the trainer while in the classroom. Data from evaluation levels 3 and 4 are typically collected by an evaluator. Input to this Obtain phase is received from two sources:

1. The data collection and analysis instruments from the Develop phase. Data collection cannot begin until the data collection instruments (survey, interview, pre-test, etc.) are in place.
2. Evaluation training records, accounting records, respondents, or others, as necessary.

Exhibit 16 shows the source (respondent or company records)of evaluation data by level.

Exhibit 16:   Source of Evaluation Data

Training Activity	Evaluation Level	When to Collect
Pilot	Levels 1 and 2	During pilots.
Ongoing training	Levels 1 and 2	Whenever training is conducted.
On-the-job performance	Level 3	As defined in the Evaluation Plan - ensure participants have had enough time to practice new skills.
Organizational impact	Level 4	When Levels 1, 2, and 3 are completed and enough time has passed for training results to be accessed - as defined in the Evaluation Plan.

The output of the Obtain phase is a completed analysis model containing results of the data collection effort. The analysis model is input to the next phase - the Analyze Phase.

Data collection is a cyclical procedure occurring at various stages of the course. When a training program is first piloted to decide its effectiveness and identify areas for improvement, evaluation Levels 1 (Reaction) and 2 (Learning) are used. This is known as initial formative evaluation. The evaluation data from the piloted program is sent to the next phase of the Training Evaluation Process to help in program improvement.

The improved training program from the initial formative evaluation is released for general attendance by the intended student population. During this time, as defined in the Evaluation Plan, Level 1 and Level 2 evaluation data are collected through ongoing formative evaluation. This data may be analyzed as deemed necessary by the organization(s) that deliver training. If the Evaluation Plan calls for a Level 3 (Behavior) evaluation, it will be performed. Level 3 evaluation cannot take place unless Level 1 and Level 2 evaluation have been completed.

Enough time must be allowed after completion of training in order for participants to try their new skills on-the-job before Level 3 data is collected. The evaluation data from Level 3 is sent to the next phase, the Analyze Phase of the Training Evaluation Process to help in program improvement.

Finally, if the Evaluation Plan calls for a Level 4 (Results) evaluation, it is initiated after completion of evaluation if the results of levels 1, 2, and 3 are positive. The Training Evaluation Process continues with the Analyze phase.

The Analyze Phase

Exhibit 17:   The Analyze Phase

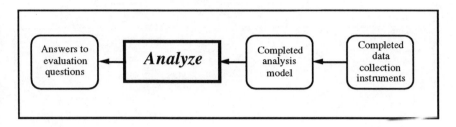

The Analyze Phase of the Training Evaluation Process uses techniques to determine meaning from data collected by the evaluation. In the Analyze Phase data that has been collected is analyzed to determine conclusions supported by the data, and the amount of support provided for these conclusions. The <u>user</u> (analyzer) of this phase could be either the course development organization or the evaluator.

There are two schools of thought pertaining to evaluator responsibility. The first believes that evaluators must only gather and summarize data while the second believes that the evaluator should also analyze the data. Many trainers and training management do not have the necessary backgrounds to analyze data. Therefore, the evaluator analyzing the data may be more beneficial to stakeholders. Evaluators should not, however, be responsible for making decisions based on the findings. Subsequent business decisions should only be made by individuals empowered to make them.

This phase, similar to the Obtain phase, is cyclical. This means that each time data are collected in the Obtain phase, the completed analysis models become input to the Analyze phase.

Input to the Analyze phase will be <u>completed analysis instruments</u> from the Obtain phase. <u>Output</u> of Analyze Phase will be answers to evaluation questions specified in the <u>Evaluation Plan</u>. In support of the answers, statistics and graphics of the data could be used to display the data created. Results can be reported in several ways such as written reports or oral presentations.

The <u>answers to the evaluation questions</u> will be an interpretation of collected data and will be used as <u>input</u> to the Reports & Decision Making phase of the Training Evaluation Process. Examples of graphics to display the results are pictorial data (graphs and charts) used to support conclusions and answers to evaluation questions. These graphics of results also will be input to phase 5, the <u>Report Evaluation phase</u>.

The Analyze phase generally begins when the minimum amount of data as defined in the <u>Evaluation Plan</u> has been collected and generally concludes after the outputs have been created but before the date the <u>Evaluation Report</u> is scheduled to be published as stated in the <u>Evaluation Plan</u>.

Report Evaluation Phase

Exhibit 18:   Report Evaluation

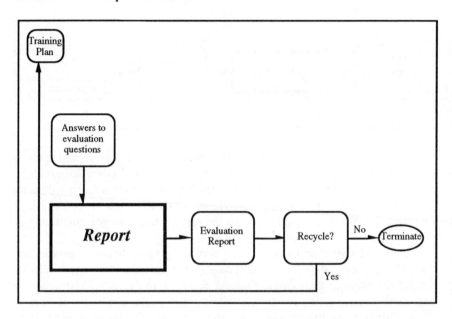

    The purpose of the Reports & Decision Making phase is to communicate training evaluation information to interested audiences which will help them use evaluation information. The <u>user</u> of this phase is the individual who will be writing the reports and drawing conclusions from the data.

    <u>Input</u> for this phase will be answers to the evaluation questions from the Analyze phase. The <u>output</u> will be an <u>Evaluation Report</u> describing the course pilot for pilot training or summative data when using Levels 3 and 4 evaluation. The <u>Evaluation Report</u> for the pilot is written for all courses and includes results of Level 1 and Level 2 evaluation for the pilot class or classes. The <u>Evaluation Report</u> for courses administering Level 3 or Level 4 is typically summative evaluation purposes. This report is designed to communicate the findings, results, and conclusions of post-training evaluation. Included in this report may be a <u>Plan of Action</u> that identifies problem area(s) within the course. It would make suggestions for correcting problem(s), recommend the organization to correct problem(s), estimate the cost of making corrections, and identify resources and dependencies associated with the problem resolution. The <u>Plan of Action</u>, depending upon problems identified, may trigger a course maintenance/development effort with another associated training evaluation. The only time, however, an evaluator writes a <u>Plan of Action</u>, is when he/she is knowledgeable about the subject or has written the course. Otherwise, an evaluator would not be in a position to make recommendations.

Evaluation Plan. If no Plan of Action has been created then the training evaluation is over. Be cautious not to over-evaluate. At times only a report from Level 1 and 2 evaluation is necessary and there is no need to continue.

Summary

The Training Evaluation Process is a series of defined work tasks associated with evaluation of commercial training programs. The process assures that work activity yields an Evaluation Plan that is executed in concert with development and delivery of corporate training programs.

The Training Evaluation Process yields data that describes the effectiveness of the course including as many as four levels of evaluation. The process is repeatable, has measurable inputs and outputs, conforms to requirements, and adds value to the training and development functions.

3. DEVELOPING AN EVALUATION PLAN

Purpose of This Chapter

This chapter provides information to perform the first phase of the Training Evaluation Process - The Planning Phase. Successful evaluations start with this phase. Planning an evaluation requires determining the customer's needs, documenting them in an understandable format and obtaining agreement with the clients for the requested evaluation. Although this phase requires tedious groundwork, a successful evaluation will not be possible without it.

This chapter outlines a practical approach to planning evaluation activities. It supplies a method of balancing theory with pragmatic business practices to achieve an effective Evaluation Plan.

Objectives of This Chapter

At the conclusion of this chapter, you will be able to:

1. Define the object (course) to be evaluated.
2. Determine whether evaluation is required for a given course.
3. Properly identify and rank evaluation stakeholders (customers).
4. Conduct interviews with evaluation stakeholders.
5. Develop an Evaluation Plan.
6. Execute the tasks necessary to obtain an agreed upon and approved Evaluation Plan.

The Training Evaluation Process provides step-by-step instructions that are easy to follow and have been practiced by the authors numerous times. Thus giving you a system that works and produces excellent evaluation results.

Developing Evaluation Plans

Exhibit 19: Developing Evaluation Plans

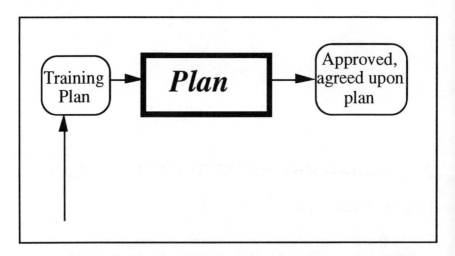

Planning an evaluation involves specifying what and how you are going to evaluate by reviewing a <u>Training Plan</u> or <u>Plan of Action</u>, identifying, ranking, and interviewing the key stakeholders, developing an <u>Evaluation Plan</u>, and obtaining agreement to that plan. The user of this phase is the course designer, developer, or evaluator. Benefits of a well planned evaluation are:

1. <u>A thorough analysis of the course(s) to be evaluated.</u> Without this data, designing an evaluation to be integrated with the training program would not be possible. Because each course differs in content and purpose, the corresponding evaluation requires changes and fine tuning. A thorough understanding of the course to be evaluated allows the techniques to be customized thus maximizing your efforts with little or no waste.
2. <u>Stakeholders, individuals or organizations who have a vested interest in the evaluation and its results, are identified and solicited for information to help in planning the evaluation.</u> This step is essential for customer satisfaction. Knowing who to interview and determining their wants and needs (requirements) permits you to plan an effective evaluation that will satisfy those needs.
3. <u>A commitment to perform a proper evaluation free of biases and political constraints</u>. By developing, sharing, and eventually getting approval for the evaluation through an <u>Evaluation Plan</u>, acceptance is gained and a commitment from those involved is gained. Acceptance and commitment are essential for a successful evaluation.

4. A written, approved, and agreed upon plan is in place before an evaluation begins. Finally, to demonstrate good business practices, no money should be spent until the plan is approved.

The Six Tasks in the Planning Phase

The Planning phase of the Training Evaluation Process, as with all phases, consists of a series of sequential work tasks that use input to produce the necessary output. To develop proper output it is essential that tasks be followed in the documented sequence. These tasks are easily followed and have consistently been proven successful. The six (6) tasks associated with planning an evaluation are:

1. Identify and define the course(s) to be evaluated.
2. Determine if evaluation is required and the appropriate levels needed
3. Identify and rank stakeholders.
4. Interview stakeholders.
5. Develop the Evaluation Plan.
6. Obtain agreement to the Evaluation Plan.

Inputs - Planning Phase

Input to this phase of the Training Evaluation Process may come in two (2) forms:

1. A Training Plan or
2. A Plan of Action from a previous Training Evaluation.

Success of the Training Evaluation Process is dependent upon its ability to use each input and their corresponding differences equally well. A Training Plan is the output from design activities and is created by the organization requesting the training. A plan provides the following information for each course to be developed, delivered, and evaluated:

1. Preliminary definition of the training need. If Evaluation Levels 3 or 4 are being planned it is essential that the business purpose for conducting the course be stated within the training need. If the need does not exist or is stated in non-business terms the design team should be consulted to clarify and document the training need.
2. Identification of the participant. Evaluation planners must know who are the intended recipients of training. This information is necessary in order to identify the target population data from non-target population data. This will facilitate an accurate picture of training and its results.
3. Number of participants. The number of individuals to complete the course

aids in the decision of what levels of evaluation to implement. For example, if only twenty people are to be trained, then Level 3 would not be applicable because the population size does not meet the Level 3 criteria.

4. The starting date. By this given date, Levels 1 and 3 evaluation instruments, analysis models, and collection procedures must be in place. These levels, as discussed in Chapter 1, are used in initial formative evaluation.

5. The predicted completion date. By this date the initial round of training should be complete and if appropriate, Level 3 evaluation may begin.

6. Best estimate of course length. The length of a course is typically a good indication of the number of Level 2 evaluation techniques that will need to be in place. Please note that this is not an exact indicator of the amount of Level 2 techniques but a good place to begin estimating the number that may be required.

7. Suggested delivery method. This data is imperative for deciding the complete evaluation strategy. For example, if the course is to be delivered by computer based training, then whole class interviews would not be a good delivery method .

8. Best estimate of development cost. As discussed in Chapter 1, course development cost is a factor in deciding whether evaluation is required. Evaluation needs to be focused on strategic programs so that data gathered by the Training Evaluation Process is used in the best business sense. Be careful not to judge course importance solely on cost alone. It should be one of many factors in deciding what courses to evaluate.

9. Organization most likely to perform course development. This information is needed by the evaluator because he/she will work hand-in-hand with the course developer in creating Level 2 instrumentality and defining Level 3 skills.

10. Best estimate of cost to deliver training. Again, this cost factor must be considered in deciding whether or not to evaluate.

11. Resources for development and delivery. The amount of company resources are committed to course design, development and delivery, are typically a good indicator of its importance.

12. Desired training outcomes stated in business terms. Documented outcomes which can be measured are essential for successful level 3 and level 4 evaluation.

13. Topical outline. This information is useful for deciding what Level 2 methods to use and, at times, what Level 3 behaviors can be expected.

A Plan of Action, the result of a previous training evaluation, constitutes the recycling efforts of an evaluation and triggers course maintenance or additional course development within the curriculum. If recycling efforts occur, additional evaluation of the new activity will be required. A Plan of Action provides the following information:

1. <u>Areas for Improvement</u> These are the areas within training that need improvement such as delivery, pace, content, instructional strategy, etc. Sometimes a problem area has been identified, but a business decision is made to not take any corrective action. This is acceptable provided the stakeholders (customers) agree.

2. <u>Recommended organization(s) to make change(s)</u>. This may or may not be included in a <u>Plan of Action</u>. If it is, it allows the evaluator to focus his/her attention on the group (individual) who are responsible for course development so that they may work together to improve course and evaluation methods.

3. <u>Approximate cost to modify</u>. These estimated costs needed for changes are considered in the decision of whether or not to evaluate.

4. <u>Timetable required for the modifications</u>. This timetable documents when evaluation activities have to be in place to support the course changes.

5. <u>Resources required to initiate the changes</u>. As with the <u>Training Plan</u>, the resources allocated for change, are an indicator as to the company's commitment to make the modifications. This is an indicator of the importance of the effort.

6. <u>Dependencies that must be met for successful modification</u>. This is the key element of the <u>Plan of Action</u>. These dependencies must be met for the changes to be considered acceptable. Evaluation needs to collect data to ensure these dependencies have been met.

TASKS -- PLANNING PHASE

1. IDENTIFY AND DEFINE THE COURSE(S) TO BE EVALUATED

This first task in planning an evaluation parallels the course development procurement activities (processes). Typically the identification procedure follows the <u>Needs Analysis</u> and <u>Training Analysis</u> activities of course development. Accurate identification and description of courses are essential to the success of evaluation activities, without a complete description of the course, successful evaluation is unlikely.

Exhibit 20 depicts the inputs, input requirements, supplier, outputs, output requirements, customer, and tasks associated with identifying and defining the course to be evaluated.

Exhibit 20: Identify and Define the Course(s) to be Evaluated

Supplier	Input	Input Req.	TASKS	Output	Output Req.	Customer
Training Plan - course designer, developer, or organization requesting the training. Action Plan - the Report Evaluation phase of the Training Evaluation Process.	Training Plan. Action Plan.	All elements of the Training Plan are included. Organizations requesting training have agreed to the plan. Action Plan written in such a manner as to document what must be done and by when. Delivery and development organizations have agreed to the Action Plan.	Determine if a Training or Action Plan exists. Determine if a Needs Analysis or Training Analysis exist. Obtain copies of relevant data. Identify course. Determine schedule for design, development and eval.	Identified course(s) for evaluation.	Course to be evaluated is named and described. Owners of design, development, and delivery are identified. Training schedule is known.	Task No. 2 Determine if evaluation is required and at what levels should be performed of the Plan Phase.

The first step is to *determine if a* Training Plan *or* Plan of Action *exist.* First, request copies of the Training Plan from course design, development, or the requesting organizations. Secondly, request a copy of the Plan of Action from the evaluator who produced the plan.

If no formal plans exist, then collect whatever information there is and in whatever form it appears. This can be done through a content analysis or by talking with key stakeholders. Caution must be taken here. When Training Plans or Plans of Action do not exist, a commitment to designing, developing, and delivering proper training may not exist. Therefore, resources, money, and time may not have been committed for training evaluation and if this exists it may be advisable at this point to consider stopping the Training Evaluation Process. When plans do exist, but are inaccessible, consideration should also be given to terminating the Training Evaluation Process.

If a Training Plan or a Plan of Action does exist and is accessible, the next process is determining *the existence of a Needs Analysis or a Training Analysis* A Needs Analysis provides a composite picture of who will be trained and an outline of the nature of training. It shows the discrepancy between what is and what ought to be.   A review of a Needs Analysis will help in deciding if evaluation is required or needed. For example, if a Needs Analysis shows a small discrepancy between desired performance and current performance, evaluation may not be practical or needed.

Training Analysis follows Needs Analysis and identifies the essential knowledge, skills, and attitudes to be included in the training program. Knowing these components allows the evaluator to decide:

1. When evaluation should be conducted.
2. What levels of evaluation need to be performed.
3. The frequency of data collection efforts.

The schedule for evaluation supports the training design, development, and delivery schedule. At a minimum Levels 1 and 2 data collection instruments and analysis models must be in place so that they are used during the Pilot Process. The skills and knowledge that training is expected to provide are valuable information when deciding if Level 3 and Level 4 are needed and if so when.

Following review of Training and Needs Analysis, proceed with the next step: deciding *what course to evaluate and who it serves?* An evaluation should be able to document and describe the course to be evaluated. Once a course has been described, it is necessary to reach agreement in writing from key evaluation stakeholders about what is being evaluated. A course description should include the following[2]:

1. Key decision makers, leaders, funders, and personnel implementing the training.
2. Goals and intended objectives for the course. Written in business terms that are measurable and therefore can be evaluated.
3. Content of the training program and resources available for performing evaluation. Problems associated with the training program.
4. Timeframes for pilot tests of the course and general availability.
5. The sequence of training within a curriculum.

The outcome of this activity is a description of the training program. A sample description could be:

"The subject of the training evaluation is a sales training course developed by Curriculum Development and being implemented by sales training organizations in regions 1 and 2. The course is a projected three-day school that gives the participants intensive product training on the XXYY System with time to work on their own presentations. Participants are sales and industry personnel from the regions' marketing organizations. Curriculum development will receive development funding from the Personnel Division to develop materials used in the course. Delivery costs will be incurred by the two marketing regions. Key organizations who have a stake in the training program are: product management, marketing, course implementation, curriculum development, and personnel. Possible levels of evaluation will be Levels 1, 2, 3, and 4."

After the course description has been written, the next step is to decide *the schedule for development, delivery, and evaluation of the Training Program.* Evaluation planning must take place at the same time as development and delivery of training. This is necessary because:

1. Level 1 and Level 2 evaluation must be performed in conjunction with the pilot program.
2. Level 3 and Level 4 evaluation must be scheduled at the optimum time (not too early or too late) to gather appropriate evaluation data.

The result of performing task 1 is a complete description of the course to be evaluated and a statement regarding evaluation activities.

-- END OF TASK 1 --

2. DETERMINE IF EVALUATION IS REQUIRED AND AT WHAT LEVELS IT SHOULD BE PERFORMED?

This step determines whether evaluation is required or necessary. If the answer is no, the Training Evaluation Process is terminated. However, if the answer is yes, the levels of evaluation to be performed are established. Exhibit 21 shows the inputs, input requirements, supplier, outputs, output requirements, customer, and tasks associated with task two.

Exhibit 21: Determine if evaluation is required. If so, what levels should be performed?

Supplier	Input	Input Req.	TASKS	Output	Output Req.	Customer
Task No. 1 of the Plan phase of the Training Evaluation.	Identified course(s) to be evaluated.	Course properly named and described.	Read evaluation policy to determine if training program meets requirements.	Evaluation decision.	Satisfies evaluation policy requirements.	Task No. 3: Identify evaluation stakeholders of the Plan phase.
		Design, development, delivery, and funding organizations identified and named.			Levels of evaluation to be performed are documented.	
		Schedule identified and documented.	Determine if a request exists for evaluation when the course does not meet policy standards.			
			Decide on evaluation levels.			

First *determination must be that the training program meets requirements.* As suggested in Chapter 2, a corporate policy should be in place stating when evaluation must be performed. Typical requirements include amount of money to be spent on training development and delivery, labor needed to develop training, or strategic initiatives specific to the company. The training development/delivery activities should be checked against the identified course and a decision made whether this training program requires evaluation. If an evaluation is not required, *special concerns beyond corporate policy exist that may require an evaluation.* For example, instances may arise when the program does not match evaluation criteria but company executives want an evaluation performed. When this happens, a decision must be made regarding whether concerns are valid and if the evaluation has utility or will be useful. If evaluation does not have utility in either case, then end the Training Evaluation Process.

If evaluation is required or requested, then *the evaluation levels that need to be performed must be selected.* Usually all courses will require both Level 1 and Level 2 evaluations. Then the decision must be made whether Level 3 or Level 4 evaluations will be implemented. A good guide to follow in making this decision would be the corporate evaluation policy. General guidelines that should be included in the corporate evaluation policy for deciding whether a Level 3 (Behavior) evaluation is needed, are the following:

1. Training will produce behaviors that are observable and measurable when participants return to their job. For example, if a training objective includes the acquisition of concepts, employers will not have a way to measure that objective.
2. Enough participants will be trained to provide a large enough sample to be significant. A predetermined sample such as one hundred, seventy-five, or fifty participants is a suggested requirement for Level 3 depending on company size.
3. Levels 1 and 2 have been performed and the results are positive.
4. Analysis of the context or setting must be performed. Factors that affect on-the-job performance that are <u>not</u> training related should be identified, eliminated or greatly reduced. For example, if there was a company strike within recent history, it could be a factor effecting both performance and absenteeism.

General guidelines for selecting Level 4 (Results) evaluation are:

1. Levels 1, 2, and 3 have been performed.
2. Level 3 evaluation suggests training behaviors have been successfully transferred to the job.
3. Appropriate experimental study techniques have been used. These techniques call for using a control group (one that does not receive training) and an experimental group (one that successfully completes training). At other times, study techniques using qualitative measures will be used.
4. Accounting records or job performance records exist and the evaluator has access to them.
5. Cost of training development and delivery can be calculated.

The result of task 2 will be decisions whether to conduct evaluation and what levels will be evaluated.

-- END OF TASK 2 --

3. IDENTIFY EVALUATION STAKEHOLDERS.

The next step during the Planning phase of the Training Evaluation Process is identification of evaluation stakeholders. The important concept during this task is the identification of <u>Key Stakeholders</u>. The key evaluation stakeholders, those individuals or organizations who have a vested interest in the training evaluation, will provide, as input to this phase, questions the evaluation will answer. Everyone associated with the training is, in one form or another, a stakeholder, however, it is impossible and impractical to, identify each stakeholder. Therefore, key stakeholders need to be identified in order to maximize the limited time for interviewing them. Exhibit 22 depicts the inputs, input requirements, supplier, outputs, output requirements, customer, and tasks associated with this task.

Exhibit 22: Identify evaluation stakeholders

Supplier	Input	Input Req.	TASKS	Output	Output Requirements	Customer
Task No. 2 of the Plan phase of the Training Evaluation Process.	Identified course to be evaluated.	Course properly named and described.	Identify stake-holders.	List of evaluation stake-holders ranked in order of imp-ortance.	All stakeholders identified.	Task No. 4: Inter-view eval-uation stake-holders of the Plan phase.
	Evaluation levels identified.	Evaluation levels meet corporate evaluation policy requirements or satisfy specifications documented by the requesting parties.	List stake-holders.		Ranking correct.	
			Rank order stake-holders.			

Typically evaluation stakeholders will be:

1. Leaders in organizations requesting the training.
2. Leaders in organizations designing and developing the course.
3. Intended participants.
4. Key personnel in organizations delivering training.
5. Key personnel in organizations funding the development of training.

Names of individuals who are assigned to the training project are *listed* along with their title, area of responsibility, and degree of influence. The first activity is to *identify key stakeholders*. Once the stakeholders are listed, the list should be *rank ordered* to establish those individuals who must be interviewed, should be interviewed, and finally those who do not need to be interviewed. Rank ordering is essential due to possible time constraints and to assure that the most important evaluation questions are answered. Therefore, if stakeholders are ranked, an evaluator can start at the top of the list and go to the bottom as time and resources allow. Rank ordering stakeholders also prevents an evaluator from making promises he/she cannot keep.

-- END OF TASK 3 --

4. INTERVIEW EVALUATION STAKEHOLDERS.

Once stakeholders have been identified and course(s) being evaluated described, the *key stakeholders are interviewed* to determine what they perceive as the purpose(s) of evaluation and to establish evaluation questions. Through interviewing procedures stakeholders are kept informed and become committed to the evaluation. Interviewing also ensures agreement with stakeholders and gives them ownership in the evaluation. Exhibit 23 depicts the inputs, input requirements, supplier, outputs, output requirements, customer, and tasks you need to properly interview stakeholders.

Exhibit 23: Interview evaluation stakeholders

Supplier	Input	Input Req.	TASKS	Output	Output Req.	Customer
Task No. 3 of the Plan phase of the Training Evaluation Process.	Rank ordered list of evaluation stakeholders.	List complete. Ranking accurately represents stakeholder importance to the evaluation.	Interview stakeholders to determine: * Purpose(s) of the evaluation * Evaluation audiences * Elements in the setting that will influence the evaluation * Evaluation questions.	Evaluation purposes(s). Evaluation audiences. Elements that may affect the evaluation. Questions the evaluation will answer.	Accurate data. Reflects stakeholders' opinion. Complete. Not biased by the evaluator.	Task No. 5 Develop the evaluation plan of the Plan Phase.

Using the rank ordered list of evaluation stakeholders, determine key stakeholders and set up interviews with them. This can be done individually or as a group interview. During the interviews a description of the evaluation, a definition of the evaluation levels, and an explanation of what is needed from each stakeholder will be given. Generally requirements for the stakeholders interviews include:

1. <u>The purpose of the evaluation</u> or the reason for wanting a training evaluation. It can be an overall single purpose for one level of evaluation or

several purposes - one for each level of evaluation.
2. The questions the evaluation will answer. These would be the major points
    of interest to the stakeholders - areas of interest where stakeholders require
    information. With this information the stakeholders can then make sound
    business decisions, regarding the course(s).

Evaluators find that different stakeholders have different reasons for wanting
the same evaluation. Conflicting agendas should be investigated and negotiated
openly so that useful information can be provided to key stakeholders. Choosing
and agreeing upon the *purpose for each evaluation level* is probably the single
most important decision initially made about the evaluation[3].
   A purpose for each level of evaluation is then defined. The stakeholders
identify what they want from each level of evaluation. The following are
examples of evaluation purposes:

1. Evaluation of the design of a training program:

       A. to clarify roles or resolve conflicts related to the design
       B. to compare alternate designs
       C. to locate problems that are keeping the design from working
       D. to find the adequacy of a given design

2. Evaluation of the implementation of a training program:

       A. to help in making incremental improvements
       B. to identify strengths and areas of concern
       C. to diagnose problems
       D. to assure the design is operating as planned

3. Evaluation of the results of a training program:

       A. to find immediate results and initial effects
       B. to find what results are appropriate to expect
       C. to find the quality of the training program

4. Assistance in the decision making process:

       A. to improve the course(s) for future implementation
       B. to determine how worthwhile it is
       C. to decide whether it is what it's expected to be
       D. to decide whether it is worth the resources it will or has consumed
       E. to establish a data base of training evaluations to compare current
           course effectiveness against past similar courses

A well written evaluation purpose is essential. The following guidelines to be used when writing an evaluation purpose[4]:

1. Clarify - The purpose must be easily understood by stakeholders and written in comprehensible terms.
2. Accessibility - The purpose must be documented and available to all interested parties.
3. Usefulness - The evaluation should be beneficial to the company and should supply data that is used in the decision making process for course improvements.
4. Relevance - information needs are identified and are in concert with corporate goals and initiatives.
5. Compatibility - the evaluation must be compatible with the goals of the training program.
6. Worthwhile - the benefits must justify the costs.

The elements in the setting that are likely to influence the evaluation. must be determined through the interview process. The setting must be stable and conducive to evaluation. The setting also influences the courses being evaluated. It is important to find out how elements in the setting such as politics, budgets, company initiatives, etc. impact the course in order to correctly interpret the evaluation results. Elements to look for in a setting are[5]:

1. Politics - or the political support of the evaluation. Even with adequate money and resources needed to carry out the training, the individuals within the power structure must support the evaluation efforts or little or no change may occur.
2. Leadership - those having control over the program must support evaluation.
3. Influences - Those having influence on the evaluation.
4. Organization - or which decision makers can influence the Evaluation.
5. Budget - or the security of the fiscal support.
6. Resources - or what resources are available to support the evaluation.

The major questions the evaluation is to answer must be identified in the interview process. Evaluation questions are the basic building block for the evaluation. These are the questions the stakeholders would like to see answered by the evaluation. Evaluation questions are the key to the whole training evaluation process. Evaluation questions for each level of evaluation and for each course must be defined. In other words, the stakeholders identify what the evaluation questions are for each evaluation levels by course.

Before an interview begins, evaluation and its four levels must be defined because most stakeholders will not be aware of the four levels or the definitions. Then, the evaluator should be prepared with his/her own list of questions as a guideline for stakeholders to add to, delete from, or modify.

Different audiences will be interested in different questions. Again, rank ordering audiences will simplify the decision on which questions will be addressed first. To generate specific questions, the general evaluation purpose must be understood, there must be some agreement about what is to be evaluated and how and when it will be reported.

Evaluation questions generate information and should be assessed in light of the quality and the type of information they produce. In assessing the evaluation questions, the four step procedure listed next should be followed:

1. Generate the evaluation questions.

   A. Identify the questions making certain that are in a question format and address a specific evaluation level.
   B. Rank order the questions by sorting them by evaluation level and then by importance within each level.
   C. The questions within each level are:

      * Relevant so that they will have significance.
      * Important so that the answers are valuable in the context of the course.
      * Comprehensive and relate to the concept being evaluated.
      * Balanced and represent all points of view.
      * Realistic and concerned only with facts and not impractical or visionary evaluation ideas.

2. Determine how data will be gathered to answer the questions.

   A. Information sources to answer the questions must be accessible and obtainable.
   B. Methods used to gather data must be practical and maintain the privacy of all individuals involved.
   C. Tools or instruments used to collect data must be either available or easy to create.

3. Determine how information will be analyzed.

   A. Qualitatively, quantitatively, or both methods must be considered.
   B. The methods chosen must be available to analyze data.
   C. Establish the criteria to judge data as worthwhile and accurately judge the worth and merit of the course.

4. Decide what will be reported. Determine how information will be:

A. Collected (Obtained)
B. Displayed
C. Interpreted
D. Reported
E. When do audiences need the report?

Examples of Evaluation Questions

Examples of evaluation questions by level are given below. An example of a typical question is given first followed by a better question for collecting evaluation data.

Level 1

Example: How did the participants feel about the quality of the participant manual?
Better: How did the participants feel about the quality of the participant manual in the areas listed below:

A. Format of the pages.
B. Tables and graphics.
C. Readability of the text.

Example: What did the participants feel about the trainer?
Better: How did the participants rate the trainer regarding:

A. Presentation skills.
B. Knowledge of the subject matter.
C. Question and answering techniques.

Example: Did the participants feel that the course objectives were appropriate?
Better: How did the participants rate the applicability of the course objectives to their current job requirements?

Level 2

Example: Did the participants learn?
Better: Comparing participant pre-test and post-test scores, what amount of learning was gained as defined in the following formula:

$$\text{Index of Learning Gain} = \frac{(Post\text{-}Test) - (Pre\text{-}Test)}{(Maximum\ Post\text{-}Test) - (Pre\text{-}Test)} \times 100$$

Example: How well did the participants perform in the workshops?

Better: After conducting an item analysis of participant performance on all workshops tasks, what changes need to be made to each workshop in the following two areas?

     A.   Rewriting work tasks so that participants have a clear understanding of what they are required to do.

     B.   Redesigning instructional content to achieve maximum participant performance on all workshop tasks.

Level 3

Example: How has training changed employee on-the-job performance?

Better: Due to successful completion of the course, how has employee job performance changed in the following areas?

     A.   How many opportunities have participants had to perform the behavior learned from the training?

     B.   How often did they do the learned behavior?

     C.   How much time did it take to complete the behavior?

     D.   What resources (tools, personnel, money, etc.) were used/consumed when doing the behavior?

     E.   Was the result of using the new behavior positive, negative, partly positive or partly negative?

     F.   What prohibited employees from using the learned behavior?

     G.   What skills, as it relates to the specific job behavior, did participants have to acquire on their own that training did not provide?

<u>Level 4</u>

Example: What is the Return-on-Investment from training?
Better: Due to the training, what expenses were incurred in designing,
             developing, and delivering training, and what was the Return-on-
             Investment from the training?

The output of task 4 should provide the following information:

1. Purpose(s) for the evaluation.
2. Identification of key evaluation stakeholders.
3. Determination of the elements within a company's environment that may
   affect the evaluation.
4. Questions the evaluation will answer.

With this output you can then proceed to the next task of the Training
Evaluation Process which is to develop the <u>Evaluation Plan</u>.

-- END OF TASK 4 --

5. DEVELOP THE <u>EVALUATION PLAN</u>.

The <u>Evaluation Plan</u> is the primary output of the *Planning* phase of the Training
Evaluation Process and is the document which guides all further actions within
the process. Once the plan is written it is submitted to individuals or
organizations identified by the evaluator as key stakeholders for their approval.
It documents all decisions made in the previous steps and clearly states the
intent, procedures, expected outcomes, timetable of events, and associated
budget. The <u>Evaluation Plan</u> must be a written agreement and included as part of
the contract when employing external evaluators. Exhibit 24 shows the inputs,
input requirements, supplier, outputs, output requirements, customer, and tasks
associated with developing an <u>Evaluation Plan</u>.

Exhibit 24: Develop the Evaluation Plan

Supplier	Input	Input Req.	TASKS	Output	Output Req.	Customer
Task No. 4 of the Plan phase of the Training Evaluation Process.	Interview data from evaluation stake-holders.	Accurate date. Reflects stakeholders' opinion. Not biased by the evaluator.	Write Evaluation Plan.	Preliminary Evaluation Plan.	Accurate, reflects wishes of evaluation stakeholders and evaluation policy directions. Understandable by the layperson. Written in timely manner.	Task No. 6: Obtain agreement to the evaluation plan of the Plan phase.

The written Evaluation Plan contains the following:

1. Object of the evaluation or a description of the course or courses to be evaluated.
2. Purpose(s) for evaluating - the rationale for conducting the evaluation. Including the following:

    A. Purpose of the training evaluation by level and course (if multiple courses will be evaluated).
    B. The reason the evaluation is being conducted.
    C. How the results of the evaluation will be used .

3. For each of the four level of evaluation, the following items are documented:

    A. Questions the evaluation will answer as identified and agreed upon by evaluation stakeholders.
    B. Data collection procedures or the methodologies that will be used to accumulate data to answer the evaluation questions.
    C. Data analysis procedures or the scheme that will be used to analyze the collected data.

4. Reporting plan or the strategy for developing and delivering written or oral evaluation reports and presentations.
5. Methods of controlling and assessing bias or the steps the evaluator(s) will follow to ensure an unbiased and truthful evaluation.
6. Timeline or the projected schedule of events with associated deadlines and time-frames for completion of critical milestones within the evaluation project. Such timelines are usually developed starting from the reporting date and working backwards to ensure completion of the evaluation.
7. Contract amendment and termination procedures or the procedures for modifying the contract between the evaluators and the individual or organization who is funding the project.
8. Budget for the evaluation or the funds necessary to conduct the evaluation, i.e., travel, salary, data processing, printing, and duplicating.
9. Signature of approval - confirmation by the funding organization(s) to spend the funds and conduct the evaluation .

A sample Evaluation Plan is provided at the end of this chapter.

-- END OF TASK 5 --

6. OBTAINMENT AGREEMENT TO THE EVALUATION PLAN.

An Evaluation Plan that is written that no one agrees to is worthless. The entire reason for planning an evaluation is to develop an approved, agreed upon plan. This final step in the Planning phase of the Training Evaluation Process solidifies the evaluation intent. The evaluation may not continue until the Evaluation Plan is approved by the funding organization and agreed upon by key evaluation stakeholders, therefore setting funds aside to be spent on evaluation. Exhibit 25 depicts the inputs, input requirements, supplier, outputs, output requirements, customer, and tasks associated with this task.

Exhibit 25: Obtain agreement to the Evaluation Plan

Supplier	Input	Input Req.	TASKS	Output	Output Req.	Customer
Task No. 5 of the Plan phase of the Training Evaluation Process.	Preliminary Evaluation Plan.	Satisfies all output requirements of task No. 5 of the Plan phase.	Distribute Preliminary Evaluation Plan to all stake-holders and funding organiza-tion(s).	Approved Evaluation Plan.	Plan approved by funding organiza-tion(s) and evaluation stake-holders	The first task of the Develop phase of the Training Eval-uation Process.
			Solicit responses to the plan.			
			Make changes as required.			
			Produce final Evaluation Plan.			

After writing the Evaluation Plan, copies must be distributed *to the funding organization and key stakeholders.* After the funding organization and key stakeholders have received a copy, a meeting is held to discuss any questions or discrepancies.   At the meeting with all concerned parties, *responses to the plan are solicited.* The responses will come in one of two forms: agreement to the plan as is, or proposed changes.If changes are proposed they must be realistic and within the boundaries of corporate evaluation direction.   At times respondents to the Evaluation Plan will propose changes that are unrealistic, too costly, or beyond the scope of training evaluation. If this happens, a meeting is held with the respondent to discuss the changes and to negotiate what should be. Then *the changes should be made as required.* For example, if a respondent submits a lengthy list of evaluation questions, the evaluator must rank order the questions and answer as many as time and money will allow.

Then the final Evaluation Plan. is written. This document will drive the evaluation effort. An agreed upon, approved plan is essential for the Training Evaluation Process to be successful.

-- END OF TASK 6 --

SUMMARY

The Plan phase of the Training Evaluation Process provides you with the

groundwork for a successful evaluation. It provides a step-by-step series of work
tasks that produce an <u>Evaluation Plan</u> that documents the evaluation project.
Exhibit 26 summarizes each task within the Plan phase and shows the output
produced by each task.

Exhibit 26: Summary of Plan Phase

Task	Output
1. Identify and define the course(s) (object) to be evaluated.	Identified courses(s) for evaluation
2. Determine if evaluation is required. If so, what levels should be performed?	Evaluation decision.
3. Identify evaluation stakeholders.	List of evaluation stakeholders ranked in order of importance.
4. Interview evaluation stakeholders.	A. Evaluation purpose(s). B. Evaluation audiences. C. Elements that may affect the evaluation. D. Questions the evaluation will answer.
5. Develop the <u>Evaluation Plan</u>.	<u>Preliminary Evaluation Plan</u>.
6. Obtain agreement to the <u>Evaluation Plan</u>.	Approved <u>Evaluation Plan</u>.

References

1. Sullivan, R. L., Wircenski, J. L., Arnold S. S., and Sarkees, M. D., (1990). *Trainers Guide - A Practical Manual for the Design, Delivery, and Evaluation of Training*, Rockville, Maryland: Aspen

2-5. Brinkerhoff, R. O., Brethower, D. M., Hluchyj, T., Nowakowski, J. R., (1983). *Program Evaluation - A Practioner's Guide for Trainers and Educators*, Boston, MA: Kluwer-Nijhoff

Sample Evaluation Plan

A PLAN FOR EVALUATING
THE DISTRICT SALES
MANAGERS' SCHOOL

ABC   Corporation
Mary T. Evaluator, Manager Training Evaluation

OBJECT OF THE EVALUATION

The subject of the evaluation is a new Sales District Managers Training course being developed by a corporation's training development department. The course will be taught in a traditional classroom mode by selected instructors from the training department. The course is projected to be a three-day program which provides the Corporation's District Sales Manager with intensive training on financial analysis of the potential market and methodology for penetrating those markets.

Key organizations who have a stake (vested interest) in the training program are;

> *Office of the Chief Executive*
> *Vice President of Marketing*
> *Training department*

Since the goals, objectives, and strategies for the training program have already been established, reviewed, and accepted by the stakeholders (as documented in the training plan), this evaluation will focus on process evaluation (is the program being implemented as designed?) and product evaluation (are we meeting the goals and objectives of the program?). The evaluation will be conducted in a formative manner by providing information to staff in order to improve the training program and to get it running as smoothly and efficiently as possible.

PURPOSE OF THE EVALUATION

The purpose of the evaluation is to determine the following:

1. *What the participants liked and disliked about the training,*
2. *The amount of learning that occurred because of the training,*
3. *To what degree participants have transferred the course skills successfully to their jobs, and*
4. *What return-on-investment has the Corporation received due to conducting the training?*

The information collected will be used in two ways:

1. *To identify and correct problems associated with the training, thus improving the program (process evaluation), and*
2. *To verify the worth and merit of the training (product evaluation).*

QUESTIONS THE EVALUATION WILL ANSWER

*All evaluation questions were obtained by interviewing key stakeholders.
Approval of the evaluation will come from stakeholders listed previously in the
plan.*

Level 1

1. How did the participants feel about the quality of the ...

   A. course materials
   B. business aids
   C. written exercises?

2. How did the participant feel about the sequence of the materials?
3. How did the participant feel about the quality of the instructor's...

   A. presentation
   B. asking and answering questions
   C. availability
   D. pace of instruction
   E. knowledge of subject?

4. How did the participant feel about the course objectives as they relate to...

   A. the participant's job requirements
   B. the degree they are willing to perform the course objectives
   C. the applicability to the participant's job?
   D. What did the participants feel were ...

      * the strong points of the course
      * the weak points of the course
      * areas that need to be added
      * areas that need to be removed
      * areas that need improvement?

5. What did the participants feel would be the problems in implementing the
   skills training has provided?

Level 2

1. By learning objective, what skills and knowledge were acquired in
   training?
2. For cognitive objectives, what amount of learning occurred in training?

3. *Given a case study and a financial analysis model, are the participants able to accurately predict the success of a specified marketing strategy while in training?*

Level 3

1. *How many times have the participants applied course objectives (behaviors) on-the-job?*
2. *Which of the following are reasons for not applying the behavior on-the-job?*

    A. *purilctpant did not acquire the knowledge and skill in training*
    B. *participant acquired the knowledge and skill in training, but has since forgotten*
    C. *participant acquired the knowledge and skill in training, but felt it was not relevant therefore, did not use it*
    D. *participant acquired the knowledge and skill in training, but the job does not require it*
    E. *the ABC Corporation work environment has not allowed the behavior to be practiced*
    F. *others, specified by the respondents*

3. *By objective, how has training impacted (positively or negatively) the participants' job performance?*
4. *What skills have participants had to learn on their own to perform a related job behavior that training did not provide?*

Level 4

1. *What expenses were incurred during the development and delivery of the training?*
2. *What value (expressed as dollars) has ABC Corporation received due to conducting the training?*
3. *What is the return-on-investment from training?*

DATA COLLECTION PROCEDURES

Level 1: Reaction

A questionnaire completed by all participants and a class interview will gather data to answer the level 1 evaluation questions. A member of the evaluation team or education management team will conduct the interview of the entire class at or near the completion of training. All participants will complete the level 1 questionnaire prior to graduation from the class. The instruments

*(questionnaire and interview) will be created by the course development
organization and certified as acceptable by the evaluation team.*

Level 2: Learning

*A pre-test and a post-test will be administered to evaluate the amount of
learning gained for all cognitive training objectives. All behavioral training
objectives will be evaluated against the standard stated in the objective by
means of observing participant performance in a workshop (practical exercise)
and recording results on a performance checklist. The instruments (pre-test,
post-test, workshop, and performance checklist) will be created by the course
development organization and certified as acceptable by the evaluation team.*

Level 3: Behavior

*A post-course questionnaire will be completed by all participants six months
after training completion. The data will be used to answer the level 3
evaluation questions and determine what changes to the training will be required
and, if necessary, what "booster" training may be necessary. In addition to the
questionnaire, ten percent of the participant population will be interviewed by
telephone to gather additional level 3 data. The instruments (questionnaire and
telephone interview) will be created by the course development organization and
certified as acceptable by the evaluation team.*

Level 4: Results

*The education proficiency system (a system that shows which district managers
have and have not completed training) will be used to extrapolate a control
group (managers who have not completed training) and an experimental group
(those managers who have successfully completed training). Candidates will be
randomly chosen to generate equal sample sizes in the control and experimental
groups. The company's sales tracking system and generated reports will be used
to analyze results of the control and experimental groups for the six month
period after training completion (value of training).*

*Existing data and accounting records will be used with permission from the
owners of the records. The cost to develop and deliver training to the
experimental group will be extrapolated from the accounting records of the
training, development and delivery department (cost). To this end, a numerator
and denominator are calculated to yield results evaluation [(value of
training)/(cost) = results evaluation.] Due to a lack of pure experimental
design, (not all group members had opportunity to participate) the evaluators
will only make judgments after comparison of the data, and will not try to
prove its statistical significance.*

DATA   ANALYSIS   PROCEDURES

Level 1: Reaction

Level 1 results will be compiled by the evaluation team for the validation (pilot) class and two subsequent classes. Participants will respond to a questionnaire and interviews. The results will be analyzed by the evaluation team and course materials will be modified as necessary. Evaluators will summarize data from the questionnaires finding an average mean score. Patterns will then be detected in the open-ended and interview questions. If 50% or more of participants responded similarly to various questions, appropriate modifications will be made. Subsequent analysis will occur every five classes.

Level 2: Learning

Level 2 results will be analyzed by the evaluation team and the course development organization at the conclusions of the pilot class or classes. Pre-test and post-test scores along with scores from performance workshops indicate participant achievement and mastery of course objectives. In order for the training program to be deemed acceptable and released for general attendance the following minimum evaluation marks must be met or exceeded:

1. *90% of the validation participants must achieve 90% or greater on their post-tests and performance workshops, and*
2. *the average percent of gain score comparing learning gained by participants must be 85% or greater.*

Calculations performed on pre-tests, post-tests, and performance workshop scores will include highest score, lowest score, range, mean, median, standard deviation, and t-score. Using a preassigned judgment (.01 level of significance), t-scores will be performed on pre-tests and post-tests to determine if the learning gain is a true representation of learning.

The percent of gain score indicates what percentage (based upon 100%) the participant could have learned. The gain score is computed as:

Gain score = [(Post test - Pre test) / (100 - Pre test)] x 100

Item analysis of pre-test results will be performed to assess what participants knew before entering the training program. Course objectives / content / test items will be modified to meet the entry level of the participant population. Post-test and performance workshop scores will have an item analysis to assess what objectives the participants could not master. Results from this analysis will then be used to modify the content and/or the test.

Level 3: Behavior

Level 3 results will be analyzed by the evaluation team, course development organization, and the course delivery organization. Level 3 data, collected six months after course completion, will be analyzed using the same process as level 1.

Level 4: Results

Level 4 results will be analyzed by the evaluation team. Raw data from the sales tracking system will be input into a statistical software package sorted by individual district results by control and experimental groups. Mean data for each individual will be calculated on the following measures:

1. *orders proposed*
2. *orders won*
3. *orders lost*
4. *close rate*
5. *win rate*

Cost of training will be divided into the following categories and summed:

1. *design cost*
2. *development cost*
3. *course development*
4. *travel*
5. *reproduction*
6. *word processing*
7. *art work*
8. *delivery cost*

    A. *participant salaries while in training*
    B. *trainer salaries while training and during preparation*
    C. *travel expenses (participants and trainers)*
    D. *airlines*
    E. *rental cars*
    F. *lodging*
    G. *meals*
    H. *facilities*
    I. *room rental*
    J. *equipment purchase*
    K. *participant materials*

Training value will be the difference between the control and experimental group results.

REPORTING   PLAN

Report   Responsibilities

There are two acceptable methods for writing both the Evaluation Report of the Pilot Program and the Final Evaluation Report.

1. *The evaluator writes the first five components with a joint effort of the evaluator and course developer writing the last two components, or*
2. *The evaluator writes the first five components and the last two are written solely by the course developer.*

Whatever the chosen method, the responsibilities of both parties must be stated in the Reporting Plan.

Evaluation Report of the Pilot Program

An Evaluation Report of the pilot, in accordance with ABC Corporation's Training Evaluation Process, will be written no later than two weeks after conclusion of the pilot class. The report will be written to the Vice President of Marketing and to all right-to-know audiences. Proposed content of the report is:

1. *Front Cover*
2. *Executive Summary*
3. *Background of the training program*
4. *Description of the evaluation study*
5. *Evaluation results*
6. *Discussion of the results*
7. *Plans of action*

Final Evaluation Report

The Final Evaluation Report, in accordance with ABC Corporation's Training Evaluation Process and outlined in this plan, will be written no later than one month after completion of the levels 3 and 4 evaluation studies. The report will be written to the Vice President of Marketing and to all right-to-know audiences. Proposed content of the report is:

1. *Front Cover*
2. *Executive Summary*
3. *Background of the training program*
4. *Description of the evaluation study*
5. *Evaluation results*
6. *Discussion of the results*
7. *Plans of action*

METHODS OF CONTROLLING AND ADDRESSING BIAS

Data Collection Bias

An outside evaluator, other than the instructor, will be used when administering level 1 instrumentation in order to avoid influence by the instructor's physical presence in the room. The outside evaluator must make certain the participants know that the program, not the participants, is being evaluated for the purpose of program improvement. A nominated participant will be responsible for passing out and collecting level 1 questionnaires and then delivering them to the proper location for analysis. Bias is generally not a concern in levels 2, 3, and 4 due to the nature of the evaluation procedures.

Analysis Bias

The course development organization and the evaluation team will perform the analysis jointly. The evaluation team will insure a true analysis is performed in light of the data available.

Reporting Bias

The evaluation team will distribute the report to all stakeholders and right-to-know audiences as identified in this plan.

TIMELINE

When	*What*
November 12	*First pilot class - level 1 and level 2 data collected*
November 19-21	*Level 1 and level 2 data analyzed and interpreted*
November 28	*Second pilot class - level 1 and level 2 data collected*
December 5-6	*Level 1 and level 2 data analyzed and interpreted*
December 10	*Evaluation Report of Pilot Program written and distributed*
June 3-24	*Level 3 data collection period*
June 25-28	*Level 3 data analyzed and interpreted*
July 15-19	*Level 4 data collection period*
July 24-26	*Level 4 data analyzed and interpreted*
August 12	*Final Evaluation Report written and distributed*

CONTRACT AMENDMENT AND TERMINATION PROCEDURES

Amendment

The agreement may be amended and modified at any time in writing, or any provisions may be waived by an instrument in writing executed by the evaluator and client or either of them in the case of a waiver.

Termination by Either Party

The agreement may be terminated by either party giving ten days written notice of termination to the other party. Termination shall not prejudice any other remedy that the terminating party may have either at law, in equity, or under this agreement.

Termination   Notices

Any notice to be given under this agreement by either party to the other may be effected by personal delivery in writing or by mail, registered or certified, postage prepaid with return receipt requested. Mailed notices shall be addressed to the parties at the addresses indicated within the contract, but each party must adopt a new address by written notice in accordance with this paragraph. Notices delivered shall be deemed communicated as of three days' after mailing.

Effect of Termination on Compensation

If this contract is terminated prior to completion of term employment specified in the contract, the evaluator shall be entitled to compensation earned prior to the date of termination as provided for in this contract computed pro rata up to and including that date. The evaluator shall be entitled to no further compensation as of the date of termination.

4. DEVELOP EVALUATION PROCEDURES

Purpose of This Chapter

The purpose of this chapter is to provide you with the ability to perform the second phase of the Training Evaluation Process -- *Develop Evaluation Procedures*. These activities encompass taking the <u>Evaluation Plan</u> and developing <u>data collection instruments</u> and <u>analysis models</u> necessary for conducting a successful training evaluation. Development of evaluation instruments and their corresponding analysis models are essential to a successful evaluation. These evaluation tools, if constructed correctly, collect and summarize course results so that you can answer the questions posed in the <u>Evaluation Plan</u>. The instruments must be easy to use and convey a sense of professionalism by the evaluator.

Objectives of This Chapter

At the conclusion of this chapter, you can:

1. Create a Level 1 questionnaire that meets the requirements defined in an <u>Evaluation Plan</u>.
2. Create a Level 1 whole class interview.
3. Create Level 2 Pre-test and post-tests. Within the body of the tests you will use the following type of test items:

   A. Multiple choice

B. True-False
C. Matching
D. Short-answer
E. Essay.

4. Create Level 2 performance tests.
5. Create the following Level 3 data collection instruments:

A. Questionnaire
B. Action Plan
C. Interviews
D. Focus Groups
E. Observation Procedures

6. For Level 4 evaluations create the following data collection instruments:

A. Develop procedures which accurately calculate the cost of training development and delivery.
B. Develop techniques to determine training value.
C. Create models (for each level of evaluation) to analyze collected data.

DEVELOPING EVALUATION PROCEDURES

Exhibit 27: The Develop Phase of the Training Evaluation Process

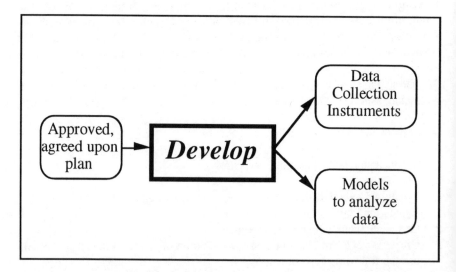

Developing evaluation procedures involves taking the input (approved, agreed upon <u>Evaluation Plan</u>) from Phase 1 and drafting the techniques, procedures, and instruments necessary to implement the plan. During the *Develop* phase, all levels of evaluation are addressed, as defined in the Evaluation Plan. For example, if the plan only calls for Level 1 & 2, Levels 3 & 4 are not addressed during this phase. The data collection instruments and analysis models are developed to ease proper summation of data. The activities associated with this phase are 1) creating data collection instruments to gather evaluation data at each level and 2) developing models to analyze data. Output of the *Develop* phase comes in two forms:

1. Instruments to collect data, and
2. Models to analyze collected data.

The data collection instruments are designed to collect data that in turn are analyzed to answer the evaluation questions. The instruments may assume a variety of forms depending upon their intent and level of evaluation. Data analysis models are input to the *Analyze phase* of the Training Evaluation Process and are designed to compliment data collection instruments. The analysis instruments and models assume a variety of forms designed by the evaluator and are a method of summarizing collected data. Models are created by the course developer or an evaluator.

DEVELOP INPUTS

Input to this phase is the approved, agreed upon Evaluation Plan from the Plan phase of the Training Evaluation Process. It documents all decisions made in that phase in a form that clearly states the intent, procedures, expected outcomes, timetable of events, and associated budget for the evaluation. The Evaluation Plan conforms to requirements stated in the Plan phase contains the following topics:

1. Object of the evaluation.
2. Purpose(s) for evaluating.
3. For each level of evaluation (1 through 4) the following items are documented:

   A. Questions the evaluation will answer
   B. Data collection procedures
   C. Data analysis procedures

4. Reporting Plan.
5. Methods of controlling and assessing bias.
6. Timeline.
7. Contract amendment and termination procedures.
8. Budget for the evaluation.

9. Signature of approval.

TASKS - DEVELOP PHASE

The Develop phase of the Training Evaluation Process, just as with the Planning phase, has a series of tasks that manipulate input into output that conforms to customer requirements. The three (3) tasks associated with developing training evaluation instruments and models are:

1. Generate data collection instruments (Levels 1-4).
2. Create models to analyze data for Levels 1-4.
3. Obtain agreement with key stakeholders to the data collection instruments and analysis models.

Each task that comprises the Develop phase follows.

1. GENERATE DATA COLLECTION INSTRUMENTS (LEVELS 1-4)

A data collection instrument is an information gathering device administered at the appropriate stages in the training process (defined in the Evaluation Plan). Instruments come in a variety of forms and are usually divided into the following categories:

1. Questionnaires
2. Interviews
3. Tests (cognitive and performance-based)
4. Observation forms

Exhibit 28 depicts all the process requirements associated with generating data collection instruments.

Exhibit 28: Generate Data Collection Instruments

Supplier	Input	Input Req.	TASKS	Output	Output Req.	Customer
The Plan phase of the Training Evaluation Process.	Evaluation Plan.	Approved and agreed upon by the key evaluation stakeholders.	Understand the use of the instrument. Generate, when required, data collection instrument for each level of evaluation specified in the Evaluation Plan.	Data collection instruments.	Meets needs defined Evaluation Plan. Satisfies all requirements of proper instrument design. Expenses are within the budget. Instruments are generated in a timely manner	Task No. 2: Create models to analyze data for levels 1-4 of the Develop phase.

Before developing a data collection instrument (independent of evaluation level), several questions must be answered. These questions provide the evaluator the ability to focus on the optimum design for the intended purpose. The questions to be answered are:

How will the data be used? Before selecting or designing an instrument, the basic purpose(s) of the evaluation is reviewed. A data collection instrument must provide data that supports the evaluation purpose and can be used to answer evaluation questions. Data that is not used in this light is worthless to the evaluation. Only collect data that supports the evaluation. At times, during business practices, your evaluation stakeholders will ask that collected data is not associated with training (i.e., success of new product or service in the market place). Be sure that data you collect is only training evaluation data. Another pitfall to avoid is using evaluation data for personnel evaluation instead of program evaluation. Do not allow collected data to infer giving grades to participants (A, B, C, 100%, 90%, 80%, etc.) or be used in performance reviews for instructional systems designers, course developers, or instructors.

How will data be analyzed? Data is collected to be tabulated, summarized, and reported to others. The types of analyses, including statistical comparisons, are considered at design time. Design data collection instruments so that data can be easily summarized and analyzed. The overriding question directing the work is *will the analysis procedures provide you with information to answer the evaluation questions?*

Who will use the information? Another important consideration is the audience for the evaluation report. Who will be reviewing the information in its raw state or summarized manner? This will help provide data that they will easily understand.

What facts are needed? Facts are needed for an effective evaluation. What are the specific costs, output, time, quality, attitudes, reactions, or observations (evaluation measures) to be collected by the instrument? An important ingredient for instrument design is to decide what is considered successful training results. This is defined as the quality goal of training. For example: at Motorola University, Level 2 Learning goals are set at eighty percent of the participants achieve a mean score of eighty percent or greater. This is known as the 80/80 rule. If the participants within a course session achieve the 80/80 goal, then the course is considered within specification or "spec" and has achieved its quality goal. Quality goals such as these are set for all levels and are used to track training quality on a session-by-session basis.

Should the instrument be tested? Testing an instrument gives the opportunity to analyze the data collected to see if there are any problems with the instrument and is an integral part of the validation process. By testing the instrument, any flaws in instrument design are corrected thus allowing you to use an instrument that will reduce biases due to improper design.

Is there a standard instrument? Sometimes standard instruments can be more effective with less cost than custom designed instruments. The chosen instruments must, however, be proven valid and reliable for its purpose. If the standard instrument is appropriate it should be used. Standard instrumentality is most common in Level 1 evaluation where a training department uses the same questionnaire for all courses.

What are the consequences of wrong answers or biased information? When evaluation data is supplied voluntarily and anonymously, the participant's biases can enter into the information. Unless opinions and attitudes are sought, the information may be unreliable. Steps should be taken to prevent this.

Once, you have addressed and answered these questions, you can begin generating data collection instruments. The steps and techniques necessary to create these instruments will be discussed.

Level 1: Reaction Instruments

Level 1 data collection instruments usually encompass one of two forms:

1. Questionnaire.
2. Group or individual interview forms.

Questionnaires are usually provided to participants at the conclusion of the course session. Yet, this is common practice but may not be the best method for gathering participant reactions. Short questionnaires at the conclusion of each course module or at the end of the day may provide better data to answer evaluation questions. The Evaluation Plan will specify when Level 1 questionnaires should be distributed to collect data. Knowing when distribution occurs greatly effects the design and generation of the instrument(s).

Questionnaire design is an important aspect to collecting accurate, reliable, and usable Level 1 data. When beginning the design of a Level 1 questionnaire use the "three column" approach. This technique is useful in sorting out good questions from bad. Start with a blank sheet of paper (or file if you are using a word processor on a computer) and divide it into three columns. The column on the left of the page contains actual questions as they will appear on the instrument. The middle column documents what program improvement techniques can be implemented if responses from participants are unacceptable and the Quality Rating is low. The right hand column contains who is responsible for implementing the changes. Exhibit 29 shows an example of this technique.

Exhibit 29:   Three Column Approach

1. The examples used in the course were helpful in allowing me to understand the material.
 	
   * Strongly agree
   * Agree
   * Disagree
   * Strongly disagree
   * No examples were used
	A. Examples may not be realistic for the participants.
	B. Examples are not matched to the course content.
	C. Examples are difficult for the participants to understand.
		Instructional Design Organization

2. The speed at which the training was delivered was . . .
 	
   *   Too fast
   *   Just about right
   *   Too slow
	A. Too much information is being delivered for the participant to comprehend at one time. Consider adding class discussion, practice work, or small breaks. to the course design.
	B. Pace needs to be quickened. Look for areas where redundancy exists and reduce or eliminate them.
	C. Counsel with the instructor on slowing down or speeding up delivery.
		A. Instructional Design Organization
		
		B. Instructional Design Organization
		C. Training Delivery Organization

As each question is written, describe in detail the procedures that should be followed if low scores are realized and who would correct it. If you cannot write sound reasons for improving the course, then this evaluation question may not be realistic or even needed. Also, be sure the procedures for improvement match the evaluation purpose and are tied to at least one evaluation question from the Evaluation Plan. Along with this format, a good practice is to group Level 1 questions in like evaluation categories. Typical categories used are:

Course Significance - this segment evaluates how the participants feel the course is applicable to their jobs or their personal needs.

Participant Scholarship - this section deals with the participants' feelings of how well they learned the material presented in the course.

Course Strategy - this portion deals with participant opinions if the instructional design and approach used were effective and offered a variety of stimulating successful learning experiences.

Instructor - this section chronicles how participants rate the instructor, if the course is taught in traditional classroom method.

<u>General Course Opinion</u> - this measure determines what participants felt about the entire learning experience.

Examples of questions dealing with <u>Course Significance</u> are:

1. *The course content met my expectations.*

   Exceeded   Met   Not Met

2. *The course has increased my capability of performing current or future job tasks.*

   Strongly   Agree   Disagree   Strongly   Unable
   Agree   Disagree   to judge

3. *With respect to my current or future job needs, the course was available to me . . .*

   Too Early   Just in Time   Too Late

4. *I had the skills or knowledge I needed to begin this course.*

   Strongly   Agree   Disagree   Strongly   Unable
   Agree   Disagree   to judge

Examples of questions dealing with <u>Participant Scholarship</u> are:

5. *The degree to which I feel I met the course objective on Designing a Training Evaluation is . . .*

   Very   High   Low   Very
   High   Low

6. *The degree to which I feel I met the course objective on Analyzing and Interpreting a training evaluation is . . .*

   Very   High   Low   Very
   High   Low

Examples of questions dealing with <u>Course Strategy</u> are:

7. *The examples presented for me to understand the content were . . .*

   Very   Helpful   OK   Not   Useless   Unable to
   Helpful   Helpful   Judge

8. *The variety of course activities was . . .*

    Too Much   OK   Not Enough

9. *The course activities, simulations, or games were . . .*

    Very   Helpful   OK   Not   Useless   None
    Helpful   Helpful   Used

10. *The course was taught in a logical sequence.*

    Strongly   Agree   Disagree   Strongly
    Agree   Disagree

11. *The time allotted for me to practice what I learned was . . .*

    Too Much   OK   Not Enough   Not Applicable

12. *The time allotted for questions was . . .*

    Too Much   OK   Not Enough

13. *The course length was . . .*

    Too Long   OK   Too Short

14. *The information in the Participant Guide is easy to read and understand.*

    Strongly   Agree   Disagree   Strongly
    Agree   Disagree

Examples of questions dealing with the <u>Instructor</u> are:

15. *All the information included in the Participant Guide was presented in the*
    course.

    Yes   No   Unable to Judge

16. *The instructor was well prepared.*

    Strongly   Agree   Disagree   Strongly
    Agree   Disagree

17. *The speed at which the instructor provided information was . . .*

    Too Fast   OK   Too Slow

18. The subject matter knowledge of the instructor was . . .

   Outstanding   Above   OK   Poor   Unsatisfactory
                  Average

19. The instructor's presentation skills are . . .

   Outstanding   Above   OK   Poor   Unsatisfactory
                  Average

20. The instructor's ability to communicate the material was . . .

   Outstanding   Above   OK   Poor   Unsatisfactory
                  Average

Example of a question dealing with <u>General Course Opinion</u> is:

21. Overall, I was satisfied with the course.

   Yes   No

Questionnaire Design

Level 1 questionnaire design allows you to enhance the validity of the data collected. When designing a questionnaire, follow the recommendations listed below[1]:

1. Word the questions on the instrument to maximize the validity of the data gathered.
2. Design the questionnaire to ensure data are gathered anonymously.
3. Inform the participant of the questionnaire's purpose.
4. Construct the instrument so that it relates positively to evaluation purpose/questions.
5. Write no questions until you have thought through the evaluation purpose.
6. Ask yourself *"Why do I want to know this?"*
7. Present all reasonable alternatives for closed questions. A closed question is one in which there are a finite series of ways the respondent can answer. For example, *"The pace of this course was..." a. too fast, b. just right, c. too slow.*
8. Use words the participant will understand.
9. Add memory clues thus improving the quality of the data collected. An example of a poor question is, *"The workshop was..." a. excellent, b. average, c. poor, etc. "The workshop Monday afternoon in which we installed this computer system was..." a. excellent, b. average, c. poor,* becomes a much better question simply by adding the memory clues.
10. Use open-ended questions to gain the participants' feeling in their words

when a finite set of responses is impractical. For example,
"The following areas need to be added to improve the training program:"

_____

_____

11. Order the questions. Start with easy, non-threatening questions first, move from general questions to more specific questions, finally complete questions on a single topic before moving on to a new topic. For example, discuss the quality of the instructor, then quality of the materials, then quality of the program, etc.

12. Arrange the types of questions to increase variety and reduce redundancy in responding. For example, do not arrange the best answers in a line whereby participants can keep checking the same response without reading the question.

13. Use filter questions - questions asked to branch to areas of the instrument to handle all contingencies. For example:

Exhibit 30: Filter Question

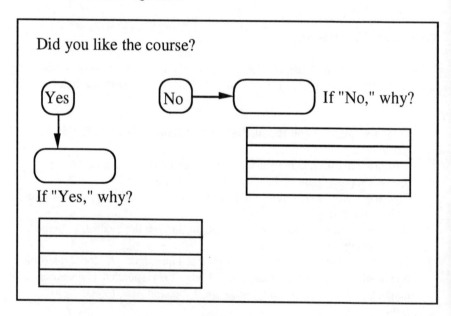

In this example, if the participant responds "Yes" they are asked to provide additional data. However, if the participant responds "No," the instrument directs them to another area on the questionnaire. Proper design of a Level 1 questionnaire allows for gathering accurate, timely data that simplifies analysis. After the initial design of the instrument, address formatting the questionnaire. Formatting a Level 1 questionnaire looks at the appearance of the instrument. Properly prepared and professionally looking instruments enhance the accuracy of collected data.

Therefore, when formatting Level 1 questionnaires, they should:

1. Look easy to answer and professionally designed and printed.
2. Include the date, title of evaluation, and the name of the organization conducting the evaluation on the first page of the instrument.
3. Include an area to gather participant background information. For example, job description, years with company, years of experience, etc.
4. Provide proper spacing (white space) to avoid crowding.
5. Use sufficiently large and clear type.
6. Have each question numbered and each subpart lettered.
7. Do not split a question between two pages.
8. Do not exceed two pages printed front-to-back.
9. Provide directions with distinctive type. For example, the instructions could be in *italics* and the questions in standard type.
10. End with a thank you. Show appreciation for their time and effort.

Remember, a properly formatted questionnaire enhances the collected data. Once general design and formatting techniques have been considered, actual preparation of the questionnaire can begin. The steps taken to create Level 1 questionnaires are to:

1. Decide what information is needed - this is provided in the Evaluation Plan.
2. Conduct a search of old files and other organizations for existing instruments, specific questions and rating scales. Reusing existing, successful questionnaires will have a significant impact on the quality of the data collected, analyzed, reported, time expended, and budget.
3. Draft new questions/revise old.
4. Sequence the questions.
5. Format the questionnaire - be sure questions deal with participant feelings and are formatted and worded in such a way to extract participant reactions on the topic. For example, *"how did you feel...," "my opinion of...," "I believe..."*
6. Obtain peer evaluation - have another evaluator or participant critique the instrument.
7. Revise draft and test on pilot class - this is the first test of the questionnaire on the targeted population.
8. Revise after pilot to ensure the best instrument is available.
9. Implement as defined in the Evaluation Plan.

As with any work task, review what has been done to decide if it meets or exceeds standards established for that work. For Level 1 questionnaires, the Training Evaluation Process standards:

1. Use questions that relate to one idea, topic, or concern. If more than one idea is used, the participant may not know how to respond if they feel differently about each topic. If both ideas need to be evaluated, then generate two questions - one for each topic.
2. Ensure each question is under twenty (20) words. Questions that are longer tend to be confusing and yield evaluation data that is biased or skewed. Try to keep questions as simple as possible.
3. Use only familiar words on the form. The most common mistake is to use the language of the training business on the form. For example, a Level 1 question using training nomenclature is: *I felt I mastered the course objectives.* The terms . . . *mastered the course objectives* are training terms and are very understandable to the training specialist but may be confusing to the participant. Rewording the question to: *I felt I understood the course material* is a simpler and more direct approach.
4. Use no words or phrases that are likely to influence responses are on the instrument.
5. Ensure questions are related in positive terms. Don't use a question where to answer affirmatively the response is negative. For example, a question that breaks the standard is:

    The instructor was not prepared.

    Strongly   Agree   Disagree   Strongly
    Agree   Disagree

6. Ensure each question does not encourage or discourage an answer. A well written questionnaire will solicit participant responses in an unbiased manner.
7. Ensure questions permit responses that show lack of knowledge or opinion without demeaning the participant. Typical responses to satisfy this requirement are:

    A. Unable to judge
    B. Not applicable
    C. Does not apply

Using standards such as these reduces the effects the instrument has on the data collected. Another area to consider when developing a Level 1 questionnaire, are the types of questions. Two types of questions can be used:

1. Closed response.
2. Open response.

Closed response questions ask questions and provide a finite set of responses for the participant to choose from. Open response questions require the participant to respond in their words. With closed response questions rating scales supply the participant with their responses. Different scales are used with different types of questions. The following scales are examples used with closed response questions:

<u>Frequency Scales</u> - used to find how often a participant perceived or has performed an activity. For example:

| Almost Always | Usually | About 50% of the time | Seldom | Never |

| Always | Frequently | Sometimes | Seldom | Never |

| Most of the time 75%-100% | Often 50%-75% | Sometimes 25%-50% | Seldom 0%-25% |

<u>Satisfaction Scales</u> - used to measure the level of satisfaction an activity has provided a participant. For example:

| Satisfied | Dissatisfied | Unable to Judge |

Completely Satisfied .... Completely Dissatisfied
   7 6 5 4 3 2 1

<u>Quality Scale</u> - used to decide how the participant perceived the quality aspect of an activity. For example:

| Outstanding | Good | Poor | Unsatisfactory |

<u>Agreement Scale</u> - used to report the intensity of the participant's feelings about an activity. For example:

| Strongly Agree | Agree | Disagree | Strongly Disagree |

<u>Semantic Differential</u> - a series of adjectives and their antonyms listed on opposite sides of the page with seven "attitude positions" in between used to collect participant reactions.

For example:

THE PACE OF THE INSTRUCTION WAS... (check the appropriate space)

FAST ____ ____ ____ ____ ____ ____ ____ *SLOW*
      7   6   5   4   3   2   1

This scale measures effect (participants' positive and negative feeling toward a statement about the course).

An example of a Level 1 questionnaire used at Motorola University is provided on the next two pages. This form is also designed to be scanned by an optical reader. The participants respond by filing in the circles on the form that are then read by an optical scanner, stored in a computer file, and finally loaded into a data base for storage, analysis, and reporting.

The example is the Participant Assessment form used at Motorola University and provided to assist in designing Level 1 questionnaires for training classes. This form was created using the "three column" approach mentioned earlier in this chapter.

Exhibit 31: Level 1 Questionnaire (page 1 of 2)

MOTOROLA UNIVERSITY

PARTICIPANT ASSESSMENT

Course Name: _____ Instructor Name: _____ Course Date: _____

CONTROL NUMBER

○ AIEG ○ UDS

○ CODEX ○ PTS

○ LMPS ○ SPS

○ CORP ○ SUPPLIER/CUSTOMER

○ GEG ○ OTHER

○ GSG/CELLULAR

My job matches the description located on the last page of the Participant Guide.

Yes ○   No ○   Expect To Match Within 1 Year. ○

Directions: Please fill in the circle which most closely describes your reactions to the training program you have just attended. Your feedback is important to Motorola University as we continually strive to reach total customer satisfaction. Thanks very much for your participation!

1. The course content met my expectations.

Exceeded	Met	Not Met
○	○	○

2. The course has increased my capability of performing current or future job tasks.

Strongly Agree	Agree	Disagree	Strongly Disagree	Unable to Judge
○	○	○	○	○

Please help us to understand why you disagree or strongly disagree?

_____
_____
_____

3. With respect to my current or future job needs, the course was available to me . . .

Too Early	Just in Time	Too Late
○	○	○

4. I had the skills or knowledge I needed to begin this course.

Strongly Agree	Agree	Disagree	Strongly Disagree	Unable to Judge
○	○	○	○	○

5. The degree to which I feel I met the course objectives is . . .
(See last page of the Participant Guide for description of objectives)

	Very High	High	OK	Low	Very Low
Objective #1	○	○	○	○	○
Objective #2	○	○	○	○	○
Objective #3	○	○	○	○	○
Objective #4	○	○	○	○	○
Objective #5	○	○	○	○	○

6. The examples presented for me to understand the content were . . .

Very Helpful	Helpful	OK	Not Helpful	Useless	Unable to Judge
○	○	○	○	○	○

7. The course activities, simulations, or games were . . .

Very Helpful	Helpful	OK	Not Helpful	Useless	None Used
○	○	○	○	○	○

If you responded not helpful or useless, how would you improve them?

_____
_____
_____

8. The variety of course activities was . . .

Too Much	OK	Not Enough
○	○	○

Please continue on the other side.

Exhibit 32: Level 1 Questionnaire (page 2 of 2)

9. The course was taught in a logical sequence.

Strongly Agree ○   Agree ○   Disagree ○   Strongly Disagree ○

10. The time allotted for me to practice what I learned was . . .

Too Much ○   OK ○   Not Enough ○   Not Applicable ○

11. The time allotted for questions was . . .

Too Much ○   OK ○   Not Enough ○

12. The course length was . . .

Too Long ○   OK ○   Too Short ○

13. The information in the Participant Guide (Class Materials) is easy to read and understand.

Strongly Agree ○   Agree ○   Disagree ○   Strongly Disagree ○

14. All of the information included in the Participant Guide was presented in the course.

Yes ○   No ○   Unable to Judge ○

15. The instructor was well prepared.

Strongly Agree ○   Agree ○   Disagree ○   Strongly Disagree ○

16. The speed at which the instructor provided information was . . .

Too Fast ○   OK ○   Too slow ○

17. The subject matter knowledge of the instructor was . . .
18. The instructor's presentation skills are . . .
19. The instructor's ability to encourage participation during the class was . . .
20. The instructor's ability to communicate the material was . . .

Outstanding ○ Above Average ○ OK ○ Poor ○ Unsatisfactory ○
○ ○ ○ ○ ○
○ ○ ○ ○ ○
○ ○ ○ ○ ○

21. The training facility or laboratory provided a quality environment to support the training experience.

Strongly Agree ○   Agree ○   Disagree ○   Strongly Disagree ○

22. The appearance and format of the printed materials was . . .

Outstanding ○   Above Average ○   OK ○   Poor ○   Unsatisfactory ○

23. Overall, I was satisfied with the course.

Yes ○   No ○

24. What would you consider to be the **strong points** of the course? _____

_____

25. What part (s) of the course do you feel need to be **expanded?** _____

_____

26. What area (s) do you feel should be **removed** from the course? _____

_____

27. What do you feel should be **added** to the course to make it better? _____

_____

28. GENERAL COMMENTS: _____

_____

This questionnaire is used in all Motorola University courses. The questionnaire contains some unique features that enhance evaluation data by it. These features being:

1. A provision to capture whether or not the participant believes they are part of the target population of the course. On the last page of the Participant Guide (course materials) the description of who the course is intended for is provided. The participant reads the description and marks one of three responses:

   A. Yes, I am part of the target audience.
   B. No, I am not part of the target audience.
   C. I expect to be part of the audience within one year. This is the proper response when the participant is in training for developmental purposes.

   The process for analyzing this data is to count the frequencies of participants choosing the three options, but to only include in the detailed analysis reports the individuals who responded "Yes" or "Expect to be within one year." This is done so that evaluation data and subsequent analysis is performed only on the defined participant.

2. Filter questions are used in questions 2 and 7. This provides further data when the participants rates the item low.
3. Question 5 allows the course to rate five learning objectives. The objectives are placed in the Participant Guide for the respondent to read and rate their learning. This allows analysis of learning on five sections of the course versus one or two.
4. Page two of the questionnaire contains five open-ended questions to gather course specific qualitative data.

Associated with this Level 1 questionnaire is a supporting three column document used in the development of the instrument. A portion of this document is shown in exhibit 33. The instructions which accompany the Motorola University Participant Assessment Analysis (three column document) are:

In order to effectively conduct a Level One Evaluation (participant reaction), the business must be cognizant of how the data collected from the Participant Assessment Form may be used for program improvement. As training professionals, we are all responsible for adding value to the training experience. However, some of the items in the Participant Assessment may be best investigated by a particular function and/or group.

This is the purpose of the following '3 column approach' to Level One Evaluation. The first column lists the assessment items and their corresponding response choices (The choices which have been defined as defects are underlined).

The second column offers suggestions on how to improve the program based on the responses received on the assessment item. The third column lists the functions/groups that may best be able to affect the program or situation change/modification. Our goal with Level One as a subset of all four levels of evaluation (Level 2: Learning, Level 3: Behavior, Level 4: Results) is simply TOTAL CUSTOMER SATISFACTION.

Exhibit 33: Participant Assessment Analysis

(M) MOTOROLA UNIVERSITY *Participant Assessment Analysis*		
Assessment Item	**How Data May be Used for Program Improvement**	**Suggested Area of Responsibility for Program Improvement**
1. The course content met my expectations. Exceeded Met Not Met	To initiate investigation as to possible content changes in terms of practical, job-related terms and examples. To initiate investigation as to possible discrepancies with content not matching the target population's assigned job tasks .	Course Designers/ SME's.
2. The course has increased my capability of performing current/future job tasks. Strongly Agree Agree Disagree Strongly Disagree	To begin analysis to determine which content areas are not perceived as mastery. Validate these perceptions against Level 2 evaluation data. Consider redesign of course content and instructional strategies.	Course Designers Instructors Course Developers

Level 1 Group or Individual Interview

Another form of level 1 data collection is interviewing selected participants or the entire class at completion of training. This is performed by someone other than the trainer and is usually the trainer's manager, group leader (supervisor), or evaluator.

The interview is conducted at the conclusion of training and follows selected topics determined by the interviewer. The purpose of the interview is to obtain additional Level 1 data from participants above and beyond the Level 1 questionnaire. An effective procedure for integrating Level 1 questionnaires with interviews is to:

1. Administer the Level 1 questionnaire during the last morning of training.
2. Give the results (completed questionnaire) to the scheduled interviewer.
3. Have the interviewer scan the Level 1 questionnaires looking for positive and negative patterns (not just one or two positive or negative responses).
4. The interviewer supplements the standard Level 1 interview form using the patterns found.
5. The instructor introduces the interviewer and explains the reason for the interview. The instructor then excuses themselves from the class and leaves.
6. Have the interviewer conduct the interview.

To conduct a successful interview, follow these guidelines.

1. Conduct interview as soon as possible or as defined in the Evaluation Plan.
2. Use a standard interview to obtain consistent Level 1 data.
3. Supplement the interview with additional questions unique to this course.
4. Review Level 1 questionnaire responses before conducting the interview. This will allow you to target the interview questions to areas that need further investigation.
5. Ensure the trainer is out of the classroom when the interview is conducted and allow participants to express their feelings in an open non-threatening atmosphere.
6. Have the interviewer introduce themselves and the purpose of interviewing ensuring that they stress to participants that this evaluation technique is for program improvement.

An example of a class interview form is on the next two pages.

Exhibit 34: Level 1 Whole Class Interview (page 1 of 2)

(M) **MOTOROLA UNIVERSITY** *Whole Class Interview*

Course Name: ——————— *Instructor* ———————
Course ——————— *Name:* ———————
Identification ——————— *Date:* ———————
Number: ——————— *Interviewer:* ———————

1. How well did you feel the class was set up when you arrived?
    What could be done to improve it?

2. Was all the equipment necessary to run the class operational?
    If no, specify:

3. How do you feel about the depth with which the instructor covered
    the topics?
    What topics needed more depth?
    What topics needed lees depth?

4. How do you feel about the length of the course?
    What sections should be shortened?
    Lengthened?

5. Was the information presented useful?
    What sections were very useful?
    What sections were not very useful?
    How would you change them to make them useful?

6. Was too much information presented at one time?

Exhibit 35: Level 1 Whole Class Interview (page 2 of 2)

(M) **MOTOROLA UNIVERSITY** *Whole Class Interview*

---

7. Was the information too redundant?

8. How would you change the lecture segment to make it more effective?

9. Were the discussions helpful?

10. Did the exercises provide effective practice for the skills presented?

11. Did the examples help you learn the steps (procedures) needed to do the exercises?

12. Were the exercise relevant?

13. Would the exercise be more effective if you worked in groups?

Course Specific Questions:

14. _____

    _____

15. _____

    _____

<u>Level 1 Instruments Summary</u>

Creation of Level 1 evaluation instruments, when done properly, establishes the cornerstone for successful training evaluations. With good Level 1 instruments in place, it is possible to move to Level 2: Learning Evaluation and beyond.

Level 2: Learning Instruments

Level 2 evaluation assesses how well the course provided participants with the ability to obtain the skills and knowledge contained in the training program. It is not just administering tests, critiquing presentations, conducting performance-based tests, and assigning grades. Although these activities are integral elements in Level 2 evaluation, they are simply the data collection portion of Level 2 evaluation. The real purpose is to assess that the course provides participants with the ability to master the course objectives and which objectives participants are unable to achieve. With this data, the course can be modified to increase the amount of learning gained by participants. Level 2 evaluation consists of some subset of the following activities:

1.   Administering written quizzes and tests (for cognitive objectives).
2.   Administering performance-based tests (for behavioral objectives) such as:

    A. Workshops
    B. Hands-on activities
    C. Presentations
    D. Demonstrations

    Performance-based tests, depending upon instructional design, are performed by participants individually, in small groups, or as whole class work. Level 2 evaluation does not create the exercises used in the course. This is done by the instructional designer and course developer. Level 2 evaluation simply develops data collection instruments to decide if participants have "arrived" at the desired learning level. In other words, the evaluation instruments surround the performanced-based tests already in place within the course.

3.   Evaluating participant attainment of course objectives using the test measures.
4.   Performing Pre-test/Post-test comparison.
5.   Conducting item analysis.

    Before constructing Level 2 evaluation instruments you must understand in what way the information gathered by instruments will be used. It is imperative that evaluation data be analyzed in the spirit of program improvement and not participant or trainer evaluation. Level 2 evaluation, along with other levels, generates large amounts of quantitative data. It is imperative that the data is not used to evaluate participants, instructional designers, course developers, or instructors. Correctly establishing an environment where all parties view the data in light of program improvement allows evaluations to be successful and build towards high quality training.

Level 2 evaluation determines the success of the course in providing the participants with the ability to attain the principles, facts, techniques, and skills presented in training. Data collection is performed by having participants complete mastery testing activities. Each participant's learning is measured so quantitative results can be determined. For proper Level 2 evaluation, learning is measured on an objective-by-objective basis where instructors or participants themselves measure participant achievement on each objective. Analysis of results provides insight as to possible program improvements.

However, all courses are not candidates for Level 2 evaluation. Certain conditions must be met in order for a course to be evaluated at Level 2. If the conditions are not met, the Training Evaluation Process will have a difficult time in providing accurate and usable information. To be a candidate for Level 2 evaluation, the course must:

1. Contain course objectives that are written in criterion-referenced-instruction form by stating:

   A. Condition
   B. Action
   C. Standard

   For example, a well written objective is:

   Given a blank floor plan of the building, the participant will label the following in the appropriate blanks on the map:

   - *Front desk*
   - *Rest rooms*
   - *Auditorium*
   - *Dining room*

   All locations will be labeled correctly and filled in from memory.

   Training departments typically use Criterion Referenced Testing that provides information on how a participant performs relative to a specific standard (course objective).

Types of tests typically used are:

A. Selected response tests:

* Multiple choice
* True/false
* Matching

B. Constructed response tests:

* Essay
* Short answer
* Oral response

C. Performance-based tests (work simulations or practice exercises):

* Workshops
* Hands-on activities
* Presentations
* Demonstrations

2. Evaluate all terminal (major) objectives.
3. Focus on the individual participant. At times, due to course design, participants will perform as part of a team or group. The evaluation effort must focus on individual participant learning versus the group experience. The only time evaluation can assess group learning is when:

A. The objective clearly states the learning as a group achievement.
B. Instruction, content, and performanced-based exercises are all group related.
C. On-the-job performance will always be performed as part of a group.

Development of Level 2 instruments depends upon the learning objective and content being tested. The instrument must match the measure stated in the objective and conform to the condition articulated. In other words, the objective directs the type and amount of Level 2 Learning instrument developed and implemented.

As with construction of any evaluation instrument, there is a step-by-step process to follow. The process for constructing Level 2 instruments is to:

1. Meet with the instructional designer, course developer, and/or subject matter expert to review the Instructional Design Document and course materials.
2. Decide objectives to be evaluated by reviewing the Training Plan, design

document, and course materials.

3. Develop a blueprint for the instrument. This is a general approach to what will be collected, how it will be obtained, and what is considered acceptable and deficient results.

4. Describe skills to be measured as discussed in the course objective to included:

   A. Nature of question or situation.
   B. Key dimensions of correct and incorrect responses.

5. Develop the data collection instrument.
6. Have the instrument reviewed by the instructional designer, course developer, and/or subject matter experts.
7. Obtain peer evaluation.
8. Validate the instrument during pilot class.
9. Perform item analysis.
10. Revise test as necessary.
11. Implement.

Let's look at the various types of instruments that can be used in Level 2 evaluation.

Pre-test/Post-tests

Pre-test and Post-Tests are used to evaluate participant attainment of the cognitive (knowledge) objectives of the course. They are basically individual paper and pencil tests. Tests are made up of various different types of items. Choice of the item depends upon the knowledge being tested. Several test items follow.

Multiple Choice Test Items

Multiple choice items are used to evaluate both knowledge and various types of intellectual skills. A multiple choice item has a stem, which presents a problem situation, and several alternatives, which provide plausible solutions to the problem. The stem may be a question or an incomplete statement. The alternatives include the correct answer and several wrong answers called distracters. Good examples of this type of test item are:

Which of the following is not a goal of Preventive Maintenance? Circle the most appropriate answer.

A. Eliminate downtime
B. Reduce variation in performance
C. Prevent major equipment repair costs

D. Maximize machine operating time

Listed below are several good reasons why you should generate an implementation plan for a software metrics program. Which of these is the most important objective for generating a plan? (choose the answer that best applies)

A.   To ensure the success of the metrics program
B.   So that you don't leave out steps that may cause it to fail
C.   To make sure that you collect appropriate data
D.   To ensure that results are fed back to the proper personnel
E.   To ensure that product, process, or project improvements occur

When writing a multiple choice test item be sure the test item:

1.   Matches the objective and content being tested.
2.   Uses a single problem in stem.
3.   Uses simple clear language.
4.   Provides as much wording as possible in the stem.
5.   Has a stem stated in positive form.
6.   Emphasizes NEGATIVE wording in stem.
7.   Has alternatives that are grammatically correct with the stem.
8.   Includes no verbal clues that point to correct the answer or elimination of incorrect alternatives.
9.   Uses alternatives of nearly equal length.
10. Does not use "all of the above," "none of the above," "a and b only," etc.
11. Varies the position of the correct answer.

True-False Test Items

The true-false test item is simply a declarative statement that the participant must judge as true or false. Whenever there are only two possible responses, the true-false item is likely to provide the most effective evaluation procedure. Good examples of this type of test item are:

True or false?   The following statement is a component of the our definition of Uncompromising Integrity.   (Circle the T if the statement is true or F if it is false)

T   F   ". . . to maintain the highest standards of honesty, integrity, and ethics . . ."

At times, you can combine multiple True/False items into one test question. The following example illustrates this concept.

The following are benefits of a metric program. If the statement is truly a benefit, circle the T (true), if the statement is not a benefit, circle the F (false).

T   F   Improved resource management
T   F   Quality of the product is improved
*T   F   Data collected will show where the process needs to be
          streamlined*

To create a successful True-False test item, ensure that the item:

1. Matches the content and objective being tested.
2. Uses one idea in the statement.
3. Is worded to only be true or false.
4. Is short with simple clear language.
5. Does not use double negatives.
6. Has no clues to the correct answer.

<u>Matching Test Items</u>

The matching test item is a modification of multiple choice items. A series of stems called premises are listed in one column and the responses are listed in another column. An example of matching test item is:

Column A contains tools used with manufacturing cycle management. Column B lists the function the tools provide. To the left of Column A match the function that best describes the tool. Selections from Column B may be used once, more than once, or not at all.

Column A - Tools   Column B - Function

____ *Assembly Flow Chart A. Shows the flow of material through a*
____ *Flow Diagram   manufacturing process*
____ *Flow Process Chart   B. Listing of all material used in the manufacturing*
                             process
                          C. Maps the overall flow of the production process
                          D. Maps five different process activities

For successful construction of matching test items, confirm that each item:

1. Matches the objective and content being tested.
2. Uses uniform material in matching items.
3. Consists of a short list. If more matches are required, create two matching questions.
4. Provides a brief response on the right.
5. Has a larger or smaller number of responses than premises.
6. Permits responses being used more than once or not at all.
7. Provides adequate directions on how to respond.

Short-Answer Test Items

Short-answer items restrict the content and form of an answer. Answers are usually one or several phrases or sentences. Examples of short answer questions are:

Within our definition of Integrity five (5) stakeholders are Identified. In the space below, list three (3) stakeholders.

A. _____
B. _____
C. _____

The best measure of <u>manufacturing performance</u> is: _____ .

Short-answer items are best used when the participant needs to show knowledge or the use of knowledge in simple situations. Successful short-answer items will ensure that they:

1. Match the objective and content being tested.
2. Are clear and free of ambiguity.
3. Are free of clues.
4. Specify to the participant the form and content of answers.
5. Require a brief relevant response.

Essay Test Items

Essay test items allow the participant more freedom to prove competence in selecting, organizing, originating, and expressing ideas than short-answer items. They require the participant to present thoughts coherently. Essay test items are best used when the objectives require the participant to demonstrate the ability to perform the following:

1. Formulate ideas.
2. Select, interpret, and apply information.
3. Organize facts and data.
4. Diagnose and solve problems creatively.
5. Evaluate information.
6. Write clearly and logically.

An example of a good essay test item is:

Using 300 words or less, for a course that you are developing, prepare a complete plan for evaluating participant achievement of course objectives. Be sure to include the procedures you would use, the instruments you would use, and the reasons for your choices.

Essay test items, to be appropriate Level 2 evaluation instruments, should:

1. Match the objective and content being tested.
2. Be clear and free of ambiguity so that the participant knows exactly what is expected of them.
3. Be focused on one topic, concept, or idea.
4. Include limits for time and length of answer.
5. Specify evaluation criteria used to determine if the participant has successfully mastered the objective.

Pre-test/Post-test Introductions

Another key component of using Pre-test and Post-Tests is the introduction and instructions included on the instrument. These instruments are used for *program improvement not personnel evaluation*, therefore your introduction and instructions must convey this. An example of a proper introduction with instructions is:

Instructions

The following is a check of your understanding of the concepts and ideas that will be presented in <u>Understanding Integrity</u>. Please answer each question to the best of your ability. If you do not know the answer, please do not guess - simply leave the question blank. This information will be used to decide the effectiveness of the course in providing you and other participants with understandable material. Your score will not be shared with anyone except the personnel who design and evaluate our courses.
Please complete the following information:

Participant Number: _____ *(supplied by your instructor)*
Date course began: _____

*This course is intended for all managers, supervisors, or employees who interface with external customers, suppliers, and agencies. **Are you part of the target audience for this course?**   (check the response that best describes you)*

____ Yes   ____ *Will be within the next 12 months*
____ No

Level 2 Post-Test Example

The example on the next few pages shows the components of a good Level 2 evaluation Post-Test. This test was developed for a software metrics course used at Motorola University.

Instructions

The following is a check of your understanding of the concepts and ideas presented in Software Metrics. *Please answer each question to the best of your ability. **If you do not know the answer, please do not guess - simply leave the question blank**. This information will be used to decide the effectiveness of the course in providing you and other participants with understandable material. Your score **will not be shared with anyone** except the Motorola University personnel who design and evaluate our courses.*

Please complete the following information:

Participant Number: _____ *(supplied by your instructor)*
Date course began: _____
Course control number: _____

Are you part of the target audience for this course?

____   *Yes*
____   *No*
____   *Will be within the next 12 months*

(check the response that best describes you)

1. *The following are benefits of a metric program. If the statement is truly a benefit, circle the T (true), if the statement is not a benefit, circle the F (false).*

      T   F   Improved resource management
      T   F   Quality of the product is improved
      T   F   Data collected will show where the process needs to be streamlined
      T   F   Improved communications with customers
      T   F   Tracking resources will provide the necessary data for allocating appropriate time and resources

2. _____ *are people or groups that have a vested interest in the product, process, or project. (fill in appropriate word)*

3. *When identifying improvement goals for the product, process, or project three categories of issues are identified. In the space below, list the three (3) categories identified when developing a goal matrix.*

    A. _____
    B. _____
    C. _____

4. *By using the Goal Matrix, a set of requirements is determined. Identify at least three (3) criteria to be used for subjectively determining the final priority of requirements.*

    _____
    _____
    _____

5. *In the context of the GQM process, a _____ is a statement of desired outcome. (fill in the blank)*

6. *List at least three (3) sources that you can use as input when developing improvement goals and associated problems, opportunities, and requirements.*

    _____
    _____
    _____

7. *The GQM Models provide tools that assist you in generating questions mapping process and product improvement goals. Identify these tools.*

    _____
    _____
    _____

8. *Which of the following are correct actions in defining the metrics for questions? (circle Y if the statement is a correct action or circle N if it is not)*

     Y   N   *Develop a formula(a) which will determine the answer*
                    to the questions
     Y   N   *Identify personnel performance review requirements*
     Y   N   *Quantify the key words*
     Y   N   *Identify the key words in the question*

9. *What are the primary steps in determining a quantitative baseline using metrics? (place your answer in the space below)*

     _____
     _____
     _____

10. *In the space below, list the steps for identifying process changes for achieving goal values.*

     _____
     _____
     _____
     _____
     _____
     _____

11. *From the list below select the items which are good reasons for developing an implementation plan.*

     A.   *To ensure the success of the metrics program*
     B.   *So that "who does what and when" is identified*
     C.   *To avoid formality*
     D.   *To avoid having to analyze your own data.*
     E.   *To ensure that product, process, or project improvements occur*

Performance Testing

If a course objective requires application of learning, the instructional designer and course developer will typically create a performance test where the participant performs the task(s) and their ability to do each task is rated against a defined criterion in the course objective. Examples of performance tests used in training are:

1. Repairing a machine.
2. Setting adjustments on a piece of equipment.
3. Running and interpreting diagnostics.
3. Writing a computer program.
4. Installing and configuring software.

5. Giving a sales presentation.
6. Running demonstration software.
7. Pricing a system.
8. Performing in role plays.

The list of performance testing is endless and limited only by the creativity of the designer and developer. As an evaluator it is not your responsibility to develop these performance-based tests but rather to create data collection instruments that encompass the test. These instruments need to answer the question: *When do we know the participant has arrived at the desired learning level?*

When establishing whether the participant has achieved the objective, create a criterion check list (based upon the tasks to be performed) to decide if tasks have been achieved. The following guidelines are used when creating performance-based data collection instruments:

1. Consult with the Instructional Systems Designer, Course Developer, and Subject Matter Expert to generate a list of tasks to be mastered by the participant.
2. Arrange the tasks into a logical sequence of work activities.
3. Ensure performance tasks match the objective(s) being tested by reviewing the Design Document and/or course materials. For example, an objective requiring the participant to "list the following..." would be a cognitive test as opposed to "doing an activity" which would be a performance test.
4. Describe in detail exactly how the performance test fits into the course and how it is administered. This is accomplished again by consulting with the Instructional Systems Designer, Course Developer, and Subject Matter Expert.
5. Establish the standards for successful completion (demonstration of the task). For example, "participants will be able to adjust the machine within two minutes to .05 calibration level."
6. Ensure instructional content adequately covers the tasks so participants can successfully complete the test.
7. Decide the best way to score participant results. Realize that depending upon the instructional design, learning results may be evaluated at the individual participant level or a group of participants working together. There are three (3) basic ways to collect learning results on a performance test:

    A. <u>Scored by the instructor</u>: With this method the instructor will determine if the participant or group has mastered the content.
    B. <u>Self-scored by the participant</u>: This technique calls for the participant to judge whether they have achieved the desired learning level. Another variation of this activity is to have one participant score

another participant's work.

C. Scored by a group of participants: This method is used when the
    performance test is based around group work. Usually a group leader is
    assigned who, with help from members of the group, scores their
    results. Another variation is to have one group score another group's
    work.

Developing Performance-based Data Collection Instruments

Performance-based Data Collection Instruments accumulate results of
participants work in the course and complement the instructional strategy being
used. The instrument must be easy to use and add very little time to the course
with minimum disruption. When developing a Performance-based Data
Collection Instruments, include the following formatting considerations:

1. Title of the course and exercise.
2. Objective being evaluated.
3. Instructions to the individual who will be scoring the instrument on how to
    record the data and what to do with it after filling it out.
4. List the tasks that they have to perform and places to determine if mastery of
    the task has been achieved.

Examples of data collection instruments for performance-based check used at
Motorola University are provided on the next few pages.

Exhibit 36: Performanced-based Check Example 1

   *Participant Results*
Exercise 1

Goal: To ensure you have properly identified all key stakeholders associated with the case study presented in Exercise 1.
Instructions: Read the case study and complete the accompanying worksheet. Read each question below and compare it against the answer provided by your instructor . Decide if your work matches the correct answer. If it does, check the "Yes" box to the right of the question. If it does not, check "No." Return the completed form to your instructor.

1. Did you identify stakeholders who have a vested interest in the process, product or project?   (Yes) (No)

2. Did you identify problems, opportunities, and requirements based on the stakeholders' perspective?   (Yes) (No)

3. Did you rank the stakeholders and requirements based on importance, certainty, urgency, payoff and cost?   (Yes) (No)

4. Did you examine the requirements and group them based on some measure of functional commonality?   (Yes) (No)

5. Did you formulate subgoals and goal statements that are statements of desired outcome? Do they fulfill a requirement, take an opportunity, or solve a problem?   (Yes) (No)

6. Did you identify what type of goal statements you created: product, process, or project?   (Yes) (No)

In this example, the instructional design called for the following flow:

1. The instructor provides twenty minutes of lecture on the correct procedure for this portion of the course.
2. Each participant reads a case study and completes a worksheet in which they complete questions about the case.

3. After all participants have completed their work, the class is debriefed by the instructor as to the correct responses.
4. During the debrief, each participant judges their work against the data collection instrument.
5. The data collection instrument is collected by the instructor and returned to the evaluator for input into the appropriate data analysis model.

Please note that no participant names or identification numbers are used on the instrument. Completion of the instrument is anonymous therefore reinforcing the approach of program evaluation versus personnel evaluation.

Exhibit 37: Performanced-based Check Example 2

	Participant Results
(M) **MOTOROLA UNIVERSITY**	*Participant Results Exercise 2*

Instructor Notes:
In the column titled "Participant Number," enter the unique number identified for each participant. Examine each participant's case study model and identify if the following concepts are in their work. If present, enter "Y"; if the component is missing, enter "N."

Concept	Participant Number						
1. Correct use of attributes in either the Quantity produced field, Cycle Time field, or both, on the singulation process.							
2. Correctly entered the Percent rule on the inspection operation.							
3. Use of a multiple quantity variable to record the number of part failures in the rework operation.							
4. Use either a multiple quantity machine, delay buffer, or conveyor to represent the wave solder process.							
5. Correctly preempted labor from singulation operation, or the cafeteria, to the final assembly operation.							
6. Limit the number of pallets available to the system, and correctly have them circulate.							

With this example, participants complete work individually and the results are viewed by the instructor. The instructor records the results of each participant's work on the data collection instrument. This information is then forwarded to the evaluator for inclusion into the Data Analysis Model (the next phase of the the Training Evaluation Process).

Exhibit 38: Performanced-based Check Example 3 (page 1 of 2)

 **MOTOROLA UNIVERSITY**   # Introduction to Programming Robots

Participant Instructions

Terminal Goal: To demonstrate your ability to program a robot using a sequence of instructions to achieve a desired result with zero errors.

Instructions:

1. After the appropriate unit of instruction, the instructor will assign a lab activity. Use the instructions in the Participant Guide to program the robot. Upon completion, run the program.

2. If the robot performs as required during the first run, check the "Yes" box in the <u>Completed? Yes or No</u> column and enter 1 in the <u>Number of Attempts</u> column.

    If the robot does not perform as required, record one "tick" in the <u>Number of Attempts</u> column.

3. Re-program the robot and ask the instructor to observe until the robot performs as required. Add a tick mark each time you try the activity. When you successfully complete the activity, the completed column is marked "Yes." If the activity was not completed, mark "No."

4. Record your comments regarding problems in the <u>Comments</u> column.

Exhibit 39: Performanced-based Check Example 3 (page 2 of 2)

(M) **MOTOROLA UNIVERSITY**			Introduction to Programming Robots	
Control Number: ☐☐☐☐☐☐			Date: _____	
Participant Number: ☐			Page 1 of 3	
Lab Activity #	Completed? Yes or No		Number of Attempts	Comments
1	Yes	No		
2	Yes	No		
3	Yes	No		
4	Yes	No		
5	Yes	No		
6	Yes	No		
7a	Yes	No		
7b	Yes	No		
7c	Yes	No		
7d	Yes	No		
8	Yes	No		
9	Yes	No		
10	Yes	No		
11	Yes	No		

Example 3 depicts Level 2 evaluation scored by the participant. The defect associated with this instrument was any participant who did not complete an individual exercise. The number of times to complete the exercise or comments were not used in the defect/opportunities for error calculations. They were, however, reviewed by the instructional design staff during formative evaluation.

Course Control Document

An evaluation tool (instrument) useful in recording participant progress through a course is the Course Control Document. The Course Control Document is a structure used to log participant progress during class through the Level 2 data collection instruments. It may be used as input into the analysis portion of the Training Evaluation Process but is also an excellent method for the instructor to maintain a history of what participants have completed what evaluation procedures. For traditional lecture courses (ones taught in the classroom), the Course Control Document is typically a paper recording device. For computer based or computer managed courses, the training program (software) usually performs the recording of participant progress.

Course Control Documents assist course delivery and training evaluation by forcing trainers to record participant Level 2 results, therefore enhancing the data collection effort.

A Course Control Document is simply a fancy word for a gradebook. For reasons of legality gradebooks are not used in training programs. Instead course objectives are either met or not met to prevent the termination of participants who may receive a "poor" grade. Trainers will also find that participants are not opposed to being tested, but do not like to be graded or made to feel as though they are in high school again.   Exhibit 40 shows an example of a Course Control Document.

Exhibit 40: Course Control Document

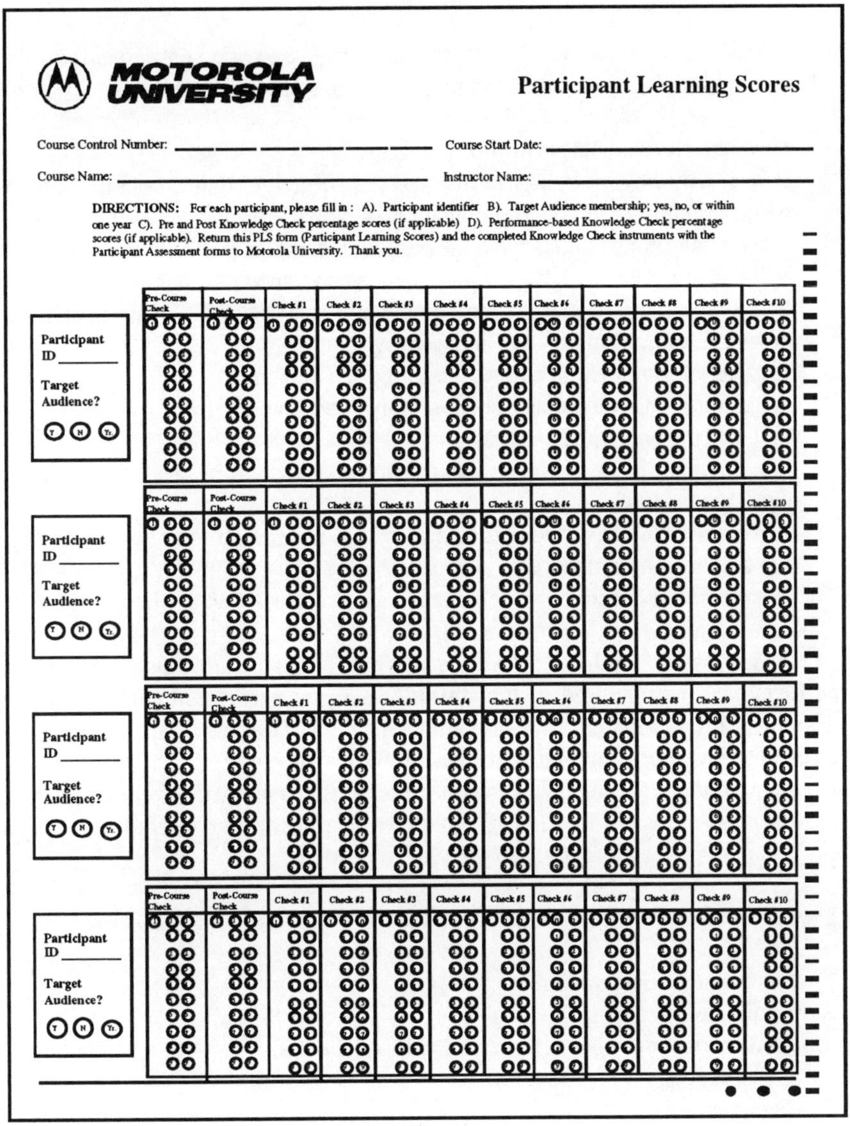

MOTOROLA UNIVERSITY

Participant Learning Scores

Course Control Number: ______ Course Start Date: ______

Course Name: ______ Instructor Name: ______

DIRECTIONS: For each participant, please fill in : A). Participant identifier B). Target Audience membership; yes, no, or within one year C). Pre and Post Knowledge Check percentage scores (if applicable) D). Performance-based Knowledge Check percentage scores (if applicable). Return this PLS form (Participant Learning Scores) and the completed Knowledge Check instruments with the Participant Assessment forms to Motorola University. Thank you.

	Pre-Course Check	Post-Course Check	Check #1	Check #2	Check #3	Check #4	Check #5	Check #6	Check #7	Check #8	Check #9	Check #10
Participant ID ______ Target Audience? Y N Yr												
Participant ID ______ Target Audience? Y N Yr												
Participant ID ______ Target Audience? Y N Yr												
Participant ID ______ Target Audience? Y N Yr												

LEVEL 3: BEHAVIOR - INSTRUMENTS

Level 3 evaluation measures the effect of training based upon participants on-the-job performance. Level 3 attempts to answer the following questions:

1. Have the participants performed the behavior?
2. If not, why have they not performed the behavior (is it a course problem, environmental issue, or a combination of both)?
3. How many opportunities have the participants had to perform the behavior?
4. With what frequency have the participants performed the course objectives?
5. What was the result from performing the new behavior (was it positive, negative, somewhat positive and negative)?
6. How much time was spent in attempting the behavior?
7. What additional resources (people, money, equipment, tools, etc.) were used in doing the behavior?
8. What impact have the behaviors (objectives) learned in class had upon the participants' job?
9. What behaviors have the participants had to acquire on their own to do their job that training did not provide?
10. What corrective action needs to take place to correct any problems?

The answers to these questions are compared to anticipated employee performance documented in the training analysis performed early in course design and development and documented in the Training Plan. Once these questions have been answered, a Plan of Action, if required, can be created to modify training. The modifications need to fit the "real" world requirements of participants' jobs or to identify to the appropriate organization why the environment is not allowing the behavior to occur.

Level 3 evaluation encompasses some subset of the following activities:

1. Post-course questionnaires (surveys)
2. Participant Action plans (contracts)
3. One-on-one interviews (in-person or by telephone)
4. Observations
5. Focus groups

Level 3 evaluation provides the extrinsic value training has provided to the company. Training is only performed to change employee knowledge, skill, or attitudes. Level 3 evaluation must provide data on how well employees are using their new skills on-the-job. When performing Level 3, several guidelines are followed to ensure true, unbiased data is collected. These guidelines are:

1. Use a before-and-after appraisal of on-the-job performance if possible. During the needs analysis phase of course design, a Level 3 instrument could collect current employee levels of performance. Training is then developed and delivered followed by administering the same Level 3 instrument after training; therefore giving a before-and-after approach. You may not have enough time or budget to perform the pre-design data collection effort. If this happens, contact the instructional systems design personnel and request access to their needs analysis instruments and subsequent results.

2. Query the following individuals:

    A. Participant
    B. Participant's superior(s)
    C. Participant's subordinates
    D. Participant's peers

    Most evaluators collect data from the participant (self-report). This data is valuable but at times may be contaminated due to biased answering or reporting. To validate self-report data, collect data from one additional source. At times, the type of behavior being evaluated may dictate data collection from additional sources. For example: if training taught first level managers new coaching and counseling techniques, the appropriate audience from which to collect data is the manager's employees to decide if the new techniques were being used.

3. Analyze and organize data so that a comfort level is achieved when describing what skills have been transferred to the job and more importantly what skills have not.

4. Measure some time after training thus allowing participants to practice what they have learned. A fine line exists between collecting data too early and too late. If data is collected too early, the participants may not have had sufficient opportunities to attempt the skill. Collecting too late will add external elements such as discussion with peers that will affect work behavior. Also, the type of training dictates when data collection occurs. For example: sales personnel will typically attempt new skills very soon after training. Thus, data collection can occur earlier than installation personnel whose work behaviors are reactive to successful sales.

5. If possible, use a control group who does not receive training and compare their job performance with employees who did complete training (experimental group).

Post-course   Questionnaires

Level 3 questionnaires present information to a respondent in writing and require a written response. All Level 3 instruments have advantages and disadvantages.

The advantages of questionnaires are:

1. They provide answers to a variety of questions in a short, simple, cost-effective manner.
2. They are compiled at the convenience of both evaluator and respondent.
3. The respondent has time to think before responding thus enriching the data collected.
4. They can be mailed.
5. Uniformity of data can be obtained, due to the format of the questionnaire.
6. The cost to implement is the lowest of Level 3 data collection instruments.

The disadvantages of questionnaires are:

1. Due to their format they are inflexible because the respondent must answer the questions asked.
2. People express themselves better orally than by the written word.
3. People do not return the instrument.

Whether to use a questionnaire or not depends upon the type of information being requested, the experience and reading level of the respondent, the evaluation budget, and the time constraints associated with the evaluation. If the information being collected lends itself to easily tabulated data (quantifiable), then a questionnaire is an appropriate choice. If the experience and reading level of the respondent is low, then the questionnaire may not be the best instrument. If the evaluation budget is tight, then questionnaires are clearly the best Level 3 alternative. Finally, if the schedule for the evaluation is short, the questionnaire approach may not be appropriate. However, if a questionnaire is chosen, then it must be designed properly to collect accurate evaluation results.

When designing Level 3 questionnaires decide how often, when, and to whom the questionnaires will be distributed. Next, alert respondents that you will be collecting data and for what reasons. Write questions based upon course objectives or tasks the participants are expected to perform on the job. Seek the following:

1. Occurrence, frequency, and duration of the behavior.
2. Form the behavior assumed.
3. Amount of participant involvement.
4. Impact upon the participant's job.

5. Resources expended to perform the behavior.
6. Success of the work.
7. Barriers that stopped or hindered the behavior from being properly executed.

Try to make the instrument easy to understand, fill out, and return. Design the instrument for a minimum amount of investment (time) on the respondents part. The design and format elements discussed for Level 1 questionnaires are also applicable to Level 3 questionnaires except they can exceed one page.

Exhibit 41: Level 3 Questionnaire

Behavior: Using Structured Design Techniques

1. How many times have you had the <u>opportunity</u> to perform this behavior since completing the *ENG500 Structured Design* course?

I have had ⬭ opportunities.
Is this value greater than 0? ⟶ (Yes)(No)   Please go to the next behavior on page 3.

Continue with question 2.

2. From all the opportunities to perform this behavior, what percentage did you actually attempt to do it? *Indicate the percentage in the box below (100% = all the time, 50% = one-half of the time, etc.)*

⬭% of the time.
Is this value greater than 75%? (Yes)(No)   Place a check mark ✔ next to the reasons why you were not able to complete the behavior.

Continue with questions 3 through 5.

Reasons:
☐ Learned it in training but forgot.
☐ Learned it in training but felt it was irrelevant.
☐ Did not learn it in training.
☐ My job has not required me to do it.
☐ My work environment has not allowed me to try this behavior. *Please describe what has blocked your attempts:* _____

_____

3. When you completed this behavior, typically how long did it take?
☐ hours

4. How would you rate the result of doing this work?

▫ Positive ▫ Positive ▫ Negative ▫ Don't know yet
          & Negative

5. Would you try this again? (Yes)(No)

If "No," what would have to change for you to try it?

Exhibit 41 shows an example of a Level 3 questionnaire. This form targets actual use of behavior and is geared toward a self-report by the employee. Notice the use of filter questions to obtain further data based upon how the employee responds. The questionnaire is actually made up of several pages with one page for each behavior being evaluated.

Participant Action Plans

The participant Action Plan approach is another method for obtaining Level 3 evaluation data. The Action Plan approach requires the participant to develop action plans listing the behaviors they want to try when they return to the job. The plans are based on the content of the course. After a set time, the participant is contacted to see what changes they have implemented.

These action plans contain detailed steps in accomplishing specific objectives related to the course. The approach produces data that answers such questions as:

1. What happened on the job because of the course?
2. Are the improvements the ones expected by the course designers?
3. What may have prevented the participants from doing specific action items?

With this information, education organizations can decide if a program should be modified and in what ways, while management can assess the findings to evaluate the worth of the course. A typical participant action plan is prepared on a printed form such as the one shown in the exhibit 43. The development of an action plan requires two phases:

1. Determining the areas for action.
2. Writing the action items.

Graphically the action plan process looks like:

Exhibit 42: Action Plan Process

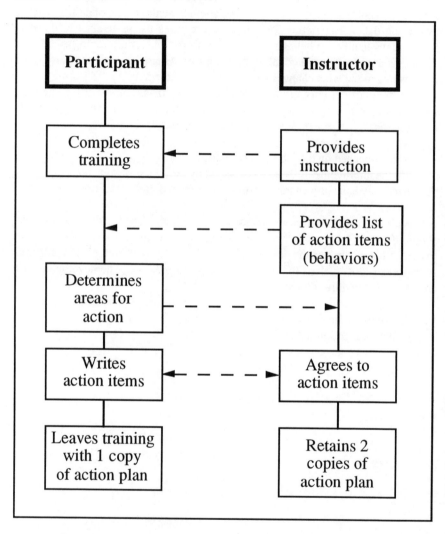

The process calls for the instructor to provide training while the participant completes the program. At the conclusion of the course, the instructor gives each participant a copy of the action plan which lists possible behaviors they may plan. The participant then decides which behaviors to attempt and writes the first draft of the action plan. The instructor reviews the draft and negotiates any changes they feel are necessary for the participant to be successful in the workplace. The participant leaves with a copy of the action plan while two copies are maintained by the training department for follow-up.

The areas for action come from the objectives presented in the course and, simultaneously are related to on-the-job activities. A list of potential activities is generated by the course development organization and provided to the instruction organization. The following questions should be asked when developing an action plan:

1. How much time will the action take?
2. Are the skills, tools, and resources for accomplishing the action item available?
3. Who has authority to implement the action plan?
4. Will this action have effect on other individuals?
5. Are there any organizational or environmental constraints preventing this action item from occurring?

The most important characteristic of an action item is that it is written so that everyone involved will know when it occurs. One way to achieve this goal is to use specific action verbs shown below[2].

<u>Mental Skills</u> - state, name, describe, relate, tell, write, express, recount, learn, identify, demonstrate, discriminate, classify, generate, apply, solve, derive, prove, analyze, evaluate.
<u>Physical Skills</u> - execute, operate, repair, adjust, manipulate, handle, manufacture, calibrate, remove, replace.
<u>Attitude</u> - choose, volunteer, allow, recommend, defend, endorse, cooperate, accept, decide to, agree.

Exhibit 43: Participant Action Plan

Participant Action Plan Worksheet

No.	Objective (goal)	Action to be taken (what will be done)	Target Date	Actual Date
1	Create a Level 1 Questionnaire.			
2	Create a Level 1 whole class interview.			
3	Create a Level 2 Pre-Course Knowledge Check.			
4	Create a Level 3 Data Analysis Model.			

Instructor:_____Participant:_____

Each action item has a date for completion and shows other individuals or resources required for completion. Planned behavior changes must be observable and be obvious to the participant and others when it happens. The action plans are reviewed by the trainer before the end of the course checking for accuracy, feasibility, and completeness.

To decide results obtained from action plans, a follow-up is conducted - usually four to six months after the course has been completed. The follow-up reveals and documents what progress has been made toward planned action items and reviews the detailed steps that were planned. It can be done through questionnaires and optional interviews. Questionnaires are gathered directly from every participant. Other options that can be just as effective:

1. Contacting only a sample of the participants.
2. Obtaining input from the participant, the participant's manager, the participant's subordinates, or the participant's peers.

The questionnaire is mailed to the participant when the previously defined time after course completion has elapsed. The questionnaire gathers the following data per action item (similar to the standard Level 3 questionnaire):

1. How the participant tried to implement this item, including, as appropriate, the following information:

   A. What they did
   B. How they did it
   C. What resources were expended
   D. How often they tried it

2. What happened when they tried to implement this item, including:

   A. What was the result
   B. How they rated the success (positive, negative, partly positive and partly negative, or don't you know yet?)

3. What they are doing differently than before attending the course.
4. Problems in trying out the action item.
5. Skills and/or knowledge additionally needed to carry out the action item.
6. Will they continue to try out this action item?
7. Would they like to participate in an optional telephone interview?

Interviews

Interviews are another method of obtaining Level 3 evaluation data. Interviews can secure data not available in performance records, or difficult data to obtain through written responses or observations. Participants may be reluctant to describe their results in a questionnaire but will volunteer the information to a skillful interviewer who probes for it. The interview process can uncover changes in reaction (Level 1) and behavior (Level 3). The interview also serves to verify other sources of information.

A major disadvantage of the interview is that it is time consuming. It also requires the training or preparation of interviewers to ensure that the process is conducted in an effective manner.

Interviews usually fall into two basic types: (1) structured, and (2) unstructured. The structured interview is much like a questionnaire. Specific questions are asked with little room to deviate from desired responses. The primary advantages of the structured interview over a questionnaire are that the interview process can ensure that the questions are completed and the interviewer understands the responses supplied by the participant. The unstructured interview allows for probing for more questions. This type of interview employs a few general questions that can lead into more detailed information as data is uncovered. Typical probing questions are:

1. Can you explain that in more detail?
2. Can you give me an example of what you are saying?
3. Can you explain the difficulty that you say you encountered?

The effectiveness of the interview process can be improved with the following guidelines:

1. List the basic questions to be asked. This information should be part of the Evaluation Plan written during the *Plan* phase of the Training Evaluation Process. Using the 'three column approach' that is used during the development of Level 1 questionnaires can be used here.
2. Draft the first portion of the interview. Be sure that all questions posed in point one are covered.
3. Decide how the interview sounds, tape record yourself reading the questions as you would if you were conducting the interview. Play the tape back and listen to the interview for flow, completeness, and whether or not is makes sense.
4. Review the interview with the subject matter expert.
5. Try out the interview on peers. Either have the peer read the interview or actually conduct the interview.
6. Try the interview out on one or two from the target population. This allows you to decided if the interviews works whiles allowing you to practice.
7. Train interviewers. Interviews besides being skillful in drawing out information from respondents must be familiar with the subject matter they are evaluating. Training provides this element along with how to conduct the interview and fill out the data collection instrument.
8. Give clear instructions to the person being interviewed.
9. Document written interview guidelines and procedures.

Exhibits 44, 45, 46, and 47 are examples of an interview developed and conducted by the Motorola University Evaluation department.

Exhibit 44: Level 3 Interview (page 1 of 4)

High Performance Work Team Resource Guide User Survey

Organization's Commitment to High   Interview Date:
Performance Work Teams   _____

Highly   1   2   3   4   5   Highly
Committed   Uncommitted

Is there a documented plan in place to support the use of the
HPWT concepts? (Yes)(No)→ If No . . .
                       Continue with the next page.

(Yes)(No)→ If No . . .
           What reference material or training
If Yes . . .   strategy does the plan include?
Continue with the next page.

→ Why do you feel your organization is uncommitted to the
HPWT concept?

What do you feel are the organizational barriers preventing
the use of High Performance
Work Teams?

Exhibit 45: Level 3 Interview (page 2 of 4)

Receipt/Review of Resource Guide

Did you receive the HPWT Resource Guide sent out by Motorola
University? (Yes) (No) ➤ If No ...
                              (End the interview and thank the
     If Yes ...   *participant for their time)*
Do you recall the date that you received
the Resource Guide? _____

Did you share the Resource Guide with anyone else? (Yes) (No)

If Yes ...
With whom did you share it?

May we contact him/her?
Phone Number: _____

Did you read any portion of the Resource Guide? (Yes) (No)
If Yes ...
Approximately what percent of the Resource Guide have you
read to date?

_____ Less than 25%
_____ 26% - 50%
_____ 51% - 75%
_____ 76% - 100%

How would you describe the way in which you read the
Resource Guide?

_____ I read each section as sequenced in the guide.
_____ I skimmed the guide and read only the sections relevant to
my interests/needs.

Exhibit 46: Level 3 Interview (page 3 of 4)

High Performance Work Team Resource Guide User Survey

Approximately how many days after receiving the Resource
Guide did you get an opportunity to read the material?

_____ 1 - 7 days   (1 week)
_____ 8 - 14 days   (2 weeks)
_____ 15 - 21 days   (3 weeks)
_____ more than 22 days   (more than 3 weeks)
_____ unknown

Overall, please rate how easy the Resource Guide was to read.

Easy to   Difficult to
   Read 1   2   3   4   5 Read

Utilization of the Resource Guide

Have you used any portion of this Resource Guide? (Yes No)

If No . . .
Please respond with a Yes or No if any of the following reasons
describe why you did not
use the guide. **(Following the response, complete the interview
and thank participant for their time.)**

Y   N   The opportunity has not been available.
Y   N   There has been no time.
Y   N   My organizational environment does not allow me to
          apply those concepts.
Y   N   The document does not adequately provide the
          information I need.
          If so, what could be added to meet your needs?

          Are there other reasons? If yes, please describe.

Exhibit 47: Level 3 Interview (page 4 of 4)

High Performance Work Team Resource Guide User Survey

Please respond with a Yes or No if the following were
beneficial to developing HPWT.

Y N Getting an overall view of 'life cycle' of High
        Performance Work Teams.
Y N Determining the skill/knowledge needs of various
        people within the organization.
Y N Identifying possible sources for training courses.
Y N Seeing roadmaps built by other business locations.
Y N Getting leads for diagnostics and videos.
Y N Explanation of teams and how they develop to line
        managers.
Y N Knowing who to contact to get additional materials.
        Were there other benefits? If yes, please describe.

   The object of the evaluation is a resource guide on High Performance Work
Teams (HPWT) which aids in the training of HPWT. This telephone interview
is divided into four basic areas: 1) commitment of the respondents organization
to the evaluation object, 2) receipt and reading information, 3) utilization of the
resource guide, and 4) results from using the guide.

Observations

Observing participants in the workplace is another form of Level 3 evaluation. This involves observing the participant either before, during, or after a training program to record changes in behavior. The effectiveness of the observation process can be improved with the following guidelines:

1. The observers must be fully prepared by equipping and training them on the instrument which is used.
2. The observation should be systematic.
3. The observers should know how to interpret and report what they see.
4. The observer's influence should be minimized.

To plan a systematic observation first decide what behavior(s) will be observed and prepare forms for the observers to use. Next, select the observers, prepare a schedule for observing, and train observers on what to and not to observe. Inform participants of the planned observation with explanations, conduct the observations, and summarize the observation data.

Training observers is a vital ingredient in successful Level 3 observations. Without proper training, the observer will prejudice the data collected. To minimize bias, be sure that observers understand their role and the importance of the activity, understand what behavior(s) should and should not occur, practice, and are instructed on how to complete the instrument(s). Two basic forms of observation instruments are used in the Training Evaluation Process. The behavior check list can be useful for recording the presence, absence, frequency, or duration of a participants' behavior as it occurs. The check list is useful, since an observer can identify exactly which behaviors should or should not occur. Exhibit 48 is an example of an observation check list.

This check list is developed from the model used in a Motorola University course titled "MGT106 Effective Interactions with Employees." The behaviors which are observed are based upon the model taught in the course.

Exhibit 48: Observation Check List

Effective Interactions with Employees

Training Observation Check List

Instructions: Use this check list when observing a manager in a coaching discussion with an employee. Listed below are the six steps that are used during a coaching discussion. Within each step are the behaviors a manager is expected to use. When you observe a listed behavior place a check mark to the left of the behavior. If additional behaviors are exhibited during the discussion record them in the **Other** area on the check list.

Opening

__Actively listens
__Appears calm
__Is supportive

Defining the Issue

__Asks what is wrong
__Further qualifies issue
   details
   ____ Who
   ____ What
   ____ Where
   ____ When
   ____ How much

Exploring Alternatives

__Seeks proposals
__Defines each proposals
__Identifies positive
   proposal effects
__Identifies negative
   proposal effects

Developing Preferred Solutions

__What can be done
__Reduce negative
   effects
__Maximize positive
   effects

Mutual Agreement

__Mutual agreement
   obtained

Obtaining Commitment

__Opportunity
   to change
__Date/time
   for next
   discussion

Other

Another method requires the observer to record all behavior on a form in specified codes (coded behavior record). This method is more time consuming because a code is entered that identifies a specific behavior. Such a record is useful when it is intended to document what happened. Exhibit 49 is an example of a coded behavior check list.

Exhibit 49: Coded Behavior Check List

Scoring Sheet for Discussions						
Key skill for this type of discussion are:	Seeking Information	Seeking Proposals	Building	Summarizing	Testing Understanding	Sharing
Opening						
Defining the issue						
Exploring Alternatives						
Developing preferred solutions						
Obtaining commitment						

This observation sheet records not only the occurrence of the behaviors but also rates (codes) the success of using the skill. The observer records a code indicating the effectiveness of the seven key skills listed across the top of the matrix as they occur during the five steps (left column) of the discussion.

LEVEL 4: RESULTS INSTRUMENTS

Level 4 evaluation closes the loop on the training process by evaluating the effects training has had upon the results of the organization. Level 4 attempts to answer questions similar to the ones listed below:

1. What modification can be made to the course when the financial benefits of the course are compared against the cost of training (design + development + implementation)?
2. Was the business purpose of the program (higher average sales per customer, increased sales person productivity, reduced turnover, fewer errors in the development process, etc.) met?
3. With this information what changes, if any, need to be made to the training program, company environmental issues, or both?

Many experts suggest Level 4 evaluation is impossible to execute due to outside factors that affect performance beyond training. At times this is true. Still, this is not a valid reason for not attempting Level 4 evaluation. We have found that this level of evaluation can be done, is easy to do, and more importantly should be done. Training, as with any company activity, must account for its expenses by showing the return it has provided. With this information, program changes can be made.

The most significant benefit of Level 4 evaluation is the summative information it provides. For example: the sales training department of a company had initiated a new strategic selling skills course. Yet, only 40% of the sales force had completed training. The reason for this was that various Vice Presidents of the marketing regions were not convinced that the course was needed or beneficial. In performing the Level 4 evaluation, a control group (sales personnel who did not receive training) and an experimental group (employees who did complete strategic selling) were used. Sales results for both groups were tracked for one calendar year.

The results were outstanding. Level 4 evaluation proved that training had a return-on-investment of 233%. Which states that for every dollar spent on training, the return to the company was $2.33 in increased order value. With this data, the marketing vice presidents were convinced that the course could increase the sales and subsequently enrollment soared.

Successful Level 4 evaluations require specific guidelines be followed. These guidelines are:

1. Use a control group (one that does not receive training) and compare its results against an experimental group (one that receives training) over the same period of time.
2. Use an established baseline (before training) and compare it against after training results if a control group cannot be employed.
3. Establish a baseline by using a before-and-after comparison of results.
4. Design the evaluation to eliminate non-course influences (management practices, new pricing information, new diagnostic routine, improved marketing information, demographic data, etc.) from the results.
5. Use only existing accounting records to calculate the cost of training and the business results associated from training. If data records do not exist, do not initiate a data collection effort to gather the data. This training course is not a candidate for level 4 evaluation.

Exhibit 50: Criteria for Level 4 Evaluations

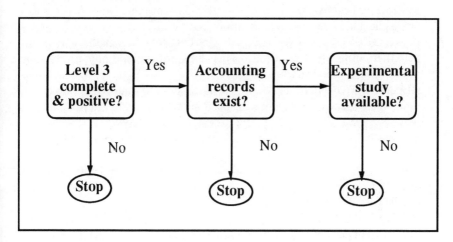

Exhibit 50 shows the criteria for conducting a Level 4 evaluation. Three basic points must be met to perform Level 4 studies. First, Level 3 evaluation is completed and the results are positive. This indicates that employees have successfully transferred training skills to the job. Second, accounting records which document training results are currently in existence and the evaluator has access to them. This reduces the cost of evaluation and increases the acceptance of findings. Finally, control and experimental group business results are evaluated to determine the value of training.

The process for conducting a Level 4 evaluation is comprised of two steps:

1. Determine the value of training in dollars.
2. Calculate the return-on-investment (ROI).

Knowing this process is important at this stage of the Training Evaluation Process thus allowing proper development of the data collection instrument. To perform a Level 4 evaluation, the first activity is to calculate the Total Cost of Training by developing an analysis model to calculate costs. This includes costs to design, develop, deliver, maintain, and evaluates training. To accurately develop an analysis model to cost training, the following elements of developing and delivering training must be known:

1. NUMBER OF PEOPLE TRAINED - the total number of individuals who received the specified course.
2. WORKING DAYS PER YEAR OF PARTICIPANTS - the number of days in each year that the employees who received training worked. This excludes weekends, holidays, allotted vacation and sick days, etc.
3. MEAN ANNUAL PARTICIPANT COST - the total average yearly cost of each employee trained. This includes gross salary, company contributions

to whatever benefits the employees receive, and any other fringe benefits that are applicable to the cost of each employee.

4. LENGTH OF TRAINING SESSION (IN DAYS) - the length, in days, the actual training class required. This does not include any travel time associated going to and from the class.

5. RELATED TRAINING TRAVEL TIME (IN DAYS) - the average amount of time, in days, each participant will spend in transit to and from training.

6. MEAN COST FOR ONE PARTICIPANT TO TRAVEL - the average allowance for air fare, rental car, mileage reimbursement, etc., to the course site. This does not include hotel accommodations, food and other expenses.

7. MEAN COST OF ACCOMMODATION FOR ONE PARTICIPANT - the average allotment for hotel accommodations, food, and other expenses for one day per participant. This does not include travel expenses.

8. WEEKLY COST OF INSTRUCTIONAL DESIGN - the weekly cost (fully burdened) of performing instructional systems design.

9. ANNUAL COST OF INSTRUCTOR - the estimated yearly cost of the training personnel who deliver the course. The cost includes gross salary and any other associated overhead. It does not include overhead such as the costs for the training center.

10. WEEKLY COST OF COURSE DEVELOPMENT - the weekly expenses required to develop the course. This does not include the cost of the actual classroom materials used by the participants or equipment. This entry is the up-front development costs.

11. COURSE DEVELOPMENT RATIO - the number of hours of course development required to produce one finished hour of course materials.

12. INSTRUCTIONAL DESIGN RATIO - the number of hours of instructional systems design hours required to produce one finished hour of course materials.

13. PARTICIPANT PACKAGE COST - the total cost of materials for each participant. Examples of these types of materials are binders, pens, reference manuals, handouts, etc.

14. PARTICIPANT/INSTRUCTOR RATIO - the average number of participants per class, assuming there is only one trainer per class.

15. WORKING DAYS PER YEAR FOR INSTRUCTOR - the average number of days per year a trainer will work.

16. ANNUAL CLASSROOM COST - the yearly amount to maintain a classroom (rental, audio visual equipment, etc.) for this course.

17. EQUIPMENT COST - the yearly amount of funds expended for course equipment (computer systems, maintenance rates, etc.).

18. TRANSLATION COST - the amount required to translate this course into local language, if this requirement exists.

19. NUMBER OF TRANSLATIONS REQUIRED - the number of times course materials will be translated into local language.

20. EVALUATION COST - the budget specified in the Evaluation Plan.

If these elements cannot be found, then this training program is not a candidate for Level 4 Results evaluation. Still, if they are known, you must build a data collection instrument to record them and calculate the Total Cost of Training. This instrument can be paper-and-pencil calculations or a computer spreadsheet. The spreadsheet is recommended because the instrument needs to be built only once and can be reused from evaluation to evaluation. The cost areas of training that are calculated are:

1. Design
2. Development
3. Participant salary while in training
4. Participant travel and expense associated with training
5. Participant course materials (package) cost
6. Trainer salary while teaching and preparing
7. Cost to rent classroom space
8. Special course equipment cost
9. Cost to translate course materials to local languages for international companies
10. Evaluation costs

Exhibit 51 shows a typical instrument used to collect costs of training. This data collection instrument allows the evaluator to gather all the necessary parameters used in calculating or estimating the true cost of training. Once collected, this data is input into the analysis model which generates the total cost of training.

Exhibit 51: Cost of Training Data Collection Instrument

Level 4 Evaluation Training Development Costs Worksheet

Course ID: _____

Competency Center: _____

Instructional Systems Designer: _____

Number of participants (to be) trained: _____

Working days per year of participants: _____

Mean annual participant cost: _____

Length of training sessions (in days):   _____

Related training travel time (in days):   _____

Mean cost for one participant to travel: _____

Mean cost of accommodations for

one participant: _____

Weekly cost of Instructional Design: _____

Annual Cost of Instructor: _____

Weekly cost of course development: _____

Course development ratio: _____

Instructional Designer ratio: _____

Participant Package cost: _____

Participant/Instructor ratio: _____

Working days per year for Instructor: _____

Instructor preparation ratio: _____

Annual classroom cost: _____

Equipment cost: _____

Translation cost: _____

Number of translations: _____

Number of translations required: _____

Evaluation cost: _____

The formulas used in analysis models to calculate the cost to develop and deliver training are discussed later in this chapter. The second step in Level 4 evaluation is to figure out the value of training in dollars. The goals of the training program provide you with how this data can be calculated. Typical course goals state[3]:

<u>Value of Increased Output</u> - Changes in output are the goal of many training programs. In most situations the value of increased output can be easily calculated. Examples which may be calculated (before and after training):

1. Average sales,
2. Average profit per sale, and
3. Increased productivity.

<u>Value of Time Savings</u> - Many training programs are aimed at reducing the time for participants to perform a function or a phase. Time savings are important because employee time is money (salaries and benefits paid directly to the employee). Several economic benefits are:

1. WAGES/SALARIES. Savings = hours saved x labor cost per hour.
2. BETTER SERVICE. When production time, implementation, construction time, or processing time is reduced so that product or services are delivered to the client or customer in a shorter period, there is better customer satisfaction, the value of which can be quantified.
3. PENALTY AVOIDANCE. Reductions in time can avoid penalty.
4. OPPORTUNITY FOR PROFIT. A benefit of time savings is the opportunity to make additional profit. Example: if a salesperson reduces the average time spent on a sales call, then there is time for additional sales calls.
5. TRAINING TIME. Using new instructional technologies [CBT (computer-based participant), IVI (interactive video instruction), self-instruction, etc.] to deliver traditional classroom training can reduce the time to conduct training.

<u>Value of Improved Quality</u> - Training is developed to overcome deficiencies in employees that are evident by low-quality output or an excessively high error rate. Calculating improved quality has several components:

1. SCRAP/WASTE. Scrap and waste translate into a dollar value that can be used to calculate the impact of improved quality.
2. REWORK. Many mistakes and errors result in costly rework to correct the mistake. This value is very expensive and can be quantified.
3. CUSTOMER/CLIENT DISSATISFACTION. Customer dissatisfaction is difficult to quantify, and attempts to arrive at a dollar value may be impossible. Usually, the judgment and expertise of sales and marketing management is the best source to try to measure the impact of dissatisfaction.
4. PRODUCT LIABILITY. Premiums for product liability insurance have soared due to an increase in lawsuits brought against businesses. Better quality can result in fewer customer complaints; so, fewer lawsuits and lower

premiums.
5. INTERNAL LOSSES. Employee mistakes such as an overpayment to a vendor can cause a loss. It does not result in rework or produce waste, but it does cost the company money.
6. EMPLOYEE MORALE. When mistakes are made, usually other employees have to suffer the inconvenience or perform extra work.
    Value of Soft Data - While soft data are not as desirable as hard data, they are important. There are several approaches to convert the soft data to a dollar value, such as:
7. EXPERT OPINION. Expert opinions are possibly available to estimate the value of soft data. The experts may be within the organization, within the industry, or specialists in a particular field.
8. PARTICIPANT ESTIMATION. The participants can estimate the value of an improvement.
9. MANAGEMENT ESTIMATION. Another technique for assigning a value to soft data is to ask management to evaluate the program.

Depending upon the course goals and the accessibility the evaluator has to accounting records, you may not have to develop a data collection instrument to decide value.

The final step in developing Level 4 instruments is to establish the formula for return-on-investment (ROI). The term "return-on-investment" originates from the finance and accounting field and usually refers to the pre-tax contribution measured against controllable assets. In formula form:

$$ROI = \frac{\text{pre-tax earnings}}{\text{average investment}} \times 100$$

It measures the anticipated profitability of an investment and is used as a standard measure of the performance of divisions or profit centers within a business. For training program evaluation, the return may be expressed in the following way:

$$ROI = \frac{\text{net program value (or savings)}}{\text{program costs (or investments)}} \times 100$$

The investment portion of the formula represents capital expenditures such as development and delivery costs. The original investment figure can be used, or the present book value can be expressed as the average investment over a period of time. If the training program is a one-time offering, then the figure is all the original investment. However, if the initial cost is spread over a period of time, then the average book value is more appropriate. This value is essentially half the initial cost since, through depreciation, a certain fixed part of the investment is written off each year over the life of the investment.

In many situations a group of employees are to be trained at one time, so the investment figure is the total cost of analysis, development, delivery, and evaluation lumped together for the bottom part of the equation. The value is then calculated assuming that all participants attend or have attended the program.

To keep the calculations simple, it is recommended the return be based on pre-tax conditions.

The calculation of the return for a training program is not always feasible. Usually, the ROI calculation should be used when program values can be clearly documented and substantiated, even if they are subjective.

Data Collection Instrument Summary

The first task of the Develop phase of the Training Evaluation Process involves generating the data collection instruments. It is imperative data collection instruments are developed quickly, within the evaluation budget constraints, and will collect data in an unbiased accurate method. The *Develop* phase of the Training Evaluation Process continues with task 2.

- END OF TASK 1 -

2. CREATE MODELS TO ANALYZE DATA FOR LEVELS 1-4

Once all the data collection instruments have been developed, the next activity is to create the models necessary to analyze data after it is collected. A model to analyze data is created for each data collection instrument and is designed to help in answering the evaluation questions. Models may be in various forms that could include:

1. Paper and pencil tabulation.
2. Spreadsheet on a PC (personal computer).
3. Customized programming from the data processing department.
4. Computer statistical analysis program.

Analysis models, as with all Training Evaluation Process tools and instruments must meet or exceed specific standards. The first measure of a good analysis model is to keep it simple and easy to record data from the collection instrument. Secondly, design into the model use of methods that help in answering the evaluation questions and validate the data. Finally, test the model for accuracy and ease of use.

Exhibit 52 depicts the input, input requirements, supplier, output, output requirements, customer, and tasks associated with developing data analysis models.

Exhibit 52: Create Models to Analyze Data for Levels 1-4

Supplier	Input	Input Req.	TASKS	Output	Output Req.	Customer
Task No. 1 of the Develop phase of the Training Evaluation Process.	Data Collection Instruments.	Meets the needs defined in the Evaluation Plan. Satisfies all requirements of proper instrument design. Funds for generation are within the Evaluation Plan budget.	Obtain copies of data collection instruments. Understand use of data collection instruments Search records for existing analysis models. Generate, models to analyze data.	Models to analyze data.	Meets needs defined in the Evaluation Plan. Proper analysis model design. Funds are within Evaluation Plan budget. Models are easy to use and include instructions .	Task No. 3: Obtain agreement to the data collection instruments and analysis models of the Develop phase.

The first activity you perform is to obtain copies of data collection instruments that have been generated for this evaluation. Simultaneously, be sure you have a copy of the Evaluation Plan. The Evaluation Plan will help in determining analysis models by providing the evaluation questions and time frames for answering those questions. Compare the collection instruments with the Evaluation Plan to ensure the instruments are in concert with the plan.

Next, understand the use of the data collection instruments. To create accurate and usable analysis models, the intention of each data collection instrument must be thoroughly understood. This understanding can be gained by reading the Evaluation Plan and the instructions which accompany the instruments.

Once a thorough understanding of the data collection instruments is achieved, search existing records for analysis models that have been successfully used in the past and can be used with this evaluation. By exploring past analysis models, you can in essence reduce the development effort, time, and cost. Previous analysis models may be:

1.   Used as is, or

2. Modified to meet the unique characteristics of the data collection instrument.

Next, generate, when required, models to analyze data for each data collection instrument. What form (paper-and-pencil, spreadsheet, etc.) the model assumes depends upon:

1. The data being collected.
2. The sophistication of the user.
3. Time, resources, and budget established for this evaluation.

Guidelines for creating analysis models are:

1. Create the report format first. Knowing what the output is to look like greatly effects the form of the model.
2. Ensure all items on the data collection instrument are covered by the data analysis model.
3. Test the model to ensure it works as designed.
4. Ensure they satisfy the requirements specified in the Evaluation Plan. Do this by comparing the report that will be generated by the model(s) and decide if all evaluation questions are addressed.
5. Generate one or two lines of summation data for each item on the evaluation instrument. For example, suppose the Level 1 Reactionary questionnaire has the following question on it:

The quality of the participant material was ...

    1=Excellent 2=Good 3=Poor 4=Unsatisfactory

The summation line in the analysis model for this question could be:

The quality of the participant material was ...

1=Excellent	2=Good	3=Poor	4=Unsatisfactory	
N=102	N=34	N=15	N=5	Total=156
65.3%	21.7%	9.6%	3.2%	

This summation shows two (2) basic elements:

1. The number (N=) of participants who chose a given response.
2. The percentage (based upon 100%) of participants who chose the response.

Level 1 Analysis Model Example

At Motorola University, the Level 1 data collection instrument is the questionnaire previously discussed in this chapter. The data analysis model is a custom written computer program to hold all the evaluation data. The computer system is titled **AdEPT** (**Ad**vanced **E**valuation **P**articipant **T**echnology). The AdEPT system is a series of computer programs that:

1. Scan the questionnaire (Participant Assessment) and stores the results in a temporary computer file.
2. Import the scanned data from the temporary file and place it into a computer relational database for storage, retrieval, sorting, and report generation.

The AdEPT system maintains historical Level 1 data for all course sessions taught at Motorola University. Exhibits 53, 54, 55, and 56 illustrate some of the features associated with the system and are examples of a typical Level 1 analysis model.

Exhibit 53: Level 1 Analysis Model Example (page 1 of 4)

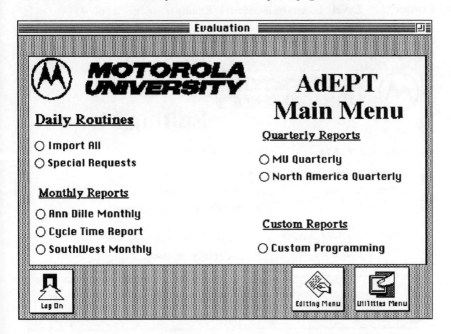

Exhibit 53 shows the main menu from the Motorola University Level 1 analysis model: AdEPT. The functions built into this system are that it is a "point and click" process where the operator, using a computer mouse, points to the function they wish to perform and clicks the mouse to execute the program. As indicated by the screen display, various programs are available which allow the operator to service data requests.

Exhibit 54: Level 1 Analysis Model Example (page 2 of 4)

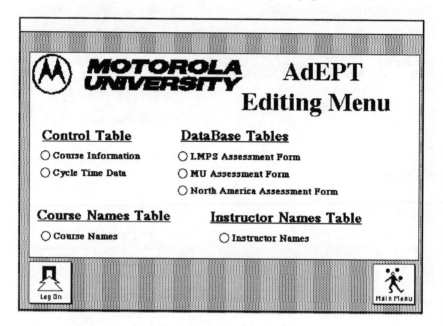

This submenu allows the operator to maintain the integrity of the database. The database is actually comprised of several separate but interrelated data tables. The data tables maintained in the system are:

1. Control Table which holds course information (Motorola University control number, course date, teaching region, etc.) and Cycle Time Data (the elapsed time from when a course is conducted until the analysis model has imported the results).
2. Course Names Tables which contains course identification codes and corresponding names.
3. Database Tables which are the tables where the actual results from scanning Participant Assessment forms are stored.
4. Instructor Names Table which holds, for each instructor, an instructor identification code and their name.

Exhibit 55: Level 1 Analysis Model Example (page 3 of 4)

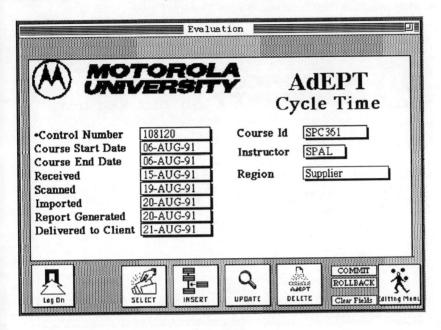

Exhibit 55 is an example of one of the AdEPT editing programs. With this particular program the operator can interrogate the information in the database with respect to Cycle Time. After viewing the data, the operator has the options to:

1. Choose additional information to view.
2. Add a new record to the database.
3. Delete an existing record from the database.
4. Change existing data.

Exhibit 56: Level 1 Analysis Model Example (page 4 of 4)

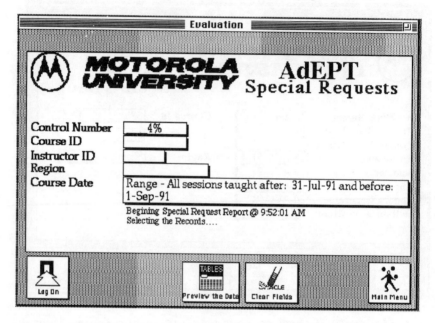

Finally, this screen is one of the program used to generate Level 1 Evaluation Reports. This program, titled <u>Special Requests,</u> is used to produce a report on a single session of a course, a group of sessions for a course, courses taught by a given region or all regions, etc. The parameters for this program allow Level 1 evaluation to be reported depending upon client requests.

These last four exhibits are included to show the type of data analysis models that are used in industry today. This is only one such program. A variety of programs exist to meet the needs of the company with respect to the storage and reporting of Level 1 results.

Level 2 Analysis Model Examples

Exhibit 57: Level 2 Pre-test/Post-test Analysis Model

Motorola University
Evaluation of Learning: Pre/Post Course Test Analysis

Course Title:	Structured Design Techniques
Date:	June 1, 1992
Instructor:	John Doe
Control Number:	123456

Number of Participants: 15

Participant Number	Pre-Test	Post-Test	Index of Learning Gain
1	12	100	100%
2	25	95	93%
3	32	79	69%
14	5	98	97%
15	11	96	95%
Mean	13	90	84%
High Score	32	100	100%
Low Score	5	79	69%
Range	17	21	30
Standard Deviation	0.83	0.70	0.54
t score	2.96		
Level of Sig.	.01		

No. of Participants:	15
No. of Participants $\geq 80\%$	14
% of Participant $\geq 80\%$	93.3%
Quality Goal Achieved?	Yes

Note: The Quality Goal for this course is a Post-Course score of $\geq 80\%$ by $\geq 80\%$ of the participants.

Exhibit 57 is an example of the Pre-test/Post-test analysis model used at Motorola University. This is only a portion of the model, additional data such as results per questions for each participant are also held. The data is maintained in a personal computer spreadsheet. The design of the model is:

1. The result of each item on the test (right or wrong) is entered into the model for each participant.
2. The spreadsheet calculates the distribution of right and wrong for each participant and the right and wrong answers by item for all participants.
3. A Pre-Test and Post-Test score (based upon 100.0%) is calculated for each participant.
4. The Index of Learning Gain score is also calculated by the spreadsheet.
5. The summative statistics (shown in exhibit 57) are calculated.
6. An detailed item analysis of which items (questions) were answered right and wrong is generated.
7. A report, detailing the entire evaluation data, is printed.

This model is used for all courses that employ Pre-test and Post-tests as an evaluation technique. The model is flexible enough to be used for Pre-test or Post-Tests only.

Besides tracking evaluation data with the Pre-test/Post-test model, analysis models for performance-based testing are used. Exhibit 58, illustrates the type of analysis model employed.

Exhibit 58: Performance-based Analysis Model

 **MOTOROLA UNIVERSITY**   Date: 30-Jun-92

Programming Robots Level 2 Data Analysis

Lab Activity Number	% of Participants Completed	% of Participants Not Completed	Mean Number of Attempts
1.	95	05	1.2
2.	100	00	1.1
3.	100	00	2.4
4.	75	25	14.7
5.	55	45	10.9
6.	62	38	12.5
7.	100	00	1.2
8.	100	00	2.0
9.	100	00	1.1
10.	100	00	1.5
11.	100	00	2.2
12.	100	00	1.1
13.	100	00	2.7
14.	90	10	1.2
15.	100	00	1.0

This analysis model captured the number of participants who completed a given lab and the participants who did not. The data is further broken down into the corresponding percentages for completions versus non-completions. This data is an example of an analysis of the items on the performance test. Another portion of this model analyzes the data based upon participant results.

Level 3 Analysis Model Example

Another type of analysis model are those that deal with Level 3 evaluation studies. As before, these models support the purpose and questions documented in the <u>Evaluation Plan</u>. Exhibit 59 is an example of a computer spreadsheet analysis model and summarizes the data collected by a Level 3 questionnaire.

Exhibit 59: Level 3 Analysis Model Example

Evaluation of Training Impact On-the-job

Behavior: Using Structured Design Techniques
Population size = *105*

1. How many times have you had the opportunity to perform this behavior since completing the ENG500 Structured Design course?   *Yes   =   103   Total count = 1,125*
                                 No   =   2   Mean = 10.9

2. From all the opportunities to perform this behavior, what percentage did you actually attempt to do it?   *85%*

3. If you did not complete the behavior, what are the reasons?

    * Learned it in training but forgot   *85%*
    * Did not learn it in training   *72%*
    * Learned it in training but felt it was irrelevant   *23%*
    * My job has not required me to do it   *12%*
    * My work environment has not allowed   *14%*
       me to try this behavior

4. How would you rate the result of doing this work?

Positive	*71*	*69%*
Positive & Negative	*11*	*11%*
Negative	*13*	*13%*
Don't know yet	*8*	*8%*

5. Would you try this again?

Yes	*103*	*100%*
No	*0*	*0%*

Level 4 Data Analysis Model Examples

Level 4 Evaluation consists of two data analysis models - one to analyze the total cost of training and the other to analyze the value of training between the control and experimental groups. When developing an analysis model to calculate the total cost of training, the specific cost areas documenting earlier in this chapter are considered.

The cost areas of training that are calculated are:

1. Design.
2. Development.
3. Participant salary while in training.
4. Participant travel and expense associated with training.
5. Participant course materials (package) cost.
6. Trainer salary while teaching and preparing.
7. Cost to rent classroom space.
8. Special course equipment cost.
9. Cost to translate course materials to local languages for international companies.
10. Evaluation costs.

The following formulas are used by the Training Evaluation Process to calculate the cost to develop and deliver training:

1. **Design Cost** = (course length / 5) x (weekly design cost) x (instructional Design ratio)

2. **Development Cost** = (course length / 5) x (weekly development cost) x (course development ratio)

3. **Participant Salary Cost** = (participant annual salary / # of working days) x (course length + travel time) x (# of participants to be trained)

4. **Participant Travel and Expense Cost** = { (travel cost) + [(course length + travel time) x (accommodation cost)] } x (# of participants to be trained)

5. **Participant Course Materials Cost** = (package cost per participant) x (# of participants)

6. **Trainer Salary Cost (teaching)** = (trainer annual salary / trainer working days) x (course length) x (# of classes)

    where # of classes = (total # of participants / # of participants per class)

7. **Trainer Salary Cost (preparing)** = (trainer annual salary / trainer working days) x (course length x trainer preparation ratio)

8. **Classroom Cost** = { (# of classes x course length) / 260 } x (annual classroom cost)

where the number of classes = total # of participants / Trainer to participant ratio

9. **Special Course Equipment** Cost = { (# of classes x course length) / 260 } x (equipment cost)

where 260 is the average number of work days available in one calendar year - this value may be modified to fit your company's requirements

10. **Translation** Cost = (cost for 1 translation) x (number of translations required)

11. **Evaluation** Cost = cost from the Evaluation Plan

The Total Cost of Training is therefore calculated as:

TRAINING COST = (1) + (2) + (3) + (4) + (5) + (6) + (7) + (8) + (9) + (10) + (11)

Please note, all formulas may not be relevant according to your company's needs, therefore, only include appropriate items. The following is an example of how the formulas can be used:

A major corporation wishes to double its close rate on sales proposals. Currently their sales personnel average 20 proposals per month, closing, on average, 2 per month. A training program to double the close rate to 4 is to be implemented. The following cost elements for this program are:

Element	Cost
Number of people to be trained	*10*
Number of actual working days per year	*220*
Average employee annual cost	*$100,000*
Length of training session (in days)	*5*
Related travel time (in days)	*2*
Average cost of travel	*$500*
Average cost daily of accommodation	*$75*
Annual cost of trainer	*$50,000*
Weekly course development cost	*$1,000*
Course development ratio	*25 to 1*
Weekly instructional design cost	*$1,500*
Instructional design ratio	*15 to 1*
Participant course materials cost	*$10*
Trainer / participant ratio	*10*
Working days per year for trainer	*220*
Trainer preparation ratio	*3 to 1*
Annual classroom cost	*$1,000*

Equipment cost	*$200*
Translation cost	*$500*
Number of translations required	2
Evaluation cost	*$1,000*

The calculations for this example are:

1. **Design** *cost* = *(5 / 5) x ($1,500) x (15)*
            = *(1) x ($1,500) x (15)*
            = *$22,500*

2. **Development** *cost* = *(5 / 5) x ($1,000) x (25)*
                 = *(1) x ($1,000) x (25)*
                 = *$25,000*

3. **Participant salary** *cost* = *($100,000 / 220) x (5 + 2) x (10)*
                     = *($454) x (7) x (10)*
                     = *$31,780*

4. **Travel and expense** *cost* = *{ ($500) + [(5 + 2) x $75] } x (10)*
                      = *{ ($500) + [(7) x $75] } x (10)*
                      = *{ ($500) + [$525] } x (10)*
                      = *{ $1025 } x (10)*
                      = *$10,250*

5. **Participant package** *cost* = *($10) x (10)*
                      = *$100*

6. **Trainer salary cost** *(teaching)* = *($50,000 / 220) x (5) x (1)*
                         = *($227) x (5) x (1)*
                         = *$1,135*

7. **Trainer salary cost** *(preparing)* = *($50,000 / 220) x (5) x (3)*
                          = *($227) x (5) x (3)*
                          = *$3,405*

8. **Classroom cost** = (5 / 260) x $1,000
                          = .019 x $1,000
                          = $19

9. **Special course equipment cost** = $200

10. **Translation** cost = ($500) x (2)
                          = $1,000

11. **Evaluation cost** = $1,000

    Total cost = (1) + (2) + (3) + (4) + (5) + (6) + (7) + (8) + (9) + (10) + (11)

=   22,500 + 25,000 + 31,780 + 10,250 + 100 + 1,135 + 3,405 + 19 + 200 +
    1,000 + 1,000

= $96,389

Using these formulas, build an analysis model to calculate the total cost of training. Once the model has been created and tested, it can be used for additional Level 4 evaluation studies by simply changing the parameters used in the calculations.

Once the total cost of training model is complete, you need to develop an analysis model to assist in analyzing the value of training. This is typically the results of the control group versus the experimental group. In the Level 4 example used above to calculate costs, the control group and the experimental group are the same individuals. The results of the control group are <u>before training</u> with the experimental results being computed <u>after training</u>. This is know as the baseline approach. Using this approach, the control data for sales results were:

1. Close rate/proposal (per employee) = 2/20
2. Average value of sale (per employee) = $5,000
3. Average value of sales per month (per employee) = $10,000
4. Average value of sale per year (for corporation) = $1,200,000
5. Cost of goods (25% of sales) = $300,000
6. Cost of sales (10% of sales) = $120,000
7. Profit = $1,200,000 - $300,000 - $120,000
          = $780,000

The impact (results) received from training (experimental) was:

1. Close rate/proposal (per employee) = 4/20
2. Average value of sale (per employee) = $5,000
3. Average value of sales per month (per employee) = $20,000
4. Average value of sale per year (for company) = $2,400,000
5. Cost of goods (25% of sales) = $600,000
6. Cost of sales (10% of sales) = $240,000
7. Profit = $2,400,000 - $600,000 - $240,000

$$= \$1,560,000$$

Using this data, the value of training is:

Profit after training - Profit before training $= \$1,560,000 - \$780,000$
$$= \$780,000$$

Analysis models for Level 4 Evaluation follow this type of format and are based around the measures agreed upon in the Plan phase of the Training Evaluation Process.

-- END OF TASK 2 --

3. OBTAIN AGREEMENT TO THE DATA COLLECTION INSTRUMENTS AND ANALYSIS MODELS.

Once the data collection instruments and analysis models have been developed, the final task in the Develop phase is to obtain agreement among funding organization (client), evaluator, trainer, and key stakeholders to the data collection instruments and analysis models. This agreement is paramount to the success of the evaluation collection effort, analysis, and reporting of results. With this agreement all parties involved in the training evaluation understand what will and will not be collected and what tools will be used for analyzing data.

Exhibit 60 depicts the input, input requirements, supplier, output, output requirements, customer, and tasks associated with this activity.

Exhibit 60: Task 1 Obtain Agreement to the Data Collection Instruments and Analysis Models

Supplier	Input	Input Req.	TASKS	Output	Output Req.	Customer
Task No. 2 of the Develop phase of the Training Evaluation Process.	Data collection instruments. Data analysis models.	Meets the needs defined in the Evaluation Plan.	Provide copies of the data collection instruments and th analysis models to stakeholders.	Agreed upon and approved data collection instruments and analysis models.	Meets the needs defined in the Evaluation Plan. Satisfies all require-ments of evaluation stake-holders.	Task No. 1 of the Obtain Phase of the Training Eval-uation Process.
			Document how each instrument and model are used.			
			Solicit comments in written form.			

To obtain agreement to data collection instruments and analysis models, perform the following:

1. Provide copies of the data collection instruments and their associated data analysis models to evaluation stakeholders.
2. Include a cover letter documenting how each instrument and model are to be used.
3. Meet with key evaluation stakeholders to discuss instruments, analysis models, and their use.
4. Set a deadline for suggestions and comments.
5. Solicit comments in written form.

After receiving stakeholder comments, decide that comments are valid and incorporate them into the models. Finally, distribute models to course development and course delivery organizations for use.

- END OF TASK 3 -

In summary the Develop phase of the Training Evaluation Process creates the data collections instruments and the data analysis models used in the evaluation. These tools are supplied to the Obtain phase to collect the evaluation data at the various evaluation levels. Exhibit 61 shows the tasks and major output for each task within the Develop phase.

Exhibit 61:   Summary of the Development Phase

Task	Output
1. Generate Data Collection Instruments.	Data collection instruments.
2. Create Models to Analyze Data for Levels 1-4.	Data analysis models.
3. Obtain agreement to the Data Collection Instruments and Analysis Models.	Agreed upon and approved data collection instruments and analysis models.

References

1. Sulivan, R. L., Wircenski, J. L., Arnold, S. S., Sarkees M. D., A Practical Manual for the Design, Delivery, and Evaluation of Training, (1990), Aspen, Rockville, Maryland
2. United States Office of Personnel Management, A Guide to participant Action Plan Approach, Washington, DC
3. Phillips, J. J., Handbook of Training Evaluation and Measurement Methods, (1983), Gulf, Houston, TX
4. Phillips, J. J., Handbook of Training Evaluation and Measurement Methods, (1983), Gulf, Houston, TX

5. OBTAIN EVALUATION DATA

Purpose of This Chapter

The purpose of this chapter is to provide you with the knowledge and ability to perform the third phase of the Training Evaluation Process -- Obtain Evaluation Data. These tasks encompass administering the data collection instruments developed in the previous phase. Administration of data collection instruments entails having respondents complete questionnaires and interviews, having participants take knowledge checks, etc.

Administration of the data collection instruments (obtaining evaluation data) is carried out according to the Evaluation Plan. Data collection, due the unique time constraints associated with the four levels of evaluation, occurs in stages. During the validation portion of the course development process, formative evaluation data are collected. This is followed by collection of Levels 1 and 2 data collection during program release, which in turn is followed by the administration of Levels 3 and 4 data collection.

Objectives of This Chapter

At the conclusion of this chapter, you can:

1. Administer data collection instruments according to the Evaluation Plan.
2. Screen completed instruments for accuracy.
3. Input collected data into analysis models.

OBTAINING EVALUATION DATA

Exhibit 62: The Obtain Phase of the Training Evaluation Process

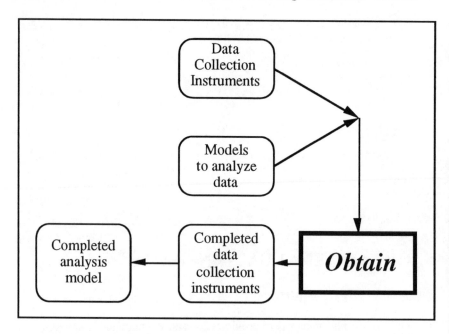

This phase of the Training Evaluation Process involves gathering information to address the evaluation questions. The method used in this phase is implementation (administration) of data collection instruments. Data sources (domains where evaluation can be obtained) include people, documents, performance data (in the training session and on-the-job), observations, and accounting records. The domains are bounded by the type of data being collected, sophistication of the respondent, and type of data collection instrument.

The goal is to obtain enough data of the right kind at the lowest cost to answer the evaluation questions. The amount of data collected and how it is obtained is explained in the Evaluation Plan. You also must report sound and credible information to audiences in order for the information to be believed and used for program improvement.

Plans for obtaining data are made after evaluation questions have been decided upon in phase 1: Plan. After the evaluation is planned and major questions drafted, the Develop phase of the Training Evaluation Process generates the instruments used in this phase. In the Obtain phase, data are systematically collected to prevent loss and simplify analysis of data. The user of this phase is the course implementation organization(s) or evaluator depending upon the Evaluation Plan and evaluation level.

OBTAIN INPUT

Input to this phase is received from three sources:

1. Phase 2: Develop which supplies the data collection instruments and analysis models.
2. The evaluation respondents. Respondents vary from evaluation level to evaluation level and according to the Evaluation Plan. For Levels 1 and 2, respondents are exclusively the participants themselves. In Level 3, the respondents, depending upon the Evaluation Plan, include the participants and others such as participants' managers, peers, and subordinates.
3. Organizational accounting records (for Levels 3 and 4).

Phase 2: Develop provides the data collection instruments and data analysis models. The evaluation respondents are individuals who have responded to the training evaluation through data collection instruments (filing out questionnaires, taking knowledge checks, etc.). Organizational accounting records provide data used in Level 3 and Level 4 evaluations.

OBTAIN OUTPUT

The output of Phase 3: Obtain is completed analysis models containing results of the data collection effort. The completed instrument is input to Phase 4: Analyze.

As discussed in Chapter 2, obtaining data is a cyclical procedure occurring at various stages of the training program. When a training program is first piloted to find its effectiveness and identify areas for improvement, evaluation Levels 1 (Reaction) and 2 (Learning) are used. The participants are the source for obtaining this data. The evaluation data from the pilot is sent to the next phase of the Training Evaluation Process to help in program improvement.

After pilot testing, the improved training program is released for general attendance by the intended participant population. During this time, as defined in the Evaluation Plan, Level 1 and Level 2 data are collected. This data is analyzed as deemed necessary by organization(s) delivering training for improving course delivery. If documented in the Evaluation Plan, Level 3 (Behavior) evaluation is performed. Level 3 cannot be done until Level 1 and Level 2 have been carried out and Level 2 evaluation results are positive.

Enough time since completion of training must pass in order for participants to try their new on-the-job skills before Level 3 data collection can occur. The evaluation data from this level is sent to the next phase of the Training Evaluation Process to help in program improvement. Finally, if the Evaluation Plan calls for a Level 4 (Results) evaluation and Level 3 evaluation is completed and results are positive, it is performed.

During these cyclical activities, the Training Evaluation Process continues with the Analyze phase. This is not a linear process, but as stated previously, a cyclical one involving constant review and reporting. Phase 3: Obtain will begin with the first pilot class and continue until its end is reached as defined in the <u>Evaluation Plan</u>. The Training Evaluation Process continues with Phase 4: Analyze. Phase 3 does not have to conclude in order for Phase 4 to commence.

OBTAIN TASKS

The Obtain phase of the Training Evaluation Process is comprised of a series of work tasks needed to collect data and place it into the appropriate analysis model(s). The five tasks identified with obtaining evaluation data are:

1. Secure copies of the <u>data collection instruments</u> and <u>analysis models</u> being used with this evaluation.
2. Understand the purpose, intended audience, and data collection timetable for each <u>data collection instrument</u>.
3. Administer <u>data collection instruments</u> according to the <u>Evaluation Plan</u>.
4. Screen completed <u>data collection instruments</u>.
5. Input data into <u>analysis models</u>.

Following is each task that makes up the Obtain phase.

1. SECURE COPIES OF THE <u>DATA COLLECTION INSTRUMENTS</u> AND <u>ANALYSIS MODELS</u> BEING USED WITH THIS EVALUATION

The purpose of this task is to acquire the <u>data collection instruments</u> and <u>analysis models</u> that are being used with this evaluation. Data collection cannot occur until these elements are secured. Exhibit 63 depicts the inputs, input requirements, supplier, outputs, output requirements, customer, and tasks associated with securing copies of the instruments and analysis models.

Exhibit 63: Secure Copies of the <u>Data Collection Instruments</u> and <u>Analysis Models</u> being used with this evaluation

Supplier	Input	Input Req.	TASKS	Output	Output Req.	Customer
The Develop Phase of the Training Evaluation Process.	Data collection instruments Data analysis models.	Meets the needs defined in the Evaluation Plan. Satisfies all requirements of the evaluation stakeholders.	Obtain, read, and understand the Evaluation Plan. Secure copies of the <u>data collection instruments</u> and the <u>data analysis models</u>	Possession of relevant <u>data collection instruments</u> and <u>data analysis models</u>.	All required instruments and models are in possession.	Task No. 2: <u>Under-stand the purpose, intended audience, and data collec-tion timetable for each data collec-tion instru-ment of the Obtain Phase.</u>

To understand and perform proper data collection you need to *obtain, read, and understand the <u>Evaluation Plan</u>*. By having a working knowledge of the <u>Evaluation Plan</u>, you will know what <u>data collection instruments</u> are to be used, when, and how. Secondly, you also need to know what <u>analysis models</u> are used with each instrument. By having this knowledge you can then *secure all <u>data collection instruments</u> and <u>analysis models</u>* that are used in the Obtain phase.

-- END OF TASK 1 --

2. UNDERSTAND THE PURPOSE, INTENDED AUDIENCE, AND DATA COLLECTION TIMETABLE FOR EACH <u>DATA COLLECTION INSTRUMENT</u>

After all instruments and models have been obtained and before using them during data collection efforts, you must know the purpose of the instrument (what evaluation question(s) it is designed to answer), who the audience is, who will complete the instrument, and when (collection timetable) the instrument is to be administered. Exhibit 64 depicts the inputs, input requirements, supplier, outputs, output requirements, customer, and tasks associated with this task.

Exhibit 64: Understand the Purpose, Intended Audience, and Data Collection Timetable for each **Data Collection Instrument**

Supplier	Input	Input Req.	TASKS	Output	Output Req.	Customer
Task 1 of the Obtain Phase of the Training Evaluation Process.	Secured copies of the appropriate data collection instruments and data analysis models.	You have the latest copy of all instruments, models, instructions, and Evaluation Plan. All required instruments and models are in possession.	Read all instructions associated with each instrument. Compare instructions with the Evaluation Plan. Develop personal timetable unique to this training program and its associated evaluation.	Personal timetable unique to this training program and its associated evaluation.	You feel comfortable with: 1) what the instrument is used for 2) who will complete the instrument 3) how it is to be administered 4) when it is to be administrated.	Task No. 3: Administer data collection instruments according to the evaluation plan of the Obtain phase.

First, *read all instructions with each instrument.* The instructions provide the information necessary to begin planning how the data collection instrument(s) are used for this specific training program. Information the instructions provide includes:

1. When is the instrument administered? For example, a Level 2 performance-based knowledge check is designed to be given at the conclusion of a specific training module.
2. How often is it administered?
3. Who completes the instrument?
4. Are there any special instructions or procedures you need to give to the respondent to implement that are beyond what is written on the instrument?
5. Are additional personnel (e.g., someone other than the trainer conducting the Level 1 interview) required? If so, who is required and when are they needed?
6. What do you do with completed instruments? Where are they sent?

Next, *compare the instructions with the Evaluation Plan.* This validates the instructions and the interpretation of them. The interpretation must correspond to the Evaluation Plan. If it does not, meet with the instrument developer and work out any inconsistencies. If this is not fixed, this problem data maybe obtained that is unwanted, not usable, or biased; therefore adversely affecting the evaluation.

When you understand the instructions and they match the Evaluation Plan, formulate a *personal timetable unique to this training program and its associated evaluation* for data collection. A personal timetable allows for establishing, by instrument, the process for collecting evaluation data. This timetable is unique for the given training program. Tips for a timetable are:

1. Level 1: Reaction - questionnaires are completed by participants at the conclusion of training. A good pattern to follow is to administer the questionnaire during the morning of the last training day. The major reason for doing this is that responses to the questionnaire can be scanned by the individual who will conduct the whole class interview, thus, providing them with possible areas for probing. If you wait to the last minute to administer the questionnaire, participants will hurry in completing the instrument because they want to go home, have to "catch" a plane, etc. By administering the questionnaire in the morning, more time can be taken thereby increasing the sincerity of the data obtained. Interviews are typically scheduled as the last training activity and are performed by someone other than the trainer. Be sure enough time (at least thirty minutes) has been set aside to conduct the interview.

2. Level 2: Learning - Level 2 data collection instruments are composed of knowledge-based checks (pre- and post-course knowledge checks) along with performance-based checking. As described earlier, the type of check depends upon the training objective being evaluated. Pre-course knowledge checks are the first event of training. Post-course knowledge checks may be final exams or small unit checks (quizzes) that comprise a final check. Performance-based checking follows the flow of training and is administered after a unit of instruction that taught the skill to be mastered. Note: Confidentiality of training scores must be maintained. Instructors must be fully aware that Level 2 evaluation is to be used only in program improvement decisions.

3. Level 3: Behavior - Level 3 instrument administration depends upon the type of instrument being used. The following list shows the recommended data collection method for a given instrument.

   A. Questionnaire: A questionnaire is mailed to participants after the period in the Evaluation Plan has elapsed. To increase the amount of returned instruments, use the following procedure:

      * Prepare (duplicate) questionnaires before the start of training.
      * After the pre-course knowledge check, pass out the questionnaire to each participant. Discuss questionnaire purpose, how to fill it out,

and how to return it.
* Distribute to each participant an envelope. Have the participants address the envelopes to themselves and "stuff" the questionnaire into the envelope.
* Pass out another envelope with prepaid postage addressed to the individual who will be collecting the completed questionnaires. Have participants "stuff" this envelope into the envelope addressed to themselves.
* Have the participants seal the envelope and return it to you. Place these into a pile and label them with the date they are to be mailed.
* When the mailing date arrives, place the envelopes into the mail.

B. Action Plan: Follow the procedure below to obtain action plan data:

* Prepare (duplicate) the Action Plan before training.
* At the conclusion of training, pass out Action Plan sheets to all participants. Discuss purpose and how to fill them out.
* Have participants complete their Action Plan. The trainer reviews each participant Action Plan and signs the document. A copy of the Action Plan is given to the participant.
* Follow the procedure for Level 3 questionnaires to obtain Action Plan follow-up data.

C. Interview: Interviewing participants is typically done by telephone. To conduct a telephone interview, perform the following:

* Call each participant to schedule a time to conduct the interview. Schedule no longer than thirty minutes. The interview MUST BE CONDUCTED AT THE CONVENIENCE OF THE PARTICIPANT not the evaluator.
* Prepare (duplicate) the interview form.
* When the agreed upon date and time arrive, call the participant and conduct the interview.

D. Observation: Observations require someone to examine participant behavior on-the-job. To conduct observations:

* Train observers and prepare (duplicate) data collection instruments.
* If more than one individual will be conducting the observations, develop an observation guide so that consistent data is obtained.
* Contact participants and their management to secure permission to observe.
* Schedule the observations and conduct them.

4. Level 4: Results   Data collection for Level 4 evaluation encompasses two
    actions: 1) using the data collection instrument to obtain cost parameters
    associated with design, development, and delivery of training, and 2)
    accessing existing accounting records to extrapolate control and experimental
    group data based upon measures agreed to in the Evaluation Plan.   Looking
    at each task individually:

    A. Using the data collection instrument developed in the previous Training
        Evaluation Process phase, meet with the individuals/organizations who
        maintain these cost parameters.   No one organization has all this data.
        Typical organizations to investigate are:

        *   Design groups - for course design costs.
        *   Development groups - for course development & maintenance
            costs.
        *   Implementation groups - for delivery costs associated with trainers,
            facilities, and course materials.
        *   Finance departments - for cost incurred by participants (salary,
            travel, etc.)

    B. Calculating the value of training requires access and copies of
        accounting records for both control and experimental groups.
        Accounting data may come in computer data files or by printed reports.
        No matter what format data is received in it will never be provided in a
        method that is totally compatible with Level 4 evaluation value
        estimations.   The data is collected in whatever form exists and is input
        into the data analysis model for calculation.

5. Establish when the data will be needed and schedule backwards in time.

    Finally, examine under what conditions the data collection instruments will
be administered.   This is known as a "context analysis".   This type of analysis
investigates the elements that surround the evaluation and course that may
influence the data gathered.   By analyzing the environment of the evaluation you
can:

1. Describe the factors that influenced or will influence results.
2. Maintain a log of any unusual circumstances such as the change in the
    General Manager position at a plant that may affect training evaluation
    results.
3. Record where the course was delivered differently than designed.

    The result of knowing and understanding proper methods for obtaining
evaluation data allows you to create your own personal timetable for data

collection. These timetables are unique for each evaluation study. Exhibit 65 is an example of a data collection timetable used at Motorola University.

Exhibit 65: Data Collection Timetable

Evaluation Timetable for Data Collection				
Training Activities	**Evaluation Levels**			
	Level 1	**Level 2**	**Level 3**	**Level 4**
Development Test	Participant Assessment with additional questions and whole class interview.	Pre-test, Performance test, Post-test.		
Pilot Test	Participant Assessment with additional questions and whole class interview.	Pre-test, Performance test, Post-test.	Participants fill out Action Plan Work-sheet.	
Ongoing course impl-ementation	Participant Assessment.	Pre-test, Performance test, Post-test.	Participants fill out Action Plan Work-sheet.	
Six months after course release			Action Plan follow-up Mail questionnaires	Calculate training cost and training value

Exhibit 65 shows a typical timetable used to prepare for collection of training evaluation data. The top column of the matrix depicts the four levels of evaluation while the left-hand column describes various events within the life-cycle of a new course. The comments within the timetable describe what actions the evaluator needs to perform. With this personal timetable created, you can proceed to the next task.

-- END OF TASK 2 --

3. ADMINISTER DATA COLLECTION INSTRUMENTS ACCORDING TO THE EVALUATION PLAN

To answer the evaluation questions, the proper data must be obtained within the specified period (outlined in the Evaluation Plan). It is imperative that data are collected in a timely systematic way. Data that is collected late is as good as no data collected at all. Data that is collected in a random, non-systematic way will be biased and incomplete. Exhibit 66 shows the inputs, input requirements, supplier, outputs, output requirements, customer, and tasks associated with this task.

Exhibit 66: Administer Data Collection Instruments According to the Evaluation Plan

Supplier	Input	Input Req.	TASKS	Output	Output Req.	Customer
Task No. 2 of the Obtain phase of the Training Evaluation Process.	Personal data collection timetable. Individuals responding are from the target population.	You have the latest copy of all instruments, models, instructions, and Evaluation Plan.	Duplicate all required data collection instruments. Administer data collection instruments.	Completed data collection instruments.	Collection carried out according to the Evaluation Plan and personal timetable.	Task No. 4: Screen completed data collection instruments of the Obtain Phase.
Evaluation respondents.	Accurate & complete accounting records. Data collection instruments, data analysis models, and Evaluation Plan.				Collected data accurately reflects the conditions associated with the course.	

Before data collection, the *instruments being used are duplicated.* This ensures no last minute hurrying that could in turn harm the data collection effort. To ensure a smooth data collection effort, estimate the number of instruments needed to collect all evaluation data. At times, you can duplicate instruments differently depending upon the respondents. For example, if a Level 3 evaluation calls for responses by participants and their managers, a good idea is to duplicate participant instruments on white paper and manager instruments on blue. This simple technique eases the chore of separating participant and manager completed instruments. Next, *administer <u>data collection instruments</u>* as defined in the <u>Evaluation Plan</u>. The next few sections describe various techniques used during data collection, by evaluation level.

Level 1 Tips on Collecting Data

<u>Questionnaire</u>

1. Administer at conclusion of training.
2. Be sure participants have enough time to answer the instrument.
3. To avoid participant fear, have a participant pass out, collect, place questionnaires in a sealed envelope, and take it to a central collection point.

<u>Class interview</u>

1. Allow interviewer access to questionnaire responses.
2. Be sure someone other than the trainer conducts the interview.
3. Ensure the trainer is not present during the interview.

Level 2 Tips on Collecting Data

<u>Pre-Course Knowledge Check</u>

1. Pass out Pre-Course Knowledge Check after class introduction and before instruction.
2. Provide adequate instructions to participants including:

    A. This is not a check of your abilities, but a check of the course.
    B. The perfect score is zero percent - you are perfectly suited to be in this course.
    C. If you don't know an answer, leave it blank or mark the I DON'T KNOW space provided. DO NOT GUESS.
    D. Stress confidentiality.

4. Collect Pre-Course Knowledge Checks from participants.
5. Score Pre-Course Knowledge Checks.
6. Record participant Pre-Course Knowledge Check scores on a Course Control Document.
7. File the checks for later use by the evaluator when they perform an item analysis.

Post-Course Knowledge Check

1. Post-Course Knowledge Checks may be a final exam or a series of small checks that when combined are equal to the Pre-Course Knowledge Check.
2. Provide adequate instructions and time to participants.
3. Collect Post-Course Knowledge Checks from participants.
4. During or shortly after training, score the checks.
5. Record participant Post-Course Knowledge Check scores on a Course Control Document.
6. File the checks for later use by the evaluator when they do an item analysis.

Performance Check

1. Performance Checks test participant mastery of a skill. Performance Checks follow a unit of instruction that taught the skill.
2. Provide proper instructions and adequate time to complete the Performance Checks.
3. Ensure all job aids, tools, equipment, etc., are in place for participants to use during the check.
4. Record participant progress against a Skills Checklist.
5. As a trainer, be available to help participants during the check.
6. Record participant scores on a Course Control Document.
7. File Skills Checklist and any examples of participant work so that the evaluator can use the data during an item analysis.

Level 3 Tips on Collecting Data

Questionnaire

1. Duplicate questionnaires before training. If more than one type of respondent is to be used (i.e., participant and participant manager), consider duplicating in different colors, different type face, etc.
2. At the beginning of training describe the purpose and procedure that will be used to collect Level 3 evaluation data. Sell the participants on the importance of this activity.
3. As described previously in this chapter, have the participants "stuff" the envelopes.
4. Mail the questionnaires as defined in the Evaluation Plan.
5. When questionnaires are returned, sort them using the duplication scheme devised in the first step.

Action Plan

1. Duplicate blank action plans before training. Action plans are duplicated in three-part paper that eases the task of filing and data analysis. One copy is given to the participant and two are retained by the trainer.
2. At or near conclusion of training, discuss the action plan approach with the participants.
3. Have participants complete the action plan.
4. The trainer reads, negotiates, and signs the action plan next to the participant signature.
5. The action plans are filed for follow up.
6. At the time specified in the Evaluation Plan, conduct the follow-up.

    A. Questionnaire is mailed to participants and they complete it and return it, or
    B. The evaluator conducts a telephone interview with the participant. During this exercise, the participant needs their copy of the action plan and the interviewer needs a copy to work from. At times, the participant will have misplaced or lost their action plan. If this happens, the evaluator sends the participant the extra copy of the action plan.

Interview

1. During training, inform participants that they will be interviewed. Discuss the purpose and reasons why this activity is so important to program improvement.
2. At the time stipulated in the Evaluation Plan, using random sampling, create a list of participants that will be interviewed.
3. Duplicate interview forms.
4. If required, train interviewers.
5. Call each participant and schedule twenty to thirty minutes to conduct the interview. The date agreed to MUST BE AT THE CONVENIENCE OF THE RESPONDENT. Try not to execute the interview now. It is best if the respondent has time to prepare before the interview. However, if the respondent insists, conduct the interview; otherwise wait until later.
6. At the previously agreed upon date and time call the respondent. Ask if the time is still convenient to conduct the interview. If it is not, reschedule. If it is convenient, conduct the interview using the following techniques:

    A. Remind the respondent of the purpose and reason for the interview.
    B. Provide instructions on how to answer.
    C. Use active listening techniques by:

1. Asking the question.
2. Recording the response.
3. Summarizing the response and repeating it to the respondent to ensure a common comprehension of the answer.
4. Passing no judgments due to a response.

D. End with a thank you.

7. File the results away so they may be input into the appropriate <u>data analysis model</u>.

<u>Focus Group</u>

1. Contact all members of the group and establish a date, time, and place for the exchange. The date, time, and place are set at the CONVENIENCE OF THE GROUP MEMBERS.
2. Meet with the focus group. Remind the group of the purpose and reason for the meeting.
3. Provide the group with instructions and procedures for participating.
4. For each question asked, do the following:

A. Pose the question to the entire group.
B. Solicit voluntary responses. Be sure not to word questions in such a way as to influence responses.
C. Record responses of the group.
D. Summarize responses to ensure understanding by all parties.

8. File the group responses for the evaluator to analyze later.

<u>Observation</u>

1. As defined in the <u>Evaluation Plan</u>, contact the participant and their immediate manager to obtain permission to observe. If permission is granted, establish a date, time, and place for the observation. The date, time, and place are set at the CONVENIENCE OF THE PARTICIPANT AND THEIR MANAGER.
2. Duplicate observation forms and if necessary duplicate the observation guidelines (when more than one observer is being used).
3. Train observers.
4. Ensure all equipment necessary for the observation is available to the observer or shipped to the observation site.
5. At the agreed upon date and time, meet with the participant and their manager to establish the routine for the observation. Try to understand what the participant will be doing. Discuss with the participant the techniques

that will be used during the observation. This will help reduce the fears and tension the participant will feel during observation.

6. Conduct the observation and record participant behaviors on the observation form(s). If additional personnel are involved while the participant is being observed, be sure to introduce yourself and discuss what and why you are observing.

7. After the observation, go over the completed forms with the participant. This will help you in filling in any gaps that occurred during the observation. Pass no judgments or give opinions as to the success of participant behavior. Only discuss what was observed and how it was recorded.

8. File the observation forms for the evaluator to analyze later.

Level 4 Tips on Collecting Data

Total Cost of Training

1. Collect the following costs:

    A. Design.
    B. Development or Purchase cost.
    C. Participant salary while in training.
    D. Participant travel and expense cost.
    E. Participant material cost.
    F. Equipment cost.
    G. Classroom cost.
    H. Trainer salary cost while conducting training and preparing.
    F. Evaluation cost.

Control and Experimental Groups

1. Identify the course being evaluated.
2. Specify the job class to be evaluated.
3. Collect personnel records to create a list of all employees within the specified job class. This is the entire population who could be trained.
4. Source training database for names of individuals who have completed training for the specified job class. This becomes your experimental group.
5. Compare the experimental group to the entire population. Employees who are listed in the entire population but have not been trained become the control group.
6. Compare the population sizes of the experimental and control groups. Usually they will be of different sizes. Randomly choose employees from one group so that the two groups are of equal sizes.

Determine the value of training

1. Ensure the following guidelines are followed:

    A. Evaluation Levels 1, 2, and 3 have been performed.
    B. Level 3 results suggest positive transfer of training behaviors to the job.
    C. Control and experimental groups can be established.
    D. Random sampling is used when creating the control and experimental groups.
    E. Accounting records exist and the evaluator has access to them.

2. Generate reports for the evaluation period from the accounting records for the control and experimental groups.
3. Input data into data analysis model(s).
4. Aggregate results for the control and experimental groups.
5. Run a statistical test and check if a .05 or less level of significance is achieved between the control and experimental group results.
6. If the significance is realized and the experimental group has outperformed the control group, determine the value of training. This can be done in one of two methods (or a combination of both):

    A. Show the value if the control group were trained (e.g., increased sales volume, reduced cycle time, etc.).
    B. Project the increased value of the experimental group into the future to expand the results.

-- END OF TASK 3 --

4. SCREEN   COMPLETED   DATA   COLLECTION INSTRUMENTS

After data collection instruments have been administered, the collected data (designated as raw data) needs to been screened (checked) for accuracy. Exhibit 67 depicts the inputs, input requirements, supplier, outputs, output requirements, customer, and tasks associated with screening data collection instruments.

Exhibit 67: Screen Completed <u>Data Collection Instruments</u>

Supplier	Input	Input Req.	TASKS	Output	Output Req.	Customer
Task No. 3 of the Obtain phase of the Training Evaluation Process.	Completed <u>data collection instruments.</u>	Collection carried out as defined in the <u>Evaluation Plan.</u> Collected data accurately reflects the conditions associated with the course. Respondents completing the instruments are from the defined target population.	The collected information is organized (coded) so that some sense can be made of it. Decide if the organized data is worth sending to the next phase.	Screened completed <u>data collection instruments.</u>	Instruments sorted properly. Data instruments that are unusable are removed from the collection effort.	Task No. 5: <u>Input data into analysis models</u> of the Obtain Phase.

First, a decision is made whether the raw data is sound enough to warrant sending it to the next task in the Obtain phase. Often, this activity is done in stages:

Stage 1: The collected information is organized (coded) so that some sense can be made of it.
Stage 2: A decision is made to determine the organized data is worth sending to the next phase.

First, *place the data into one whole unit and code as necessary.* Coding completed data collection instruments means separating the instruments into logical groups. For example, separating pre-course knowledge checks from post-course checks or dividing Level 3 participant questionnaires from management Level 3 questionnaires.

Next, *decide if the organized data is worth sending to the next task.* This action requires examining completed data collection instruments and removing all instruments that have been completed incorrectly or are in some way deficient. This ensures that data used during analysis is not tarnished or presents an untrue picture of the training program. The rules that specify what criteria remove a completed instrument from the raw data are documented in the <u>Evaluation Plan.</u> It is important that instruments that are removed are not thrown away. Analysis of these documents often shed light on training issues that may have gone overlooked.

-- END OF TASK 4 --

5. INPUT DATA INTO <u>ANALYSIS MODELS</u>

After completed data collection instruments have been divided (coded) into logical groups and instruments that do not meet defined acceptable criteria removed from the raw data, the Obtain phase continues with entering the data into the analysis model(s). Exhibit 67 shows the inputs, input requirements, supplier, outputs, output requirements, customer, and tasks associated with this task.

Exhibit 68: Input Data Into <u>Analysis   Models</u>

Supplier	Input	Input Req.	TASKS	Output	Output Req.	Customer
Task No. 4 of the Obtain Phase of the Training Evaluation Process.	Screened completed <u>data collection instruments</u>.	Instruments sorted properly. Data instruments that are unusable are removed from the collection effort.	Enter data from the completed <u>data collection instruments</u> into the <u>data analysis models</u>.	<u>Data Analysis Model(s)</u> with Levels 1, 2, 3, or 4 evaluation data.	All raw data successfully entered into <u>data analysis models</u>.	The Analyze Phase of the Training Evaluation Process.

Following the instructions documented in the <u>Evaluation Plan</u> and accompanying the analysis model, raw data (completed data collection instruments) are entered into appropriate <u>data analysis model(s)</u>. The tasks undertaken during this activity depend upon the data collected, the level of evaluation, and the <u>data analysis model</u>.

For example, if the <u>data analysis model</u> is a spreadsheet on a personal computer, the tasks to enter data are:

1. Spreadsheet program is loaded into the personal computer.
2. Screened <u>data collection instrument</u> is read by the individual who is entering the data.
3. Respondents' values are keyed into the spreadsheet.
4. Spreadsheet program is saved to the personal computer disc storage system.

Tasks such as those listed above are defined in the <u>Evaluation Plan</u>.

Summary

The Obtain phase of the Training Evaluation Process collects evaluation data and inputs it into models for analysis. This phase has various work tasks depending upon the evaluation level and type of instrument used. However, accurate, timely, and usable data is imperative to a successful training evaluation. This phase, if followed correctly, provides this data. The output of each task within the Obtain phase is:

Exhibit 69: Summary of the Obtain Phase

Task	Output
1. Secure copies of the <u>Data Collection Instruments</u> and <u>Analysis Models</u> being used with this evaluation.	Possession of relevant <u>Date Collection Instruments</u> and <u>Data Analysis Models</u>.
2. Understand the purpose, intended, audience and data collection timetable for each <u>data collection instrument</u>.	Personal timetable unique to this training program and its associated evaluation.
3. Administer <u>Data Collection Instruments</u> according to the <u>Evaluation Plan</u>.	Completed <u>Data Collection Instruments</u>.
4. Screen Completed <u>Data Collection Instruments</u>.	Screened Completed <u>Data Collection Instruments</u>.
5. Input data into <u>Analysis Models</u>.	<u>Data Analysis Models</u> for Levels 1, 2, 3, or 4 evaluation data.

The Training Evaluation Process continues with the next phase, Analyze.

6. ANALYZE EVALUATION DATA

Purpose of This Chapter

The purpose of this chapter is to provide the knowledge and skills to perform the fourth phase of the Training Evaluation Process - the Analyze Phase. Evaluation data that is accurately planned and systematically collected but is analyzed improperly is worthless. Obtained data needs to be correctly analyzed and then interpreted so that sound business decisions are made. These decisions must be supported by sound, pragmatic procedures that yield information that accurately reflects results from training and answers the evaluation questions posed in the Evaluation Plan. This phase of the Training Evaluation Process supplies the step-by-step procedures for correctly analyzing and interpreting evaluation data.

Objectives of This Chapter

At the conclusion of this chapter, you can:

1. List and define the three outputs from the Analyze Phase.
2. Identify what to look for when verifying data.
3. Answer the training evaluation questions using the information generated.

ANALYZING EVALUATION DATA

Exhibit 70: The Analyze Phase

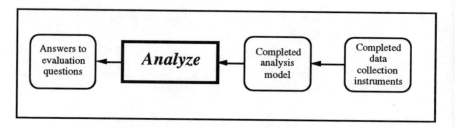

In the Analyze Phase of the Training Evaluation Process the meaning of the collected data is interpreted. This phase uses the collected data to determine the conclusions which the data supports and the amount of support the data supplies for, or against, those conclusions. The purpose of the Analyze Phase is to organize the data to answer the evaluation questions. The <u>user of this phase is the course development organization or evaluator.</u> The *Analyze* phase will begin when the minimum amount of data, as defined in the <u>Evaluation Plan,</u> has been collected and will conclude after the outputs have been created and before the date the <u>Evaluation Report</u> is due to be published.

Tasks of the Analyze Phase

As with all phases within the Training Evaluation Process, the Analyze phase is composed of a series of related work tasks. In these tasks, evaluation data are checked for completeness and accuracy, and a decision is made whether the data are sound enough to warrant an analysis. In summary, analysis of data is done in the tasks outlined below:

1. Organize and code collected data (in an easily understood format).
2. Decide whether the organized data is worth analyzing.
3. Perform a detailed analysis (to arrive at preliminary findings).
4. Answer the evaluation questions (using the synthesized findings).

Inputs to the Analyze Phase

Inputs to the Analyze Phase are the complete analysis models from the Obtain Phase of the Training Evaluation Process. These models form the basis for determining the answer to the evaluation questions and contain all data collected for this evaluation study.

Output of the Analyze Phase

The output from analyzing evaluation data is answers to the evaluation questions including statistics, graphs and tables that support those answers. The answers to the evaluation questions will be the interpretation of the collected data and will be input to the Report Evaluation Phase of the Training Evaluation Process. The statistics, graphs, charts, and tables that are used to support conclusions and answers to the evaluation questions. These entities are also input to the Report Evaluation phase.

To maintain a record of the procedures used and as a valid input for a Meta-evaluation (see chapter 8), document what you do to produce these outputs by keeping accurate and complete records.

1. **ORGANIZE AND CODE COLLECTED DATA (IN AN EASILY UNDERSTOOD FORMAT).**

Data must be properly managed and stored in preparing it for analysis. This includes coding, organizing and storing data for safekeeping and ready access. Data must be organized in ways that facilitate their use so that the information will not be lost or forgotten. This activity is an integral part of the previous Training Evaluation Process phase and may appear as repetition of previous work. However this activity assures that data has been properly prepared for analysis.

Exhibit 71 depicts the input, input requirements, supplier, output, output requirements, customer, and steps associated with organizing and coding data.

Exhibit 71: Organize and Code Collected Data

Supplier	Input	Input Req.	TASKS	Output	Output Req.	Customer
The Obtain Phase of the Training Evaluation Process.	Completed Analysis Models. Data collection instruments that have completed been by respondents.	Data collected as defined in the Evaluation Plan. All raw data successfully entered into the Data Analysis Models.	Check accuracy of coded data contained in the Data Analysis Models.	Data that is appropriately organized in the analysis models.	All data checked for accuracy and proper coding.	Task No. 2: Decide whether the Organized Data is Worth Analyzing of the Analyze Phase.

A coding system, as described in chapter 5, can be as simple as recording the data from the collection instruments by paper and pencil into a logical pattern for analysis. It can also be as extensive as creating a computer spreadsheet, relational data base, or a custom program. The coding system involves checking the accuracy of the coded data in the <u>data analysis models</u>.

To assure accurate analysis of the data, check for the following elements in coding:

1. All instruments have been entered into the analysis models. For example, does each participant have a Pre-test <u>and</u> a Post-test?
2. Instruments that were completed incorrectly or filled out incompletely have been eliminated from the models.
3. Different instrument types or different respondents with the same instrument have been separated into appropriate groups. For example, Level 1 questionnaires are not combined with Level 3 instruments or Level 3 participant responses are separate from Level 3 supervisor responses.

The above elements will verify the accuracy, completeness, and quality of the raw data. If problems with data collection arise, they may spoil the data and cause wrong interpretation of the results.

-- END OF TASK 1 --

2. DECIDE WHETHER THE ORGANIZED DATA IS WORTH ANALYZING.

When verifying evaluation data or determining if the data are worth organizing, certain problems tend to surface. Such problems may stop the Analyze Phase and cause the evaluator to step back and rework the data. This task allows the determination of the worth of the collected data. Exhibit 72 shows the input, input requirements, supplier, output, output requirements, customer, and steps associated with determining worth of evaluation data.

Exhibit 72: Decide whether the organized data is worth analyzing

Supplier	Input	Input Req.	TASKS	Output	Output Req.	Customer
Task No. 1 of the Analyze phase.	Data that are properly organized in the analysis models.	All coded data checked for accuracy and proper coding.	Examine all data and decide if it should be analyzed.	Decision whether to proceed with evaluation analysis.	Collected data accurately represents the results of the training program.	Task No. 3: Perform a detailed analysis of the Analyze Phase.

When *examining data to determine if they should be analyzed,* the processes used in collecting the data must be reviewed to assure that the data are worth analyzing. In making this determination, the following are suggested:

1. Ensure responses were complete and collection procedures were uninterrupted. Incomplete responses may be an indicator of a poorly

developed data collection instrument which in turn may yield inaccurate data. Data collection procedures that, for some reason, are interrupted may further spoil the data. If either of these two conditions exist, review the <u>Evaluation Plan</u>, development of the data collection instrument, or data collection procedures to determine if the analysis of data will result in sound information.

2. Ensure that there are no inconsistencies or coding errors.
3. Check that respondents are a true representative sample of the population. For example, if ten participants completing Level 2 tests are not part of the target population, their results need to be removed from the data set.
4. Ensure that there is a sufficient return of completed instruments. The return rate is specified in the <u>Evaluation Plan</u>. This is typically a problem for Level 3 data collections using survey as the instrumentality. If the return rate is low, there are two basic procedures to follow so that the rate specified in the <u>Evaluation Plan</u> is satisfied.

   A. Extend the data collection period, thus allowing additional time for the responses to arrive.
   B. Mail a reminder letter to the respondents to complete the instrumentality.

5. Ensure that administration procedures were implemented as planned.
6. Check to see that the numbers of unusual responses are few. A large number of unusual responses are indicators of poorly developed data collection instruments, respondents who are not part of the target population, or a combination of both concerns.
7. Check that the environment in which the data were collected has not significantly changed from the initial planning phase thus supplying the planned results.

There are a variety of procedures that can be used when verifying and checking data that has been received such as:

1. "The eyeball method": With this technique, instruments are scanned for responses, blank areas, or incorrect responses. For example, Level 1 and Level 3 evaluation interviews could be incomplete and the interview identified as short. Also in Levels 1 and 3 evaluations, the questionnaire pages could be missing. In Level 2 evaluation tests could be scored incorrectly, or trainers, feeling uncomfortable with a lesson or test, may have administered the test improperly or skipped it entirely. Within Level 4

evaluation, the accounting records that compare control and experimental groups may be incomplete or record different results.
2. "Spot-checks": Completed instruments or groups of instruments are chosen at random and checked for accuracy and completeness. If the group of instruments are accurate and complete, it can be assumed that the entire sample is accurate and complete.
3. "Audit": Information collection procedures are retraced to assure that there are no breaches in the evaluation practice. This assures properly obtained data.

The following are examples of circumstances to be aware of when verifying the value of the collected data. These will also help confirm that the data had been properly and correctly analyzed.

1. The more complex the instrument, the greater chance for errors. Therefore, data from complex instruments should be carefully examined.
2. The larger the data collection effort, the greater the chance of out of the ordinary responses. Therefore, data from a large sample, should be carefully examined.
3. Finally, criteria for verification are essential for the proper cleansing of data. The Training Evaluation Process suggests the following measures:

   A. Consistent use of established verification rules. Verification rules establish what constitutes acceptable completed data collection instruments.
   B. Documentation of the verification procedures used in the Evaluation Plan and the Evaluation Report

--END OF TASK 2 --

3. PERFORM A DETAILED ANALYSIS (TO ARRIVE AT PRELIMINARY FINDINGS).

Conducting a detailed analysis is the heart of the Analyze Phase. In this task the data are analyzed using sound procedures so that conclusions can be drawn from them. When conducting this sort of analysis, follow the steps outlined below:

1. Review the evaluation purpose and the questions to be addressed by the evaluation. This information is contained in the Evaluation

Plan.
2. Prepare the appropriate descriptive analysis and frequency distributions for each set of data and results.
3. Prepare a summary of basic issues, trends, relationships, and questions evident in the data.
4. Assess the available information relating to issues and questions to be pursued.

Exhibit 73 depicts the input, input requirements, supplier, output, output requirements, customer, and steps associated with performing a detailed analysis.

Exhibit 73: Perform a detailed analysis

Supplier	Input	Input Req.	TASKS	Output	Output Req.	Customer
Task No. 2 of the Analyze phase of the Training Evaluation Process.	Decision to proceed with the evaluation analysis.	Collected data accurately represents the results of the training program.	Review evaluation questions and purpose. Prepare statistics and frequency distributions. Prepare a summary issues, trends, relationships. Assess evidence considering issues and questions.	Descriptions, graphs, and tables that provide insight to answer the evaluation questions.	Use of proper procedures to support answers to the evaluation questions. Analysis of all levels of evaluation to provide adequate information to answer the evaluation questions.	Task No. 4: Answer the Evaluation Questions of the Analyze phase.

When performing a detailed analysis, the first step is to review the evaluation questions *or purpose of the evaluation*. The evaluation questions that guided information collection should have been identified in *Phase 1 Plan*. They are now reviewed using the following guidelines to help direct the analysis.

1. Are the questions still appropriate considering what's happened in the program and evaluation to this point?
2. Are there new questions that should be addressed?
3. Are the questions sufficiently clear to guide analysis?

It is important that key evaluation stakeholders and audiences be involved in this review. This cooperation is essential for focusing the evaluator on the task at hand. Inexperienced evaluators may over analyze data causing a state of "analysis paralysis" or not analyze enough. The evaluator needs to know when the analysis has provided sufficient information. Collaborating with key stakeholders and audiences helps in not over or under analyzing data.

Next, prepare descriptive statistics, frequency distributions, and/or narrative summaries for each set of data to display the results. Descriptive statistics are used to reduce the data so that key features become more evident. The kind of analysis used depends on the kind of

data gathered and level of evaluation being analyzed. The following
two kinds of analysis methods may be used:

1. *Quantitative   methods* - which include:

    A. Descriptions of central tendencies such as means, modes, and
       medians.
    B. Descriptions of dispersions in the data, such as range,
       standard deviations, and variance.
    C. Frequency distribution that shows the frequency of response,
       numbers of respondents who chose certain options, etc.

2. *Qualitative methods* - which provide the information in a
   narrative form based on value judgment of the evaluation or others
   who interpret the data. Qualitative methods include:

    A. A checklist analysis where yes-no decisions are made.
    B. Determining whether evaluation data contain certain
       information, a document has a key component, etc.
    C. Content analysis in which a training program's characteristics
       and content are used as a source of answering evaluation
       questions.

3. Summary analysis in which narrative data are summarized.
   Subsequently, *a summary of basic issues, trends, relationships, and
   questions evident from the data must be prepared.* The objective is
   to take the information and decide the next step. In other words,
   review preliminary analyses and decide what the data are telling
   you in relation to the evaluation questions.
4. *Assess the available evidence considering pertinent issues and
   questions.*   This is the decision point whether to proceed. The
   following are some decisions to be made:

    A. Are the issues and questions worth further analysis?
    B. Is the scope and selection of evaluation data sufficient to find
       answers to the evaluation questions?

Using Statistics in Training Evaluation

Analysis is the process of determining the meaning of collected
information. Statistical procedures can be used as one method of
analysis. The use of statistics in evaluation has three primary
purposes:

1. **Statistics are used to summarize large amounts of information.** Summarizing the information is probably the most practical use of statistics. Under this category there are two basic measures: the measure of the central tendencies and dispersion. The measures of central tendencies are the *mean, median, and mode.* A measure of central tendency is a single number, a summary of the characteristics of an entire group, such as an average absenteeism rate for a group of employees. One of the most powerful uses of dispersion is *standard deviation.* This reveals how much the individual items in a group are dispersed.

2. **Statistics provide for frequency distributions to exhibit cluster and separation of responses.** A *frequency distribution* for a particular item on a questionnaire is simply a count of the number of responses for each possible answer to the question. The distribution also can be expressed as <u>percentages</u>.

3. **Statistics provide a level of confidence that the data truly is representative of the training program.** A level of confidence indicates that the summative data shown by the statistics truly represent the results from training and are not influenced by other sources. The standard level of confidence used in training evaluation statistics is 95%. If, by using selected statistical tests, the evaluation data reaches or exceeds a 95% confidence level, then it can be stated that 95 times out of 100 the results occur as shown independent of other forces.

The question that typically arises is - what types of statistics are used with each evaluation level and corresponding data collection instrument? The next sections of this chapter give the suggestions for statistical methods recommended by the Training Evaluation Process for each evaluation level.

<u>Level 1 Statistical Methods</u>

The most common form of data collection instrument used in Level 1 evaluation is the questionnaire (survey). The questionnaire is most likely composed of several closed response questions (where the respondent selects an item from a finite list) and open-ended responses (where the respondent supply his/her own reaction in his/her own words). For open-ended responses, the evaluator usually transforms the respondents' ideas into a code. For example, if the open-ended item on the questionnaire asked the participant to list the "strong points of the course," responses are read and then coded into ideas or concepts such as:

Code   Concept

01   Case study examples.
02   Role plays.
03   Instructor debriefing after each teaching segment
04   Logical flow of information

The evaluator counts the number of participants who, in their own words, responded with something similar to the codes listed. The statistical method used shows the frequency of responses by category.

If the closed response is a Likert scale then the following statistical methods are recommended:

1. Calculate the mean for all responses. Anytime a mean is calculated, the standard deviation also is calculated and displayed.
2. Calculate and display a frequency distribution and/or frequency histogram that shows the dispersion of responses by category.

Exhibit 74 is an example of a frequency distribution for the question "*The training content was presented in logical order.*" from a level 1 instrument. The choices available to the respondent were *Strongly Agree, Agree, Neutral, Disagree,* and *Strongly Disagree.*

Exhibit 74: Frequency Distribution

The course content was presented in a logical order. N = 47		
Responses	**Number**	**Percent**
1. Strongly Agree	13	28%
2. Agree	15	32%
3. Neutral	10	21%
4. Disagree	7	15%
5. Strongly Disagree	2	4%

The frequency distribution can provide insight at a glance regarding which responses tend to cluster and the amount of separation among responses. When developing a frequency distribution be sure to include the following:

1. The question or concept being reported.
2. The total number of respondents (N = 47 in this example).
3. A description of each possible response.
4. The number of responses per anchor (the distribution).
5. The percentage of response per item. Always show the percentage as a whole number.

A **Frequency histogram** is a visual representation of frequency information. It is always advisable to show frequencies as often as possible in a frequency histogram. For example, Exhibit 75 shows the responses using a five point scale from strongly agree to strongly disagree:

Exhibit 75: Frequency Histogram

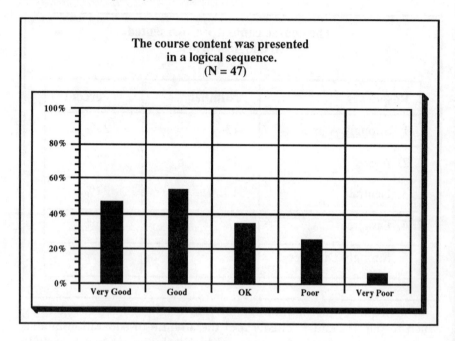

Frequency histograms fall into four basic categories:

1. Bell shaped (normal curve) where responses are equally distributed around a mean score.
2. U-shaped curve that is an inverted normal curve where most of the responses or scores fall at the extremes.
3. Positive skew curve where the scores / responses cluster to the left.
4. Negative skew curves where scores gather to the right of the mean.

Exhibits 76 through 79 graphically show these types of distributions.

Exhibit 76: Normal Curve

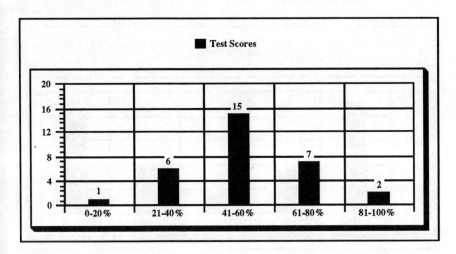

This example shows Level 2 test scores but is also very useful in depicting the distribution of data from a Level 1 or Level 3 questionnaire. As seen in exhibit 76, the dispersion of scores is distributed equally around the mean (average) score.

Exhibit 77: U-shaped Curve

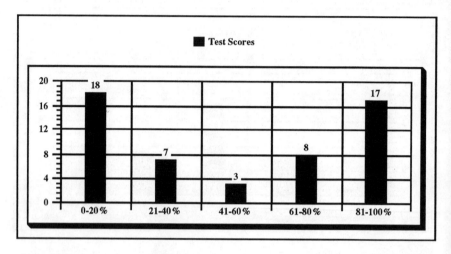

Exhibit 77 shows data where participants are distributed equally at the high end and low end of test scores.

Exhibit 78: Positively Skewed Curve

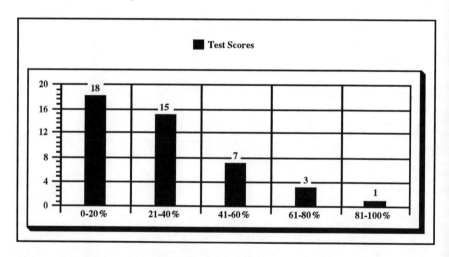

With a positively skewed curve the majority of the scores cluster to the left (low test scores).

Exhibit 79: Negatively Skewed Curve

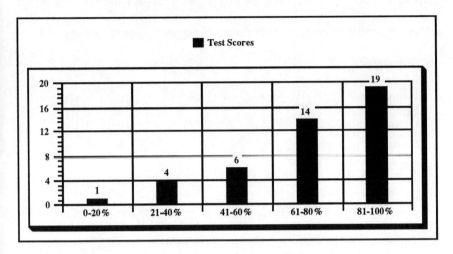

The negatively skewed curve is the opposite of the positively skewed curve. With this distribution the results (in these case test scores) are grouped to the right (high test scores).

Frequency distributions and frequency histograms are excellent ways to chart responses to level 1 (reaction) and level 3 (behavior) questionnaires. Using these statistics, the perceptions toward the training program can be tracked over time. When administering the Level 1 questionnaire at the conclusion of each course, any changes that may occur in the training program can be observed as the training continues to be offered over time.

Bigger changes in the frequency distribution over a large period of time may suggest a change in participants' perception of the training. Depending upon the nature of the change in the frequency distribution may mean modifications of the training content and structure. The evaluation results of all sessions of a given course may be combined for six months or even a year to create more stable and reliable information.

Level 2 Statistical Methods

Level 2 evaluation data collection methods require participants to complete tests. As part of the data collection effort the tests are scored either by the participant or the instructor. The first statistical method suggested is to transform each participant's raw score into a percentage. Therefore, a raw score of 32 correct answers out of a total of 38 possible answers is transformed into 84%. Note - when reporting percentages always report whole numbers (84%) versus results with decimal places

(84.21%) making it easier for the reader to interpret the results. With individual participant scores transformed into percentages, the following statistics are used to report results on a group of scores:

1. Mean score.
2. Median
3. High score.
4. Low score.
5. Range (high score - low score).
6. Standard deviation.
7. Index of Learning Gain
8. Item analysis.

For example, as discussed earlier, a method of determining level 2 evaluation (learning) is to conduct a Pre-test and Post-test comparison. Exhibit 80 gives scores from a training program.

Exhibit 80: Pre-test and Post-test Scores

Participant Number	Pre-test Score	Post-test Score
1	25	90
2	21	95
3	16	93
4	3	89
5	28	85
6	35	93
7	17	72
8	12	88
9	4	94
10	56	91
11	10	79
12	5	92
13	8	89
14	13	90
15	7	97

The data from pre- and post-test scores may be used to predict the amount of learning that has occurred in a level 2 evaluation by analyzing the data in the following three ways:

1. **Measures of Central Tendency:** The most common measures of central tendency are the *mean and median*. The *mean* is the arithmetic average of a group of numbers. It is calculated by adding all the values and dividing by the total number. The Pre-test scores (from Exhibit 80) would yield a mean value of 17.3. The post-test scores yield a mean value of 89.1. When analyzing Pre/post-test data from a successful training program, the Pre-test scores will typically be lower than the post-test scores. These two figures represent the average performance of all the participants completing the tests. The mean is *very sensitive* to extreme scores when the scores are not balanced at both ends of the distribution.

   The median is the middle score in a set of numbers - it is the centermost score if the number of scores is odd and it is the average of the two centermost scores if the number of scores is even. To calculate the median, first rank the scores from high to low, determine the total number of scores, count half the scores, and identify the middle most score as discussed above. From Exhibit 80 the median for the Pre-test scores is 13.0 and for the post-test scores is 90.0. As with the mean, the median score for the Pre-test should be lower than the post-test median in a successful training program. The *median* is *less sensitive than the mean* to unbalanced extreme scores.

2. **Measures of Variability:** Variability deals with how far scores are spread throughout the dispersion. Two measures of variability are the: *range and standard deviation*. The *range* is the difference between the highest and lowest score in the distribution. The equation is:

$$Range = highest\ score - lowest\ score$$

   The range for the Pre-test scores from Exhibit 80# is 53 (56 - 3). The range for the post-test scores is 25 (97 - 72). The range gives a crude measure of dispersion because it only measures the spread of the two extreme scores and not the spread of any of the scores in between. When analyzing, the range for the Pre-test scores should be higher than the range for the post-test scores in successful training programs.

   Standard deviation is a measure of variability that represents how data deviate from the mean of a set of scores. If the standard deviation is low, the data cluster close to the mean. Conversely, if the standard deviation is large, the scores are dispersed farther from the mean. The use of standard deviation can be used to show the evaluator how his data conform or depart from a normal curve or spread. The standard deviation is the measure of variability in most statistical operations and is the expression of variability from the mean.

3. **Measuring Learning Gain:** The Index of Learning Gain score shows the learning change of a single participant or group of learners. It is based upon the participant attainment goal of 100% of a Post-Test score. The formula used in this calculation is:

Formula:

$$\frac{(\text{Actual Post-Test}) - (\text{Actual Pre-Test})}{(\text{Maximum Post-Test}) - (\text{Actual Pre-Test})} \times 100$$

The chart below shows the concept of Index of Learning Gain.

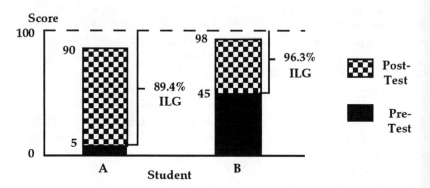

In this example, student A has a Pre-test score of 5 points and Post-Test score of 90 points (based upon a maximum of 100 points). Student A's raw gain is 85 points, but the Index of Learning Gain (ILG) is 89.4% that means they learned 89% of what they could have learned. However, student B has a Pre-test score of 45 points and a Post-Test of 98 points for a raw gain of 53 points and an Index of Learning Gain of 96.3%. If you only compare raw gain scores (A=85 points, B=53 points), A has clearly learned more. But this comparison penalizes student B for having more prerequisite knowledge. The better comparison is to contrast Index of Learning Gain scores. Using this statistic, student B gained 96.3% of what they could have learned versus student A's 89.4%. Translating this to training evaluation quality, the Index of Learning Gain is not used to compare participant to participant but as an indicator of a course's capability to allow participants to maximize their learning potential. Low aggregate Index of Learning Gains are indicators of poor instructional design.

Exhibit 81 displays the gain scores for our example.

Exhibit 81: Learning Gain Scores

Participant Number	Pre-test Score	Post-test Score	Index of Learning Gain
1	25	90	87%
2	21	95	94%
3	16	93	92%
4	3	89	89%
5	28	85	79%
6	35	93	89%
7	17	72	66%
8	12	88	86%
9	4	94	94%
10	56	91	80%
11	10	79	77%
12	5	92	92%
13	8	89	88%
14	13	90	89%
15	7	97	97%

The average gain for the total participant population can be calculated. In Exhibit 81 the average learning gain for the fifteen participants is 88%.

An item analysis shows, by test item, the number of right or wrong answers and the gain or (loss) from Pre-test to Post-test for each question. To perform a test item comparison, it may be useful to complete a chart similar to the one displayed in Exhibit 82.

Exhibit 82: Test Item Analysis

Item #7	Pre-test #	Pre-test %	Post-test #	Post-test %	Gain #
A.	5	10%	3	6%	-2
B.	2	4%	30	60%	+28
C.	3	6%	12	24%	+9
D.	1	2%	5	10%	+4
DON'T KNOW	39	78%			

This information can be compared with the objective and learning activity associated with this item to determine if and what changes will be required.

Level 3 Statistical Methods

Level 3 statistical methods are very similar to Level 1 procedures because both data sets collect similar types of data. Therefore, depending upon the data collection instrument used, the following statistical methods are suggested:

1. Mean scores, standard deviations, frequency distributions, and frequency histograms for closed response questions.
2. For open response questions, coded transformations and the associated frequency distributions and histograms.

Level 4 Statistical Methods

Data collected for Level 4 evaluations deal with two separate data sets:

1. Cost to design, develop, deliver, maintain, and evaluate the training program.
2. The value of training determined by investigating accounting records for control (non-trained) personnel and experimental (trained) personnel.

Training costs are best summed together and an average (mean) for each participant trained is calculated. Training value, depending upon the measure being evaluated, are summed for each group, a mean is calculated, and a test of significance is run to determine if the difference between the means is statistically significant.

In evaluation a hypothesis is stated such as ". . . the learning gained by the participants is due to the training program or the participants' job performance will improve because of the training program." The statement (hypotheses) is either rejected or accepted based upon measurement data, the result of statistical analysis, and a statistical test describing the level of confidence with the results.

The process of testing a hypothesis involves calculating a statistical test value and comparing it with a value from an appropriate statistical table, based upon a predetermined level of significance. One type of test of significance used in evaluation is the t-test. This test compares the scores of two groups and produces a result to determine if the difference in scores is statistically significant. If the t-test reveals that the scores are statistically different, a prediction can be made that the training probably caused the difference and the training was successful.

Level of significance is represented by such values as .10, .05, .01, etc. The .05 indicates that five times out of one hundred change was caused by chance or we can predict with 95% confidence that the training program caused the change.

For example, the numbers of sales for an experimental group of salesmen are 25% greater than for a control group. The size of each group is twenty-six salesmen. The t-test computed value is 1.708. Using a statistical table, the accepted level of significance for this measure is .05. Therefore, you can say that you can predict with 95% confidence that training caused the 25% gain in order results. For evaluations, a .05 or less level of significance is suggested for the evaluator to accept or reject the hypothesis.

Tables and Graphs to be used when Reporting Training Evaluation

Properly constructed and described tables and graphs not only convey major data summaries for a variety of written evaluation reports, they also provide the basic visual dimensions for other forms of presentations. For each evaluation question, a table or graph can be created that will effectively portray what has been found. Tables are numbers (the results of the data collection and analysis) placed in a specific format to help answer the evaluation questions. Graphs are used to (pictorially) represent the data from analysis and assist in answering the evaluation questions. The following are examples of tables and graphs used in training evaluation.

Exhibit 83: Percentage of participants responding to the question regarding the quality of materials

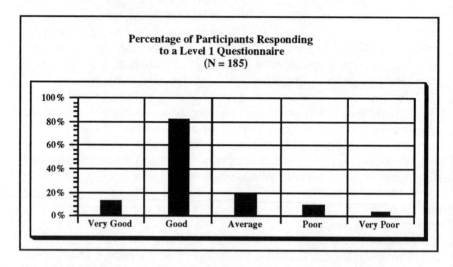

Exhibit 83 is a frequency histogram depicting the results of a question on a Level 1 survey. This type of chart is also useful when depicting Level 3 results from questionnaires. When developing this type of chart, follow the suggestions listed below:

1. Place possible participant responses on the X (horizontal) axis.
2. Develop and label the Y (vertical) axis as a percentage.
3. Draw grid lines at the major categories on the X axis and every twenty percentage points on the Y axis.
4. Title the chart with the item from the questionnaire.
5. Always list the size of the population from the data collection effort with (N = ##).
6. Use a horizontal (landscape) orientation versus a vertical (portrait) orientation.
7. Place a frame around the chart.

Exhibit 84: Table of Level 1 Results

Participant Satisfaction to Course ABC100 (N = 117)					
	Responses				
Area Measured	Outstanding	Above Average	Average	Below	Poor
Materials	18%	34%	24%	3%	1%
Objectives	19%	49%	29%	3%	0%
Sequence	18%	56%	24%	2%	0%
Overall Rating	12%	57%	27%	4%	1%

Exhibit 84 is an example of a frequency distribution that may be used with Level 1 and Level 3 evaluations. This table is useful because it shows four separate areas evaluated and allows the reader to distinguish the quality between each area. A table of this nature is useful when the areas being evaluated all use the same rating scales.

When developing this type of table, follow the suggestions listed below:

1. Place the evaluation area on the left of the table and the results to the right of each area.
2. Use percentages to show results.
3. Title the table.
4. Always list the size of the population from the data collection effort with (N = ##).
5. Use a horizontal (landscape) orientation versus a vertical (portrait) orientation.
6. Place a frame around the chart.

Exhibit 85: Pre-test / Post-test Comparison

Pre-test / Post-test Comparison (N = 215)		
Descriptive Statistic	**Pre-Test**	**Post-test**
Mean	55%	93%
Median	56%	84%
Lowest score	12%	54%
Highest score	92%	100%
Range	80 points	46 points
Standard deviation	12.5	6.9

Exhibit 85 is a table used with Level 2 evaluations that shows the results of participant learning results. When developing this table, follow the suggestions listed below:

1. Place the descriptive on the left of the table and the results to the right of each statistic.
2. Use percentages to show results for mean, median, lowest score, and highest score. Use the number of points to depict the range and display the standard deviation to one decimal place.
3. Title the table appropriately.
4. Always list the size of the population from the data collection effort with (N = ##).
5. Use a horizontal (landscape) orientation versus a vertical (portrait) orientation.
6. Place a frame around the chart.

Exhibit 86: Pre-test / Post-test Comparison

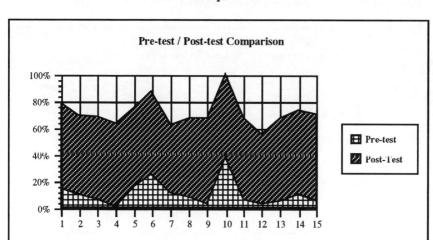

Exhibit 86 is an excellent method of depicting the difference between Pre-tests and Post-tests. When developing this graph, follow the suggestions listed below:

1. Place the participant number on the X axis and the label the Y axis as the scores based upon 100%.
2. Draw grid lines at each participant number on the X axis and every twenty percentage points on the Y axis.
3. For each participant, plot their Pre-test score and the corresponding Post-test score.
4. Label to the right the values (percentages) used to represent Pre-test scores and Post-test scores.
5. Title the table appropriately.
6. Use a horizontal (landscape) orientation versus a vertical (portrait) orientation.
7. Place a frame around the chart.

Exhibit 87: Table of Employee Responses

Table 3: In what ways has the training program helped or hindered in the selling motion?	
Comment	**Number of Responses**
Helped to focus on who was the decision maker.	69
Increased organizational skills.	27
Provided a good planning tool.	26
Identified "red flags" and ways to eliminate them.	25
Identified coaches.	21

Exhibit 87 is an example of a table used to show open-ended responses that have been transformed to coded responses. This type of table is best used with Level 1 and Level 3 evaluations. When developing this table, follow the suggestions listed below:

1. Place the comment (code) on the left of the table and the frequency to the right of each comment.
2. Title the table with the item from the questionnaire.
3. Use a horizontal (landscape) orientation versus a vertical (portrait) orientation.
4. Place a frame around the chart.

Exhibit 88: Use of Training Skills Table

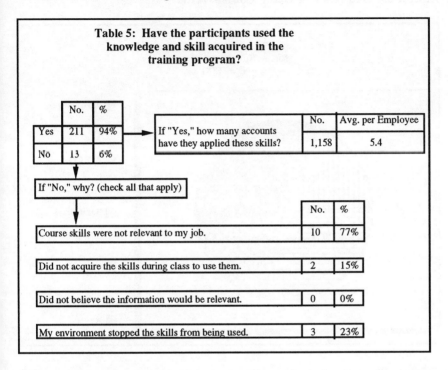

Exhibit 88 is a table that describes the results from a Level 3 questionnaire. This table shows how to depict responses to a filter question on the survey. When developing this table, follow the suggestions listed below:

1. Structure the table to represent the path followed by the respondent when answering the item.
2. Title the table with the item from the questionnaire.
3. Use a horizontal (landscape) orientation versus a vertical (portrait) orientation.
4. Place a frame around the chart.

Exhibit 89: Frequency of Using Course Skills

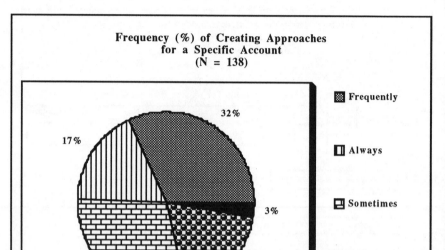

Frequency (%) of Creating Approaches
for a Specific Account
(N = 138)

Frequently

Always

Sometimes

Occassionally

Never

Exhibit 89 is a pie chart depicting a frequency distribution for Level 1 and Level 3 questionnaires. It is another method of graphically depicting frequencies. When developing this type of chart, follow the suggestions listed below:

1. Place possible participant labeled responses on the right of the chart.
2. Develop a pattern for each category that allows the reader to easily distinguish each category. Use color or different black and white patterns.
3. Label each category with the response percentage.
4. Title the chart with the item from the questionnaire.
5. Always list the size of the population from the data collection effort with (N = ##).
6. Use a horizontal (landscape) orientation versus a vertical (portrait) orientation.
7. Place a frame around the chart.

Exhibit 90: Cost of Training

Expense Category	Actual Expenses
Lease cost of training	$24,225
Participant salaries	$85,500
Travel and expenses	$30,290
Participant materials	$885
Trainer salary.	$3,988
Classroom rent	$2,288
Total cost	**$147,146**
Cost per participant	$2,581
Number of participants	57

Exhibit 90 is a table that shows the cost of training from a Level 4 evaluation. When developing this table, follow the suggestions listed below:

1. Place the expense category on the left of the table and the actual expense to the right of each category.
2. Use a horizontal (landscape) orientation versus a vertical (portrait) orientation.
3. Place a frame around the chart.

Exhibit 91: Level 4 Training Value

Measure 3: No. of Orders Won
Divided by the No. of Proposals

	PRODUCT A		PRODUCT B	
	Experimental	Control	Experimental	Control
Number of cases	21	29	41	46
Mean	76%	55%	76%	55%
Standard deviation	21.9	25.2	28.0	14.1
Level of significance	.001		.006	

Exhibit 91 is a table that compares the results of training for experimental and control groups for two separate products. When developing this table, follow the suggestions listed below:

1. Place the data being measured in the left column with the results for experimental and control groups to the right.
2. Title the table with the data being measured.
3. Use a horizontal (landscape) orientation versus a vertical (portrait) orientation.
4. Place a frame around the chart.

Summary

Task 3 takes the data from the data analysis models and summarizes it using statistical methodologies. This task also recommends development of tables, charts, and graphs to pictorially represent the results.

-- END OF TASK 3 --

4. ANSWER THE EVALUATION QUESTIONS.

Interpretation is the process of giving meaning to the results of analysis and deciding the significance and implications of what the data shows. It also involves comparing with some value, standard, expectation, or other trends. Exhibit 92 shows the inputs, input requirements, supplier, output, output requirements, customer, and tasks associated with this task.

Exhibit 92: Answer the Evaluation Questions

Supplier	Input	Input Req.	TASKS	Output	Output Req.	Customer
Task No. 3 of the Analyze phase of the Training Evaluation Process.	Narrative summaries, statistics, graphs and tables that provide insight to the evaluation questions.	Proper information to support answers to the evaluation questions. Sufficient analysis of all levels of evaluation which provides adequate information to answer the evaluation questions.	Review each evaluation question. Decide if you can answer the question or document why you cannot. Answer the evaluation questions you feel you are able to answer.	Answers to the evaluation questions.	Answers coincide with the questions documented in the Evaluation Plan. All questions answered are supported with statistics, tables, graphs, etc.	The Reports and Decision Making phase of the Training Evaluation Process.

Answering the evaluation questions means interpreting the analyzed data to see if results support or do not support the answer to the question. At times an evaluation question can not be answered. If this occurs:

1. Document why the question can not be answered and stop the analysis for that question, or
2. Decide what additional work (further data collection, additional analysis, etc.) must be completed to answer the question.

Some guidelines to use when interpreting data include:

1. Be prepared to deal with multiple and conflicting evidence.
2. Assume that statistical significance may not be the same as practical reasoning.
3. Confirmation and consistency with other sources of information strengthen the interpretation.
4. Avoid "analysis paralysis" by knowing when to stop.

5. Consider and cite the limitations of the analysis methods.
6. Ensure that norms and references are appropriate for the population of the total participants in the program.
7. Cite and provide rationale for particular references used in interpretation of the data.
8. Formulate and explain interpretations considering contextual and confirming or limiting information.
9. Use summations and holistic interpretation techniques.
10. Provide alternative explanations and interpretations.
11. Review each evaluation question by reexamining the <u>Evaluation Plan</u>.
12. Understand the intent of each question so that you can quickly and accurately answer the question when looking at the results of the analysis.

Decide if the evaluation questions can be answered and if not, document the reason. Not all evaluation questions can be answered. This may be due to: a bad evaluation question; lack of good, solid evaluation data; environmental issues that have tainted the data; or the execution of the training evaluation process.

The evaluation questions that can be answered should be addressed. For example, if the evaluation question states: *"WHAT DID THE PARTICIPANTS FEEL ABOUT THE QUALITY OF THE INSTRUCTIONAL TEXT?"* and the Level 1 analysis data from the end-of-class questionnaire is:

Question on the Level 1 Instrument	Percent Responding "Outstanding"	Percent Responding "Poor"
The quality of the printed material was . . .	97%	3%
The readability of the printed material was . . .	95%	5%
The content in the printed material was . . .	93%	7%

Then the answer to the evaluation question would obviously be "YES" with the data in the table as supporting evidence. Answering evaluation questions entails reviewing the question and looking at the summative results and providing your best response.

-- END OF TASK 4 --

Summary

Evaluation data that is accurately planned and systematically collected and analyzed properly supplies evaluation stakeholders with answers to the evaluation questions. These in turn are used to document the quality of the training program and highlight areas for possible course improvement. This phase of the Training Evaluation Process documented the step-by-step procedures for correctly analyzing and interpreting evaluation data. Exhibit 93 shows each task within the phase and its corresponding outputs.

Exhibit 93: Summary of the Analyze Phase

Task	Output
1. Organize and code collected data.	Data that is appropriately organized in the analysis models.
2. Decide whether the data is worth analyzing.	Decision whether to proceed with evaluation analysis.
3. Perform a detailed analysis.	Descriptions, graphs, and tables that provide insight to answer the evaluation questions.
4. Answer the evaluation questions.	Answers to the evaluation questions.

The Training Evaluation Process continues with the next phase: Report Evaluation.

7. REPORT EVALUATION RESULTS

Purpose of This Chapter

This chapter provides the knowledge and skills necessary to perform the fifth phase of the Training Evaluation Process - *Report Evaluation*. Once data has been collected and properly analyzed, it must be reported in a timely accurate manner. Evaluation reports are the mechanism where the results of training are communicated to key evaluation stakeholders so that they can make sound business decisions associated with the training. This phase of the Training Evaluation Process completes the work of training evaluation.

Objectives of This Chapter

At the conclusion of this chapter you can:

1. Create an Evaluation Report that accurately documents the effects of training based upon the levels of evaluation used.
2. Present the data according to the needs of diverse audiences.

Report Evaluation

The purpose of this phase is to communicate training evaluation information to interested audiences so that they can make use of the evaluation information for decision making or for purposes of accountability. This phase will generate an Evaluation Report and possibly other presentations detailing the results of evaluation and the activities necessary to correct any problems with the training program. The user of this phase of the Training Evaluation Process is the course development organization or the evaluator.

Exhibit 94: Report Evaluation

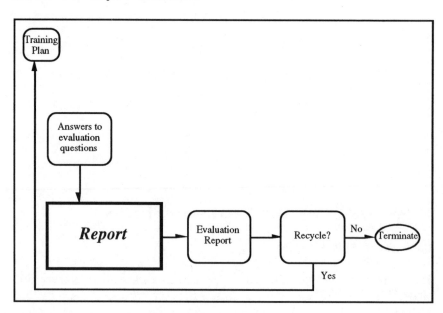

Evaluation reporting promotes the decision making process. Training evaluation does make recommendations concerning judgments and decisions concerning how and if training needs improvement. Final judgments and decisions, however, rest with key stakeholders. The Training Evaluation Process, during the *Report Evaluation* Phase, supplies key evaluation stakeholders with the information necessary to make sound business decisions in order for plans of action to be implemented to correct training problems. As in the Obtain and Analyze Phases, reporting of evaluation results is a cyclical procedure. Exhibit 95 depicts how this is accomplished.

Exhibit 95: The Training Environment

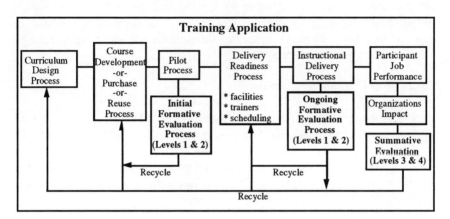

Reporting evaluation results encompasses all other phases of the training environment. During the **Curriculum Design Process,** reports are written which depict the training requirements as documented in a curriculum for a given job description and produce a <u>Training Plan</u> used in course development. The **Course Development Process** takes the <u>Training Plan</u> and begins producing, purchasing, or reusing training materials to meet the defined need. During course development, the first two phases of the Training Evaluation Process (*Planning* and *Developing*) are executed. After the training materials have been developed, the **Validation Process** is conducted during which representatives from the target population complete either all or designated parts of the training program.

During the validation process, Level 1 and Level 2 evaluations are conducted as defined in the <u>Evaluation Plan</u>. The Training Evaluation Process executes the *Obtain, Analyze, and Report Evaluation* Phases with the final output being an <u>Evaluation Report</u> documenting the results of the validation. This information is used to improve or to recycle training materials before full implementation. This form of evaluation reporting is associated with formative evaluation and requires a specific format to completely describe the results from the validation.

Once training materials are completed, a **Delivery Readiness Process** is executed that prepares training organizations to implement the training program. Next, the **Instructional Delivery Process** begins training the intended audiences. Coinciding with instructional delivery, the Training Evaluation Process executes ongoing Levels 1 and 2 evaluations by obtaining, analyzing, and reporting the effects of training in a summative mode. One or more <u>Evaluation Reports</u> are written chronicling results of the delivery process. This data is used to improve the **Delivery Readiness, Instructional Delivery Processes,** or the **Curriculum Design Process.** Summative reports are produced on regularly scheduled dates using agreed upon formats.

The results of training are changes in participant job performance and, eventually, organizational impact. The Training Evaluation Process again obtains, analyzes, and reports training effects upon these entities. The primary output being another Evaluation Report used to improve the course or curriculum. These changes then filter through the training environment by affecting all subsequent processes.

Task of the Reporting Phase

Reporting the findings of training evaluation begins when the analysis and the interpretation of the evaluation data are completed. The purpose of evaluating training is to furnish key stakeholders with information that allows them to make sound business decisions about training continuation, termination, or modification. Evaluation Reporting communicates these findings. Reporting is accomplished by performing the following tasks:

1. Verifying and adjusting the list of those who receive an Evaluation Report.
2. Deciding content to be included in the report.
3. Determining delivery methods of the reports.
4. Deciding due dates of the reports.
5. Writing and delivering the Evaluation Report(s).

Inputs to the Reporting Phase

Input to the Reporting Phase are the outputs from the *Analyze* Phase of the Training Evaluation Process that would be:

1. Answers to the evaluation questions.
2. Graphs, tables, and charts of the results.
3. Appropriate interpretation of results by evaluators.

Outputs of the Reporting Phase

The output of *Report Evaluation* Phase will be any of three possible documents:

1. Formative Evaluation Report,
2. Summative (regularly scheduled) Evaluation Reports.

    A formative Evaluation Report describing the results of training validation is written for all courses and includes outcomes of Level 1 and Level 2 evaluations. Additional formative Evaluation Reports are written for training programs administering Level 3 or Level 4 evaluation. These reports are designed to communicate the findings, results, and conclusions of evaluation Levels 3 and 4.

    Summative Evaluation Reports are produced on a regularly scheduled basis (weekly, monthly, quarterly, etc.). These reports typically provide results for ongoing Level 1 and Level 2 evaluation results.

1. VERIFYING & ADJUSTING THE LIST OF THOSE WHO RECEIVE AN EVALUATION REPORT

The Evaluation Plan includes a list of those individuals or organizations who will receive a copy of the Evaluation Report. Usually those receiving a copy of the Evaluation Plan are the persons, groups, and agencies whose information needs and interests guided the evaluation and whose actions supported the evaluation - in other words the key evaluation stakeholders are the customers of the Training Evaluation Process. The report audiences may include:

1. Funding organizations: Groups within the company who have paid for the design, development, or delivery of training.
2. Overseeing agencies: Internal company organizations such as corporate departments responsible for evaluation or quality, training boards, etc.
3. Staff and consultants: Instructional design, course development, and teaching organizations who are responsible for producing and delivering the training offerings.
4. Others: Any one with a vested interest in the evaluation.

Developing the list of potential Evaluation Report audiences allow the evaluator to better focus the content and method of report delivery so that the need of the audiences is best served. Exhibit 96 depicts the input, input requirements, supplier, output, output requirements, customer, and tasks associated for this activity.

Exhibit 96: Verifying and adjusting the list of those who receive an Evaluation Report.

Supplier	Input	Input Req.	TASKS	Output	Output Req.	Customer
The Planning Phase of the Training Evaluation Process.	Evaluation Plan.	A list of all key evaluation stakeholders and audiences who will receive a copy of the Evaluation Report.	Identify all audiences. / Rank order audiences.	The list of Evaluation Report audiences in ranked order.	The list is complete.	Task No. 2: Deciding the Content to be included in the Report of the Report Evaluation Phase.

The first task in this phase is to identify all audiences who may receive an Evaluation Report (whether formative or summative). Listed below are suggested guidelines for identifying reporting audiences:

1. Determine all organizations that may need the information. Organizational structures within each company are different. However, the following organizations typically exist in one form or another and need to be considered as potential report audiences:

    A. Instructional design.
    B. Course development.
    C. Course delivery.
    D. Funding organizations.
    E. Training boards.
    F. Business units who send personnel to training.
    G. Quality departments.

2. Attempt to differentiate audiences by function or interest in the training.
3. Rank order audiences by their importance or influence to the evaluation so that the needs of key audiences can be fully met.

Completion of this verification task will result in a rank ordered list of report audiences.

-- END OF TASK 1 --

2. DECIDING CONTENT TO BE INCLUDED IN THE REPORT

The evaluation report documents answers to the evaluation questions. To give appropriate answers, the decision has to be made regarding what content should be included in the report. Exhibit 97 depicts the input, input requirements, supplier, output, output requirements, customer, and tasks associated with making that decision.

Exhibit 97: Deciding the Content to be Included in the Report

Supplier	Input	Input Req.	TASKS	Output	Output Req.	Customer
Task No. 1: from the Report Evaluation Phase.	A ranked list of Evaluation Report audiences.	A complete and comprehensive list.	Decide what content is to be included in the report and the format to be used.	Decision of content to be included in the Evaluation Report.	Report content that provides readers with the needed information.	Task No. 3: Determine Delivery Methods of Reports for the Report Evaluation Phase.

The content of evaluation reports depends upon whether it is a formative report or a summative report. Formative reports are produced following a course validation (test) and describe the training results using Level 1 and Level 2 evaluation. Formative reports are also used for single administrations of Level 3 and Level 4 evaluations. Summative reports are generated on a regular basis and supplied to a finite set of audiences. The content of these reports is based upon the requirements of the audiences and typically reports ongoing Level 1 and Level 2 training results. A formative Evaluation Report may contain the following[1]:

1. **A Front Cover that provides:**

   A. Title of the training program and course number.
   B. Name of the evaluator(s) and organization where employed.
   C. Beginning and ending dates of evaluation.
   D. Date the report is submitted.
   E. Course design organization(s).
   F. Course development organization(s).
   G. Course delivery organization(s).

   The front cover should be attractive as well as informative because it reflects the quality of the evaluation work.

2. **Executive Summary**: This section gives a brief overview of the evaluation explaining why it was conducted and listing the major conclusions and findings. The executive summary provides information for people wanting only a summary of the full report, and it will typically be no longer than two or three pages. Content of the Executive Summary may include:

   A. The course evaluated.
   B. The reason for conducting the evaluation.
   C. The major findings concluded from the evaluation.

3. **Background Information Concerning the Training Program:** This section describes the training program and its purpose. The amount of detail in this section will depend upon the report audiences and their familiarity with the program. Content of this section may include:

   A. The source of the training program: the initiator, designer, and the developer.
   B. The location of the training program and the people who conducted the training.
   C. The purpose for the training program.
   D. The results of a formal (or informal) needs assessment if one was conducted.
   E. Objectives of the training program.
   F. Definition of the defined target population.
   G. Criteria for participant selection.
   H. Characteristics of the training materials, activities, and administrative arrangements
   I. Materials developed or purchased and the implementation procedures.

    J. Resources available such as: funds, speakers, hardware, documentation, software, subject matter, experts, and source of support.

    K. Any specific procedures for implementers.

    L. Differences between the actual and anticipated program.

    M. Staff and others involved in the training program.

3. Description of the Evaluation Procedures: This section describes the procedures of the evaluation and it's intended accomplishments. It also describes the evaluation methodology. The source of some of this information is the <u>Evaluation Plan</u>. Content of this section may include:

    A. Purpose(s) of the evaluation.

    B. The client(s) of the evaluation.

    C. Information requirement from stakeholders.

    D. Decisions for which evaluation data is needed.

    E. Evaluation design(s) composed of:

        *   Description of the design.
        *   Levels of evaluation conducted.
        *   Criteria for selection of design.
        *   Design limitations.
        *   Possible design alternatives and the reasons for their rejection.

    F. Questions the evaluation will answer for each level of the evaluation.

4. Evaluation Results: This part of the <u>Evaluation Report</u> presents results in such a way as to answer the evaluation questions. Content for this section may include:

    A. Evaluation question(s).

    B. The data needed to answer the question(s) using tables, graphs, as well as written information.

    C. Answers to the evaluation questions.

5. Conclusions: The results and findings from the training evaluation are discussed in this section with respect to the evaluation questions. Value judgments regarding the training program may be made. This section will detail relevance of answers to the evaluation question. Content for this section may include:

    A. Were results from the actual Training Program or were there other alternative explanations for training results?

    B. Did program results compare with what might have been expected had there been no training?

C. Do results compare with the standard used to judge training quality?
D. What were the perceived strengths and weaknesses of the program?

6. Appendices. Appendices contain summaries of internal data reports, copies of collection instruments, statistical summaries, and other documents that validate the report. The contents of the appendices are of enough depth and scope so that the reader may recreate the evaluator's analysis.

A summative Evaluation Report contains less verbiage that the formative report. The contents of the report show the results, by evaluation level, for the courses taught during the reporting period. Therefore, the content for each report format will differ. However, for summative Evaluation Reports, the following data is produced:

1. Level 1 or Level 2 results for a single session or single course for a group of sessions. These summative reports deal with one course for one training session or a group of sessions for the same course (e.g., all sessions of ABC Test Course taught in the second quarter). Typical content includes:

A. Course name and number.
B. Reporting period (to and from dates).
C. Location(s) where training was conducted.
D. Name of instructor(s) who delivered the course.
E. Number of participants.
F. Results for each question on the Level 1 questionnaire.
                    - or -
G. Level 2 results for each participant with summary results.

2. Levels 1 and 2 evaluation results for a specific organization. Typically delivery and design organizations wish to see Level 1 and Level 2 results of training programs that they deliver or own. Content for these reports is similar to the content discussed in the previous point.

-- END OF TASK 2 --

3. DETERMINING DELIVERY METHODS OF THE REPORTS

Decisions need to be made regarding the best way to report evaluation information. These decisions are based upon whether the report is formative or summative and the needs of report readers. Exhibit 98 depicts the input, input requirements, supplier, output, output requirements, customer, and tasks associated with the delivery of the reports.

Exhibit 98: Determining delivery methods of the reports.

Supplier	Input	Input Req.	TASKS	Output	Output Req.	Customer
Task No. 2 of the Report Evaluation Phase.	Decision on the content to be included in the Evaluation Report.	Report content that provides readers the information needed.	Determine how the report(s) will be delivered.	Decision on how the evaluator is to share evaluation results with audiences.	Decision will provide the easiest and quickest method for evaluation audiences to understand and make use of the information.	Task No. 4: Decide Due Dates of the Reports of the Report Evaluation Phase.

Guidelines for choosing report strategies are imperative to bring a training evaluation to a successful conclusion. Evaluation information must be timely and readily accessible to individuals and organizations who need the data to make sound business decisions. Disseminating the information is more than just writing and distributing a report. It must be useful and easy to understand for the evaluation to be used for training improvement. Evaluators need to hold meetings and to make presentations to key stakeholders. For the evaluation to have the most impact, explanations must be provided which will in turn facilitate decision making. When selecting report strategies the following guidelines should be considered:

1. Use strategies that accommodate multiple sensory channels, i.e., graphics, charts, tables, figures, displays in written reports.
2. Include provisions to facilitate interaction and for comprehension.
3. Be simplistic.
4. Encourage audience input.
5. Think beyond the range of paper-based reports. Deliver reports by means of computer programs or data communications.

To ensure your Evaluation Report meets the needs of key stakeholders, ensure that the following occur:

1.   The report must be understood by all audiences.
2.   The content must be accurate.
3.   The information is useful for the intended purpose.

The output of this task is the determination of the best method of presenting evaluation information. Within that decision, additional supplements to the report should be considered such as presenting the evaluation information at meetings in which training effectiveness is discussed.

Reviewers of the report should discuss the evaluation report rather than rely on one-way communication. Therefore, to further enhance usability, readability and acceptance of the Evaluation Report, the audience must be involved. The following options are ways to involve audiences:

1.   Discuss the report with key audience members.
2.   Make a presentation that accompanies the report.
3.   Submit a rough draft of the report to some audience members for editing and review.
4.   Distribute preliminary reports.
5.   Have audience members make reports, write reviews, conduct meetings, etc.
6.   Conduct panel meetings, hearings, open forums, etc.
7.   Be available to attend meetings where reports are discussed.
8.   Solicit questions, concerns, and related issues.

-- END OF TASK 3 --

4. DECIDE DUE DATE OF REPORTS

Timelines when reporting are crucial because audiences must receive reports on time. Late information serves no purpose. A reporting schedule should be in place so that the reporting is timely. The reporting schedule shows who gets what reports, when they are due, and in what form the report will be. Exhibit 99 depicts the inputs, input requirements, supplier, output, output requirements, customer, and task associated with this task.

Exhibit 99: Decide Due Dates of Reports

Supplier	Input	Input Req.	TASKS	Output	Output Req.	Customer
Task No. 3 of the Report Evaluation Phase.	Decision on the method to share evaluation information with key audiences and stake-holders.	Method will provide the evaluation audiences with an opportunity to make use of the evaluation information in a timely way.	Review the Evaluation Plan for prior committ-ment.	Reporting schedule.	The schedule matches the timetable documented in the Evaluation Plan.	Task No. 5: Write and De-liver the Eval-uation Reports of the Report Eval-uation Phase.
			Investigate the environ-ment for factors that influence need for evaluation information.		Schedule includes any other individuals who have a need for the evaluation information.	
			Decide report timelines.			

The Evaluation Report is written and distributed according to the schedule agreed upon in the Evaluation Plan. Agreements made and documented in the plan must be adhered to as much as possible. Guidelines of the plan should be followed when appropriate and any changes should be agreed upon in writing by the evaluator and the client. By following the plan, a sense of direction and professionalism is maintained.

However, the context (company environment) in which the evaluation is conducted may affect the report schedule. Careful examination of the context is essential to providing timely and useful reports. After reviewing the Evaluation Plan and conducting an environmental analysis, the decision and documentation of when the Evaluation Report needs to be delivered is made.

-- END OF TASK 4 --

5. WRITE AND DISTRIBUTE EVALUATION REPORT

The final task of the *Report Evaluation* Phase of the Training Evaluation Process is to write and distribute evaluation report(s). This task poses little difficulty if all previous tasks within this phase are completed successfully. Exhibit 100 shows the tasks associated with writing an Evaluation Report.

Exhibit 100: Write and Distribute Evaluation Reports

Supplier	Input	Input Req.	TASKS	Output	Output Req.	Customer
Task No. 4 of the Report Evaluation Phase.	Report schedule which is the output from the previous phase.	The schedule is the same as the timetable outlined in the Evaluation Plan.	Write the report and develop any other methods which may be used in a presentation. Distribute the report to all right-to-know audiences.	Evaluation Report.	Report is an accurate account of training results. Limitations of the evaluation are included in the report. Report is delivered within the report schedule.	Key stakeholders including instructional designers, course developers, and instructors. The Plan Phase of the Training Evaluation Process.

Writing the first Evaluation Report, as with any initial work task, should be a learning experience. Repetition of reporting generates more usable reports. The perfect report should not be expected on a first try or the one hundredth - perfect Evaluation Reports do not exist. Strive for the best possible report, learning from it, and thus making the next report better. The following suggestions facilitate writing reports:

1. Follow the guidelines, criteria, and standards outlined in this chapter.
2. Be as concise as possible. State the results and any other pertinent information in short paragraph form.
3. Clearly state the facts and justify the conclusions.
4. List the limitations and biases of the evaluation.
5. Provide a glossary for evaluation terms.
6. Use tables, charts, and graphs to clarify information.
7. Solicit peer review before the final distribution.
8. Use an editor when possible.
9. Do not deviate from the original evaluation questions posed in the Evaluation Plan.

A cover letter describing how to use the report and how the evaluator can be contacted if necessary, should be attached to the final report. Hand delivering the report and spending a few moments discussing it increases the chances of key stakeholders reading it and making use of the information contents.

Evaluation Report Examples

Level 2 Formative Evaluation Report - This example is a formative Evaluation Report for a Level 2 evaluation study. It is shown here as a typical example of a formative Evaluation Report within a business setting. Other formative reports for Level 3 and Level 4 evaluations are similar.

Level 2 Evaluation Report
for ABC100 - Test Course

Table of Contents

1. Description of the Evaluation

> *A. Purpose of the Evaluation*
> *B. Evaluation Design*

2. Results
3. Limitations and Bias of the Evaluation
4. Appendix

> *A. Learning Report*
> *B. Completed Data Collection Instruments*

1. Description of the Evaluation

This section contains a brief description of the evaluation study that encompasses its design and implementation.

> *A. Purpose of the Evaluation: The evaluation study conducted for ACB100 - Test Course was a Level 2: Learning formative evaluation. The evaluation purpose was to assess the course's success in providing the participants with the skills and knowledge described in the course's Instructional Design Document. This information is used, where appropriate, to improve the course so that subsequent participants will have to master course skills.*
> *B. Evaluation Design: The evaluation design included five embedded knowledge checks and one group presentation checklist to collect participant learning results. The knowledge check items are written to measure participant understanding of concepts, principles, and techniques using the content outlined in the Instructional Design Document for*

ACB100 - Test Course. The group presentation checklist items are written to measure participants' ability to apply the concepts given a description of a possible work situation as outlined in the Instructional Design Document. These 'knowledge check' instruments were criterion referenced to each of the course terminal objectives.

After consultation with the instructional systems designer, data collected to determine learning was measured at the individual participant level by the cumulative mean scores achieved on the five embedded knowledge checks. The decision was made to capture Knowledge Check scores received by each participant thereby being able to measure learning attributable to the course. A successful course being at least 80% of the participants score 80% or greater on their cumulative mean score on each of the knowledge checks.

The data collection instruments were developed to record this data. To meet the requirement of the Evaluation Department that Level 2 evaluation data is program evaluation and not personnel evaluation, each participant was assigned a number to record on the data collection instrument. The Evaluation Department and the instructional systems designer have no knowledge as to what results belong to what individuals.

2. Results

Total Number of participants: 14

(Number of participants vary for each knowledge check and is so noted in the following the statistics).

	Whole Brain	Skills/ Traits	Idea Finding	Creative Process	Summing
Mean	88%	94%	99%	97%	95%
High Score	100%	100%	100%	100%	100%
Low Score	57%	67%	83%	89%	83%
Range	43	33	17	11	12
Std. Dev.	14.67	10.84	4.81	5.02	4.63
Population	N=13	N=12	N=11	N=11	N=12

Statistical Definitions:

Mean:	*The average score for a defined population.*
High Score:	*The highest score achieved for the defined population.*
Low Score:	*The lowest score achieved for the defined population.*
Range:	*The difference between the high score and the low score.*

Std. Deviation: *The degree of variance on either side of the mean score.*
Quality Goals

Participant Number	Whole Brain	Skills Traits	Idea Finding	Creative Process	Summing	Participant Mean
1	57%	83%	100%	89%	86%	83%
2	100%					
3	100%	100%	100%	100%	100%	100%
4	100%	100%	100%	100%	100%	100%
5	86%	100%	100%	100%	86%	94%
5	100%	100%	100%	89%	100%	98%
7	100%	100%	100%	100%	86%	97%
8	100%	100%	100%	100%	100%	100%

Participant Number	Whole Brain	Skills Traits	Idea Finding	Creative Process	Summing	Participant Mean
9	86%	100%		89%	100%	
10	71%	83%	100%	100%	86%	88%
11	100%	100%	100%	100%	100%	100%
12	71%	100%	83%	100%	100%	91%
13	86%	67%	100%	100%	87%	88%
14	83%	100%	100%	100%	100%	94%

** Not a member of the target population and scores not counted in quality goal
measurement.*

Number of participants completing all five checks: 12
Number of participants with Mean Score ≥ 80%:   12
Percent of participants with Mean Score ≥ 80%:   100%
Quality Goal Achieved? :   Yes

*Detailed analysis by participant is provided in the Appendix of the Learning
Report section. Two possible actions may need to be taken to increase quality:*

1. *Review knowledge check items for validity against the course objectives.*
2. *Investigate the possibility of modifying corresponding instructional
    strategies to increase participant learning, incorporate the changes into the
    next class, and evaluate to determine success of the changes.*

The reader should consider the Limitation and Biases of the Evaluation of this report before decisions are made based upon the results of this evaluation.

3. Limitations and Bias of the Evaluation

No limitations or biases are known at this time. However, the reader should consider the following guidelines:

A   *The reader should consider that a minimum of 80% of recommended class size should be represented in a Level 2 evaluation before decisions are made based on the results of this report. Though fourteen people participated in the development test of ACB100 - Test Course, one person was not a part of the target population, and only twelve participants completed all five embedded knowledge checks.*

B.   *The group presentation was not used during development test.*

The following points need consideration when analyzing the results of this report.

1.   *Check to ensure the objectives tested are complete and match the course content.*

2.   *Review the item analysis to determine which portion of the course (design) may require improvement.*

3.   *This evaluation does not show if the objectives tested are the right objectives for today's audience or if the content is correct.*

4. Appendix

The Appendix contains two elements:

1.   *The ACB100 - Test Course.   This report is the detailed analysis of the results of the class. The report is fourteen pages in length and contains:*

   A   *Evaluation Instruments*
   B   *Summative Learning Report*
   C   *Item Analysis*
   D   *Item Analysis rank ordered by the number of incorrect responses*

2.   *All knowledge checks completed by the participants.*

Level 1 Item Analysis Report for One Quarter's Worth of Data -
This example is a Level 1 summative Evaluation Report detailing the results of
a delivery organization for one quarter. All questions on the Participant
Assessment (see chapter 4 for a copy of the survey) are reported. For this
example, only the first and last set of questions are portrayed.

Course Name:	*All courses*
Course Dates:	*Quarter 1*
Instructor:	*All instructors*
Region:	*All sites*
Training Location:	*All Locations*
Number of Participants	*3,331*
Yes:	*52%*
No:	*3%*
Within one year:	*3%*
Unknown:	*42%*

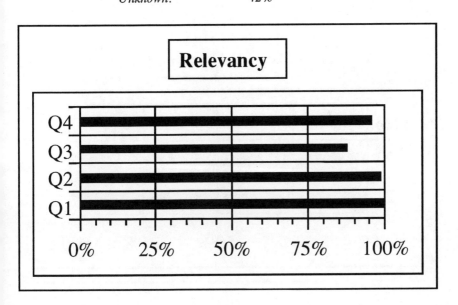

1. *The course content met my expectations.*

Exceeded	=	*30%*
Met	=	*68%*
Not Met	=	*2%*

2. *Course increased my capabilities of performing my job tasks.*
    Strongly agree   =   *22%*
    Agree   =   *72%*
    Disagree   =   *2%*
    Strongly disagree =   *1%*
    Unable to judge   =   *3%*
3. *The course was available to me . . .*
    Too early   =   *3%*
    In time   =   *86%*
    Too late   =   *11%*
4. *I had the skills and knowledge to begin the course.*
    Strongly agree   =   *23%*
    Agree   =   *69%*
    Disagree   =   *5%*
    Strongly disagree =   *1%*
    Unable to judge   =   *2%*

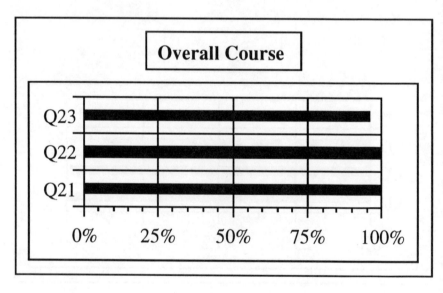

21. *The training facility provided a quality learning environment.*
    Strongly agree   =   *24%*
    Agree   =   *72%*
    Disagree   =   *4%*
    Strongly disagree =   *0%*

22. *The appearance / format of the printed materials was ...*

Outstanding	=	15%
Above average	=	43%
OK	=	42%
Poor	=	0%
Unsatisfactory	=	0%

32. *Overall, I was satisfied with the course.*

Yes	=	98%
No	=	2%

-- END OF TASK 5 --

Summary

The *Report Evaluation* Phase of the Training Evaluation Process communicates training evaluation information to interested audiences so that they are able to use the evaluation information in decision making. This phase generates an Evaluation Report which details the result of the evaluation and activities necessary to correct any problems with the training program. Exhibit 101 summarizes the tasks associated with this task and their outputs.

Exhibit 101: Summary of the Reports & Decision Making Phase

Task	Output
1. Verify and adjust the list of those individuals who will receive an Evaluation Report.	List of Evaluation Report audiences in ranked order.
2. Decide on the content to be included in the report.	Decision of report content.
3. Determine delivery methods for reports.	Report delivery format.
4. Decide upon due dates for the reports.	Report Schedule.
5. Write and deliver Evaluation Report(s).	Evaluation Reports.

References

1. Morris, L. L., Fitz-Gibbhon, C. T., Freeman, M. E.,*How to Communicate Evaluation Findings*, (1987), Sage, Newbury Park, CA

\

8. MEASURING EFFECTIVE EVALUATIONS

Purpose of this Chapter

This chapter supplies details about Meta-evaluations - an evaluation of an evaluation. Meta-evaluations close the loop on providing world class training evaluations by examining the process, techniques, and methodologies used in conducting the evaluation. With this data subsequent evaluations can be improved by identifying weaknesses in past performance and replicating strengths in previous evaluations.

The basis for performing Meta-evaluations on Training Evaluation Process activities is the text titled <u>Standards for Evaluations of Educational Programs, Projects, and Materials</u>[1]. This chapter provides the standards for the evaluation of training programs, along with an instrument that may be used in a Meta-evaluation.

Objectives of this Chapter

At the conclusion of this chapter you will be able to:

1. Define Meta-evaluations and describe how it is used in judging the effectiveness of training evaluations.
2. Determine which of the Evaluation Standards apply to corporate training Meta-evaluations.
3. Use the <u>Meta-evaluation Survey</u> instrument to judge the effectiveness of work associated with the Training Evaluation Process.

Introduction

A corporation's training evaluator or evaluation team would be remiss if they did not evaluate the effectiveness of their own evaluations. Personal bias of evaluators is always a concern and needs to be controlled and assessed to provide credibility to an evaluation. The same holds true for the technical procedures (the Training Evaluation Process) used by the evaluation team. If an evaluation does not achieve creditability with the client because of personal bias, technical inadequacy or for other reasons, both that particular evaluation and future evaluations could become suspect. Also, because program evaluation properly implemented leads to program improvement, evaluations of evaluations or Meta-evaluations give assurances that under existing circumstances the best possible information has been provided.

Meta-evaluation is an evaluation of an evaluation. These evaluations are conducted to provide assurances of the quality of an evaluation, to provide when necessary credibility to the evaluation and, to improve subsequent evaluations. Evaluations must be useful feasible, proper, and technically accurate to be creditable for the intended purpose of training program improvement. This process is discussed in the literature by Scriven, 1972, and Stufflebeam, 1975, and they provide criteria and techniques to use.

Both writers rely heavily on the The Standards for Evaluation of Educational Programs, Projects, and Material when conducting Meta-evaluation. The standards were developed in late 70's and early 80's and published in 1981 by the Joint Committee on Standard for Educational Evaluation and are presently under study for revision. The focus of the Standards as quoted from the Standards Book is as follows[2]:

> *The Standards do not encompass a particular view of what constitutes good education, nor do they present specific criteria by which to judge educational programs, projects and materials. However, they do contain advice for dealing with these vital issues. In essence, evaluators are advised to gather information that is relevant to the questions posed by clients and other audiences and yet sufficient for assessing an object's effectiveness, costs, responses to societal needs, feasibility, and worth.*

The Joint Committee attempted to recognize in the standards all types of studies used to evaluate educational materials, programs, and projects. These include internal and external, small and large, and informal and formal studies. They also include formative evaluations (evaluations designed to improve an object while it is still being developed) and summative evaluations (evaluations designed to present conclusions about the worth or merit of an object and to provide recommendations about whether it should be retained or eliminated).

In addition, the Joint Committee wrote standards that encourage the sound use of a variety of evaluation methods. These include: surveys of various reference groups, archival searches, observation of school practices, school profiles, jury trials for projects, case studies, advocacy teams to expose the strengths and weaknesses of projects, testing programs, simulation studies, time series studies, checklists, the Delphi Technique, Modus Operandi Analysis, goal-free evaluation, secondary data analysis, and quasi-experimental designs.

The Joint Committee also constructed the standards to help evaluators identify and confront political realities. Particularly the Committee sees information and money as two sources of power that may be used to corrupt evaluations. The standards, if followed, should help to ensure that evaluators and their clients will not misuse their power.

The thirty Standards are grouped into four categories according to whether they will contribute to the utility, feasibility, propriety, or accuracy of an evaluation study. The Joint Committee included with each standard an overview of the standard, guidelines for using the standard, some possible pitfalls, caveats, an illustrative case, and an analysis of the case. For easy reference, the thirty Standards are listed following with a brief explanation of each. It is suggested however, that corporate training evaluators obtain a copy of the standards for reference when conducting Meta-evaluations.

Summary of the Standards

A   UTILITY STANDARDS - The Utility Standards are intended to ensure that an evaluation will serve the practical information needs of given audiences. These standards are:

A1 Audience Identification - Audiences involved in or affected by the evaluation should be identified, so that their needs can be addressed. Within corporate training a variety of audiences exist. Typically they are composed of:

1. Training managers.
2. Instructional designers.
3. Course developers.
4. Participants.
5. Participant managers.
6. Funding organizations.
7. Corporate councils or training boards (if they exist).

A2 Evaluator Credibility - The persons conducting the evaluation should be both trustworthy and competent to perform the evaluation, so that their findings achieve maximum credibility and acceptance.

A3 Information Scope and Selection - Information collected should be of such scope and selected in such ways as to address pertinent questions about the object of the evaluation and be responsive to the needs and interests of specified audiences. These data need to be validated against the Evaluation Plan written during the Design phase of the Training Evaluation Process.

A4 Valuational Interpretation - The perspectives, procedures, and rationale used to interpret the findings should be carefully described, so that the bases for value judgments are clear. It is imperative that this data be established and set during the Planning phase so that all analysis and interpretation are clear and relevant.

A5 Report Clarity - The evaluation report should describe the course being evaluated and its context, and the purposes, procedures, and findings of the evaluation, so that the audiences will readily understand what was done, what information was obtained, and what conclusions were drawn.

A6 Report Dissemination - Evaluation findings should be disseminated to clients and other right-to-know audiences, so that they can assess and use the findings.

A7 Report Timeliness - Release of reports should be timely, so that audiences can best use the reported information.

A8 Evaluation Impact - Evaluations should be planned and conducted in ways that encourage follow-through by members of the audiences so that program or process improvement can take place.

B FEASIBILITY STANDARDS - The Feasibility Standards are intended to ensure that an evaluation will be realistic, prudent, diplomatic, and frugal; they are:

B1 Practical Procedures - The evaluation procedures should be practical, so that disruption is kept to a minimum, and that needed information can be obtained. A fine line exists between effective evaluation techniques and ones that disrupt or inhibit learning. Training evaluation procedures must always be planned to complement and enhance the learning experience rather than hinder it.

B2 Political Viability - The evaluation should be planned and conducted with anticipation of the different positions of various interest groups (departments and organizations within the company), so that their cooperation may be obtained, and so that possible attempts by any of these groups to curtail evaluation operations or to bias or misapply the results can be averted or counteracted.

B3 <u>Cost Effectiveness</u> - The evaluation should produce information of sufficient value to justify the resources expended. Wherever possible, training evaluation procedures need to be automated to reduce cycle time, errors, and cost. Funds within corporations for evaluations, at times, are difficult to obtain. Therefore, proper use of theses funds is paramount to continued evaluation functions and successes.

C <u>PROPRIETY STANDARDS</u> - The Propriety Standards are intended to ensure that the evaluation will be conducted legally, ethically, and with due regard for the welfare of those involved in the evaluation, as well as those affected by its results. These standards are:

C1 <u>Formal Obligation</u> - Obligations of the formal parties to an evaluation (what is being done, how, by whom, when, etc.) should be agreed to in writing (Evaluation Plan), so that these parties are obligated to adhere to all conditions of the agreement or formally to renegotiated it.

C2 <u>Conflict of Interest</u> - Conflict of interest, frequently unavoidable, should be dealt with openly and honestly, so that it does not compromise the evaluation processes and results.

C3 <u>Full and Frank Disclosure</u> - Oral and written evaluation reports should be open, direct, and honest in their disclosure of pertinent findings, including the limitations of the evaluation.

C4 <u>Public's Right to Know</u> - The formal parties to an evaluation should respect and assure the public's right to know, within the limits of other related principles and statutes, such as those dealing with public safety and the right to privacy. This standard, although quite appropriate for public institutions, has little use in the private sector, unless the training is associated with some government contract.

C5 <u>Rights of Human Subjects</u> - Evaluations should be designed and conducted, so that the rights and welfare of the human subjects are respected and protected.

C6 <u>Human Interactions</u> - Evaluators should respect human dignity and worth in their interactions with other persons associated with an evaluation.

C7 <u>Balanced Reporting</u> - The evaluation should be complete and fair in its presentation of strengths and weaknesses of the course under investigation, so that strengths can be built upon and problem areas addressed.

C8 <u>Fiscal Responsibility</u> - The evaluator's allocation and expenditure of resources should reflect sound accountability procedures and otherwise be prudent and ethically responsible.

D   ACCURACY STANDARDS - The Accuracy Standards are intended to ensure that an evaluation will reveal and convey technically adequate information about the features of the course being studied that determine its worth or merit. These standards are:

D1 Object Identification - The object of the evaluation (course) should be sufficiently examined, so that the form(s) (content, purpose, business requirement, etc.) of the object being considered in the evaluation can be clearly identified.

D2 Context Analysis - The context in which the course exists or will exist should be examined in enough detail, so that its likely influences on the object can be identified.

D3 Described Purposes and Procedures - The purposes and procedures of the evaluation should be monitored and described in enough detail, so that they can be identified and assessed.

D4 Defensible Information Sources - The sources of information should be described in enough detail, so that the adequacy of the information can be assessed.

D5 Valid Measurement - The data collection instruments and procedures should be chosen or developed and then implemented in ways that will assure that the interpretation is valid for the given use.

D6 Reliable Measurement - The data collection instruments and procedures should be chosen or developed and then implemented in ways that will assure that the information obtained is sufficiently reliable for the intended use.

D7 Systematic Data Control - The data collected, processed, and reported in an evaluation should be reviewed and corrected, so that the results of the evaluation will not be flawed.

D8 Analysis of Quantitative Information - Quantitative information in an evaluation should be appropriately and systematically analyzed to ensure supportable interpretations.

D9 Analysis of Qualitative Information - Qualitative information in an evaluation should be appropriately and systematically analyzed to ensure supportable interpretations.

<u>D10 Justified Conclusions</u> - The conclusions reached, if drawn by the evaluator, should be explicitly justified, so that the audiences can assess them.

<u>D11 Objective Reporting</u> - The evaluation procedures should provide safeguards to protect the evaluation findings and reports against distortion by the personal feelings and biases of any party to the evaluation.

Application of the Standards

These standards need to be applied to different settings within evaluation studies. In public educational evaluation they are applied one way whereas in private, commercial training evaluation they are applied differently. This section of the chapter discusses how to apply the evaluation standards when using the Training Evaluation Process. Exhibit 102 is a matrix which shows a phase of the Training Evaluation Process and the corresponding evaluation standards which apply.

Exhibit 102: Training Evaluation Process Phases Mapped to Standards

Training Evaluation Process Phase	Evaluation Standard	
1. Plan	A1 Audience Identification A3 Information Scope & Selection A4 Valuation Interpretation A8 Evaluation Impact B1 Practical Procedures B2 Political Viability	B3 Cost Effectiveness C1 Formal Obligation C2 Conflict of Interest C8 Fiscal Responsibility D1 Object Identification D3 Described Purpose and Procedures
2. Develop	A1 Audience Identification A3 Information Scope & Selection A4 Valuation Interpretation B1 Practical Procedures C1 Formal Obligation D1 Object Identification	D3 Described Purpose and Procedures D4 Described Information Sources D5 Valid Measurement D6 Reliable Measurement D8 Analysis of Quantitative Information D9 Analysis of Qualitative Information
4. Analyze	A4 Valuational Interpretation B1 Practical Procedures D1 Object Identification D2 Context Analysis	D8 Analysis of Quantitative Information D9 Analysis of Qualitative Information D10 Justified Conclusions
3. Obtain	A2 Evaluator Credibility A3 Information Scope & Selection C5 Rights of Human Subjects D1 Object Identification D3 Described Purposes and Procedures	D4 Defensible Information Sources D5 Valid Measurement D6 Reliable Measurement D7 Systematic Data Control
5. Report	A1 Audience Identification A3 Information Scope & Selection A4 Valuational Interpretation A5 Report Clarity A6 Report Dissemination A7 Report Timeliness A8 Evaluation Impact C3 Full and Frank Disclosure	C4 Public's Right to Know C7 Balanced Reporting D1 Object Identification D2 Context Analysis D3 Described Purposes and Procedures D4 Defensible Information Sources D10 Justified Conclusions D11 Objective Reporting

Exhibit 102 shows which standards are used to judge the quality of a training evaluation as you progress through the various stages of the process. However, two important aspects of Meta-evaluations need to be discussed: 1) who performs the Meta-evaluations and 2) what instrument(s) do they use.

Who Performs Meta-evaluation?

The individual who conducts a Meta-evaluations should be an expert in the Training Evaluation Process. The dilemma is whether you conduct the Meta-evaluate yourself or have it performed by someone else. This is preferable to have Meta-evaluation conducted by someone other than the original evaluator. The major problem associated with this tactic is the one of resources. Most companies do not have a group of evaluators who can Meta-evaluate each other. Therefore, Meta-evaluation of one's own work happens. This is still feasible, but may cause biased judgment.

What Instrument(s) Are Used?

No matter who performs the Meta-evaluation, a standard instrument should be used so that Meta-evaluators follow a set of prescribed rules when collecting data associated with a training evaluation. Exhibits 103 and 104 depict the Meta-evaluation instrument used at Motorola University.

Exhibit   103:   Meta-evaluation   Instrument

Meta-evaluation of Process Used

Date of Meta-evaluation: _____ Meta-evaluator name: _____
Course evaluated: _____ Evaluator name: _____
Evaluation period:_____

1. Evaluator Credibility: Are the evaluator(s) who conducted the   [Yes] [No]
    evaluation trustworthy and competent so that their findings
    achieve maximum credibility and acceptance?

    Have the personnel successfully completed training on the   [Yes] [No]
    Training Evaluation Process?

2. Report Dissemination: Were evaluation findings distributed to   [Yes] [No]
    clients and other right-to-know audiences, so that they can
    assess and use the findings?

3. Report Clarity: Did the Evaluation Report describe the course   [Yes] [No]
    being evaluated, including its context, and the purposes,
    procedures, and findings of the evaluation?

4. Political Viability: Was the evaluation planned and conducted   [Yes] [No]
    with anticipation of the different positions of various groups,
    so that their cooperation may be obtained, and so that possible
    attempts by any of these groups to curtail evaluation operations
    or to bias or misapply the results was averted or counteracted?

5. Conflict of Interest: Were conflicts of interests dealt with openly   [Yes] [No]
    and honestly, so that it did not compromise the evaluation process
    and results?

6   Rights of Participants: Was the evaluation designed and conducted [Yes] [No]
    so that the rights and welfare of the participants are respected
    and protected?

7. Systematic Data Control: Were data collected, processed, and   [Yes] [No]
    reported in the evaluation reviewed and corrected so that results
    of the evaluation were not flawed?

8. Formal Obligation: Did a formal obligation to the evaluation   [Yes] [No]
    (what is done, how, by whom, when) in writing exist so that all
    key stakeholders were obligated to follow the conditions of the
    agreement or renegotiate it?

Page 1

Exhibit   104:   Meta-evaluation   Instrument   (continued)

Meta-evaluation of Process Used

9. Context Analysis: Was the context in which the course exists examined in enough detail so that its likely influence on the course identified?   (Yes No)

10. Practical Procedures: Were evaluation procedures practical so that disruption to the learning event, workplace, or organization kept to a minimum?   (Yes No)

11. Full and Fair Reporting: Were oral and written reports open, direct, and honest in their disclosure of pertinent findings including limitations of the evaluation?   (Yes No)

12. Defensible Information Sources: Were the sources used to gather information described in enough detail so that accuracy of information was assessed?   (Yes No)

13. Valid Measurement: Were data collection instruments and procedures chosen, developed, and carried out in ways that assured that the interpretation arrived at is valid for the given use?   (Yes No)

14. Reliable Measurement: Were data collection instruments and procedures chosen, developed, and carried out in ways that assured that the information obtained was sufficiently reliable for the intended use?   (Yes No)

15. Objective Reporting: Were evaluation procedures safeguarded to protect the evaluation findings and reports against distortion by the personal feelings and biases of any party to the evaluation?   (Yes No)

16. Data Analysis Procedures: Were the perspectives, procedures, and rationale used to interpret the findings carefully described so that the basis for value judgments are clear?   (Yes No)

Notes:

Page 2

Exhibits 103 and 104 are the instruments used by a Meta-evaluator to collect data on the execution of the Training Evaluation Process. For training evaluation to be successful, the process must be followed with the execution of the process being reviewed periodically (Meta-evaluation) to determine:

1. Does the process work? If not, where did it falter and was it the fault of the evaluator of the definition of the process?
2. What changes need to be made in order allow the next execution of the

process to be more successful?

When using these instruments the Meta-evaluator will be making value judgments based upon what was observed and investigated. As Meta-evaluators gain experience in Meta-evaluation, their valuing of the process used will increase. It is important to allow the Meta-evaluator the opportunity mature into an experienced performer that conducts excellent Meta-evaluations.

Besides evaluating the process, the Meta-evaluator needs to investigate the specifics (<u>Evaluation Plan</u>, data collection instruments, <u>Evaluation Report,</u> etc.) for an individual evaluation. Exhibits 105 through 110 depict the instruments used in gathering Meta-evaluation data from a specific evaluation.

Exhibit 105: Meta-evaluation Instrument for a Specific Evaluation

---

Meta-evaluation Survey Instrument

Date of Meta-evaluation: _____ Meta-evaluator name: _____
Course evaluated: _____ Evaluator name: _____
Evaluation period: _____

Evaluation Planning

1. Was an Evaluation Plan written for this evaluation?   `Yes | No`
   If "Yes," please attach a copy. Does the plan meet standards by:

   A. Reflect the wishes of key evaluation stakeholders.   `Yes No N/A`
   B. Meets all requirements of corporate policy and direction. `Yes No N/A`
   C. Written in such a way so that it is understandable by the `Yes No N/A`
      layperson.
   D. Written in time for stakeholders to modify or approve.   `Yes No N/A`

Level 1 Evaluation

2. Was a Level 1 survey (questionnaire) used to gather   `Yes | No`
   participant reactions? If "Yes," please attach a copy.
   Does the survey meet standards by:

   A. Questions worded to maximize the validity of the   `Yes No N/A`
      data gathered.
   B. Data gathered anonymously.   `Yes No N/A`
   C. Constructed so that it relates positively to evaluation   `Yes No N/A`
      purposes/questions.
   D. For closed response questions, all reasonable alternatives `Yes No N/A`
      are present and match the stem.
   E. Used words the participant understands.   `Yes No N/A`
   F. Open ended questions were used.   `Yes No N/A`
   G. Questions were ordered.   `Yes No N/A`
   H. Filter questions were used.   `Yes No N/A`

3. Was a Level 1 whole-class or group interview used to obtain `Yes | No`
   participant reaction to the course? If "Yes," please attach a
   copy. Did the Interview meet standards by:

   A. Having the interviewer review Level 1 survey results   `Yes No N/A`
      prior to the interview.
   B. Instructor introduced the interviewer and left the classroom. `Yes No N/A`
   C. The interviewer described the purpose of the interview and `Yes No N/A`
      procedures for responding.
   D. The interviewer allowed all participants an equal chance of `Yes No N/A`
      responding.

Exhibit 106: Meta-evaluation Instrument for a Specific Evaluation (continued)

Meta-evaluation Survey Instrument

Level 2 Evaluation

4. Was a Pre-test administered? **[Yes | No]**
    If "**Yes**," please attach a copy. Did the test meet
    standards by:

    A. Matches course objectives. *(Yes No N/A)*
    B. Matches course content. *(Yes No N/A)*
    C. Each test item constructed to meet test standards. *(Yes No N/A)*
    D. Is equal to or similar to the Post-test. *(Yes No N/A)*
    E. Written at the cognitive level of the defined *(Yes No N/A)*
        target audience.
    F. Include instructions for administering the check. *(Yes No N/A)*
    G. Includes a scoring strategy. *(Yes No N/A)*

5. Was a Post-test administered? **[Yes | No]**
    If "**Yes**," please attach a copy. Did the test meet standards by:

    A. Matches course objectives. *(Yes No N/A)*
    B. Matches course content. *(Yes No N/A)*
    C. Each test item constructed to meet test standards. *(Yes No N/A)*
    D. Is equal to or similar to the Pre-test. *(Yes No N/A)*
    E. Written at the cognitive level of the defined target audience. *(Yes No N/A)*
    F. Include instructions for administering the check. *(Yes No N/A)*
    G. Include a scoring strategy. *(Yes No N/A)*

6. Were any skill based Performance Checks administered? **[Yes | No]**
    If "**Yes**," please attach copies of all Checks. Did the
    Check(s) meet standards by:

    A. Matches course objectives. *(Yes No N/A)*
    B. Matches course content. *(Yes No N/A)*
    C. Each task composed of work tasks. *(Yes No N/A)*
    D. Written at the cognitive level of the defined target audience. *(Yes No N/A)*
    E. Include instructions for administering the check. *(Yes No N/A)*
    F. Includes a scoring strategy. *(Yes No N/A)*

Exhibit 107: Meta-evaluation Instrument for a Specific Evaluation (continued)

Meta-evaluation Survey Instrument

Level 3 Evaluation

7. Was a Level 3 evaluation questionnaire administered?   `Yes | No`
    If "**Yes,**" please attach a copy. Did the questionnaire
    meet standards by:

    A.   Matching the purpose outlined in the Evaluation Plan.   (Yes)(No)(N/A)

    B.   Gather participant work performance in the following areas: (Yes)(No)(N/A)

       *   Specifically defined work task(s) attributable (Yes)(No)(N/A)
          to training.

       *   Number of opportunities the participants have (Yes)(No)(N/A)
          had to practice the behavior.

       *   The actual of number of times the behavior was tried. (Yes)(No)(N/A)
       *   The duration of performance. (Yes)(No)(N/A)
       *   Additional resources (tools, personnel, money, (Yes)(No)(N/A)
          etc.) used in performance.

       *   Success of the performance. (Yes)(No)(N/A)
       *   Barriers that hindered performance. (Yes)(No)(N/A)
       *   Elements that contributed to successful performance. (Yes)(No)(N/A)
       *   Time frame since completing training. (Yes)(No)(N/A)
       *   Skills participants had to learn on their own that (Yes)(No)(N/A)
          training did not provide.

    C.   Data was gathered anonymously. (Yes)(No)(N/A)

8. Was a Level 3 evaluation interview/focus group administered?   `Yes | No`
    If "**Yes,**" please attach a copy. Did the interview/focus group
    meet standards by:

    A.   Matching the purpose outlined in the Evaluation Plan. (Yes)(No)(N/A)

    B.   Gather participant work performance in the
       following areas:

       *   Work task(s) attributable to training. (Yes)(No)(N/A)
       *   Number of opportunities the participants have (Yes)(No)(N/A)
          had to practice the behavior.

       *   The actual of number of times the behavior was tried (Yes)(No)(N/A)
       *   The duration of performance. (Yes)(No)(N/A)
       *   Additional resources (tools, personnel, money, etc.) (Yes)(No)(N/A)
          used in performance.

       *   Success of the performance. (Yes)(No)(N/A)
       *   Barriers that hindered performance. (Yes)(No)(N/A)
       *   Elements that contributed to successful performance (Yes)(No)(N/A)
       *   Time frame since completing training. (Yes)(No)(N/A)
       *   Skills participants had to learn on their own (Yes)(No)(N/A)
          that training did not provide.

Meta-evaluation Survey Instrument

Level 3 Evaluation (continued)

9. Was a Level 3 evaluation interview/focus group administered? `Yes | No`
    If "**Yes**," please attach a copy. Did the interview/focus group
    meet standards by (continued):

    C. The interviewer/facilitator was trained in how to   Yes No N/A
        conduct the session.
    D. The respondents are from the defined target population. Yes No N/A

10. Was a Level 3 evaluation observation conducted? `Yes | No`
    If "**Yes**," please attach a copy. Did the observation meet
    standards by:

    A. Matching the purpose outlined in the Evaluation Plan.   Yes No N/A
    B. Gather participant work performance in the following areas:
        *   Specifically defined work task(s) attributable   Yes No N/A
            to training.
        *   Number of opportunities the participants have had to Yes No N/A
            practice the behavior.
        *   The actual of number of time the behavior was tried. Yes No N/A
        *   The duration of performance.   Yes No N/A
        *   Additional resources (tools, personnel, money, etc.) Yes No N/A
            used in performance.
        *   Success of the performance.   Yes No N/A
        *   Barriers that hindered performance.   Yes No N/A
        *   Elements that contributed to successful performance. Yes No N/A
        *   Time frame since completing training.   Yes No N/A
        *   Skills participants had to learn on their own that   Yes No N/A
            training did not provide.
    C. The observer was trained in how to observe the session. Yes No N/A
    D. The observation was conducted with full knowledge and   Yes No N/A
        support of the participant their manager.

Exhibit 109: Meta-evaluation Instrument for a Specific Evaluation (continued)

Meta-evaluation Survey Instrument

Level 3 Evaluation (continued)

11. Was a Level 3 evaluation action planning process administered? **Yes | No**
If "Yes," please attach a copy. Did the action planning process meet standards by:

   A. Matching the purpose outlined in the Evaluation Plan. (Yes)(No)(N/A)
   B. Gather participant work performance in the following areas:
      * Specifically defined work task(s) attributable to training. (Yes)(No)(N/A)
      * Number of opportunities the participants have had to practice the behavior. (Yes)(No)(N/A)
      * The actual of number of time the behavior was tried. (Yes)(No)(N/A)
      * The duration of performance. (Yes)(No)(N/A)
      * Additional resources (tools, personnel, money, etc.) used in performance. (Yes)(No)(N/A)
      * Success of the performance. (Yes)(No)(N/A)
      * Barriers that hindered performance. (Yes)(No)(N/A)
      * Elements that contributed to successful performance. (Yes)(No)(N/A)
      * Time frame since completing training. (Yes)(No)(N/A)
      * Skills participants had to learn on their own that training did not provide. (Yes)(No)(N/A)
   C. The evaluator conducted a follow-up to track success of the action plan. (Yes)(No)(N/A)

Meta-evaluation Survey Instrument

Level 4 Evaluation

12. Was a Level 4 total cost of training calculated? **Yes No**
    If "**Yes**," please attach a copy. Did the total cost of
    training calculation meet standards by:

    A. Matching the purpose outlined in the Evaluation Plan — Yes No N/A
    B. Gathering the following training cost parameters:
        * Number of participants trained — Yes No N/A
        * Working days per year of participants — Yes No N/A
        * Mean annual participant cost — Yes No N/A
        * Length of training session (in days) — Yes No N/A
        * Related travel time (in days) — Yes No N/A
        * Mean cost for one participant to travel — Yes No N/A
        * Mean cost of accommodation for one participant — Yes No N/A
        * Weekly cost of instructional designer and/or
          subject matter experts — Yes No N/A
        * Annual cost of of instructor — Yes No N/A
        * Weekly cost of course developer — Yes No N/A
        * Course development ratio — Yes No N/A
        * Instructional design ratio — Yes No N/A
        * Participant package cost — Yes No N/A
        * Participant/instructor ratio — Yes No N/A
        * Working days per year for instructors — Yes No N/A
        * Annual classroom cost — Yes No N/A
        * Equipment cost — Yes No N/A
        * Translation cost — Yes No N/A
        * Number of translations required — Yes No N/A
        * Evaluation cost — Yes No N/A

13. Was the value of training calculated? If "**Yes**," please attach a **Yes No**
    copy. Did the value of training calculation meet standards by:

    A. Establishing control and experimental groups. — Yes No N/A
    B. Random sampling was used to create the control and
        experimental groups. — Yes No N/A
    C. The measures (metrics) used to calculate value were
        agreed to by evaluation stakeholders. — Yes No N/A
    D. Accounting records were used to collect training
        value data. — Yes No N/A
    E. The level of significance between the two group results
        is $\leq.05$. — Yes No N/A
    F. The size of the control and experimental groups was
        equal. — Yes No N/A

Summary

By using the survey instruments shown in this chapter, the evaluator can begin
to judge the merit and worth of their own work - training evaluations. Meta-

evaluation is viewed in the same light as training evaluation by judging the effect of the program (evaluation) and not the person (evaluator). Striving to increase the accuracy, feasibility, and credibility of training evaluation through Meta-evaluation is not a luxury but a necessity to further the art and science of training evaluation.

References

1. The Joint Committee on Standards of Educational Programs, Projects, and Materials. Standards for Evaluations of Educational Programs, Projects, and Materials (1981), McGraw-Hill, New York, NY
2. The Joint Committee on Standards of Educational Programs, Projects, and Materials. Standards for Evaluations of Educational Programs, Projects, and Materials (1981), McGraw-Hill, New York, NY, pp. 7.

Action plan A documented approach on what changes need to take place to improve a training program.

Agreement scale A scale used to report the intensity of the participant's feelings about an activity - e.g., a scale that gives choices as Strongly agree, Agree, Disagree, Strongly disagree.

Analysis bias A consistent alignment with one point of view.

Audit An independent examination and verification of the quality of an evaluation plan, the adequacy with which it was implemented, the accuracy of results, and the validity of conclusions.

Behavior checklist A record of all behavior on a form using specified codes.

Closed response A set of questions that provide a finite set of responses for the participant to choose.

Coding system Translating a set of data into a set of quantitative or qualitative symbols. This can be as simple as recording the data from the collection instrument by paper and pencil or as extensive as creating a computer spreadsheet.

Control group A group equivalent to an experimental group (one that is exposed to a program, project, or instructional material), and exposed to all the conditions of the investigation except the program, project, or instructional material being studied.

Course control document A document used to record participants' progress through a course.

Course designers Individuals who, using an instructional design process, create the instructional strategy to be used with a given course.

Course development process The process of developing a new training course or the selection and maintenance of an already developed training course.

Course developers Individuals who create the course materials from an Instructional Systems Design Document.

Criterion reference tests Tests whose scores are interpreted by referral to specifically defined performances, rather than by referral to the performance of some comparable group of people.

Customer The recipient of the results (output) of any phase of the Training Evaluation Process.

Data analysis model A pre-defined methodology for summarizing collected evaluation data.

Decision making process The procedure within any company where resolution is obtained related to a specific program, process, or concept.

Delivery readiness process The procedure for preparing training organizations to teach courses.

Develop phase The component of the Training Evaluation Process where data collection instruments and data analysis models are created.

Evaluation phobia At times' evaluations are a threat to personnel involved. Evaluation describes personnel who do not want to be a part of an evaluation because they fear they may lose their job or that the results will adversely effect them.

Evaluation plan A plan that guides all activities of an evaluation and is a formal obligation between the evaluator or evaluation team and the client.

Experimental group A group of subjects assigned to receive a treatment (independent variable) the effects of which are measured (dependent variable). Often comparisons are made between these effects and those observed for a comparison (non-treatment) group.

Focus group A group interview with a set of participants who have completed a training program. Usually used with Level 3 evaluations.

Formative evaluation Evaluation designed and used to improve an object, especially when it is still being developed.

Frequency scales Scales used by an evaluator to determine how often a participant has perceived or has performed an activity.

Input The product required to perform the work tasks associated any task of the Training Evaluation Process.

Instructional design document A paper that details the instructional strategies to be used in developing and delivering training.

Instructional delivery process The method of providing training to participants.

Key Stakeholders Sponsors of the training program or anyone with a vested interest in the program.

Level 1 evaluation - Reaction Evaluate to learn participants' perception to the training program.

Level 2 evaluation - Learning Evaluate to determine whether participants have mastered the course subject matter.

Level 3 evaluation - Behavior Evaluate participants' use of newly acquired job skills on the job.

Level 4 evaluation - Results Evaluate the organizational impact of training on company's workforce.

Measures of central tendency Measures to determine the central most measure in a set of scores. The most common such measures are the mean and the median.

Measures of variability A statistical method that deals with how far scores are spread throughout a dispersion. Two such measures are range and standard deviation.

Merit The excellence of an object as assessed by its intrinsic qualities or performance.

Needs analysis The process of determining the demand and necessity of training.

Negative skew curves A distribution of evaluation results where a large percentage of the results clusters to the right.

Object What one is evaluating; e.g., a program, a project, or instructional material.

Observation check list A form used to record behaviors observed during an observation using specific codes (a coded behavior record).

Obtain phase The component of the Training Evaluation Process that collects evaluation data.

Open response Using questions in collecting data where the participants are required to respond in their own words.

Output The results of performing a Training Evaluation Process task.

Participant assessment analysis The techniques used to interpret results from Level 1 evaluation questionnaires.

Participant assessment form The Level 1 evaluation questionnaire used by Motorola University.

Performance based check A Level 2 evaluation technique used to test participant mastery of skills.

Pilot class The "dry run" or test of a newly developed training program.

Pilot process The method of testing a course during pilot.

Plan phase The component of the Training Evaluation Process that develops and distributes an Evaluation Plan.

Post-test A test to determine performance after the administration of a program, project, or instructional material.

Pre-test A test to determine performance prior to the administration of a program, project, or instructional material.

Qualitative methods Presenting information using facts and claims presented in narrative rather than numerical form.

Quality scale A scale used to determine how a participant perceived the quality aspect of an activity.

Quantitative methods Presenting information using facts and claims represented by numbers.

Recycling decisions Decisions as to whether to continue a training program, restructure it, or to discontinue it based on information from a training program evaluation.

Satisfaction scales Measures the level of satisfaction an activity has provided a participant in a training program.

Semantic differential A series of adjectives and their antonyms listed on opposite sides of the page with seven "attitude positions" in between used to collect participants' reactions.

"Shelf life" The determination of how long a training program design is effective for its purpose.

Stakeholders Any persons affected by the training or projects.

Summative evaluation Evaluation designed to present conclusions about the merit or worth of an object and recommendations about whether it should be retained, altered, or eliminated.

Supplemental courses Training deemed necessary to increase participant skill or knowledge.

Supplier The person or process which provides the input for a Training Evaluation Process task.

Target audience Those persons for whom the training is designed.

Training analysis An analysis conducted to determine where training can improve employees' competence and to determine the best type of training to achieve expectations.

User The individual who executes a Training Evaluation Process task.

Worth The value of an object in relationship to a purpose.